WHAT DO
WOMEN
WANT?

ALSO BY ERICA JONG

WHAT DO WOMEN WANT?

ESSAYS BY
ERICA JONG

JEREMY P. TARCHER/PENGUIN
a member of Penguin Group (USA) Inc., New York

JEREMY P. TARCHER/PENGUIN
Published by the Penguin Group

Penguin Group (USA) Inc., 375 Hudson Street, New York, New York 10014, USA • Penguin Group
(Canada), 90 Eglinton Avenue East, Suite 700, Toronto, Ontario M4P 2Y3, Canada (a division of Pearson Penguin
Canada Inc.) • Penguin Books Ltd, 80 Strand, London WC2R 0RL, England • Penguin Ireland, 25 St Stephen's Green,
Dublin 2, Ireland (a division of Penguin Books Ltd) • Penguin Group (Australia), 250 Camberwell Road,
Camberwell, Victoria 3124, Australia (a division of Pearson Australia Group Pty Ltd) • Penguin Books India Pvt Ltd,
11 Community Centre, Panchsheel Park, New Delhi–110 017, India • Penguin Group (NZ), 67 Apollo Drive,
Rosedale, North Shore 0745, Auckland, New Zealand (a division of Pearson New Zealand Ltd) • Penguin Books
(South Africa) (Pty) Ltd, 24 Sturdee Avenue, Rosebank, Johannesburg 2196, South Africa

Penguin Books Ltd, Registered Offices: 80 Strand, London WC2R 0RL, England

Previously published in 1998 by HarperCollins Publishers
First Jeremy P. Tarcher/Penguin edition 2007

Copyright © 1998, 2007 by Erica Mann Jong

Grateful acknowledgment is made to the following periodicals and books in which some of these essays originally appeared (in somewhat different form):

The Boston Globe; The Independent on Sunday (London); *Lear's; Marie Claire; The Nation; The New Republic; The Sunday Times* (London); *The New York Observer; The New York Times Book Review; The New York Times Magazine; The Times Literary Supplement* (London); *Travel & Leisure; A Place Called Home,* edited by Mickey Pearlman, St. Martin's Press, 1998; *Introspections,* edited by Robert Pack and Jay Parini, University Press of New England, 1996; *In Their Own Voices,* produced by Rebekah Presson and David McLees, Rhino Records, 1996; *Jane Eyre* by Charlotte Brontë, introduction by Erica Jong, Penguin Books, 1997; *Reservoirs of Dogma,* edited by Richard Collins and James Purnell, Institute for Public Policy Research, London, 1996; *The Best of the Best,* edited by Elaine Koster and Joseph Pittman, Penguin Putnam, 1998; *The Oxford Mark Twain,* edited by Shelly Fisher Fishkin, Oxford University Press, 1996; *The Source of the Spring,* edited by Judith Shapiro, Conari Press, 1997; *Witches,* by Erica Jong, Abrams, 1997; National Public Radio; *Talk Magazine*

Most Tarcher/Penguin books are available at special quantity discounts for bulk purchase for sales promotions, premiums, fund-raising, and educational needs. Special books or book excerpts also can be created to fit specific needs. For details, write Penguin Group (USA) Inc. Special Markets, 375 Hudson Street, New York, NY 10014.

Library of Congress Cataloging-in-Publication Data

Jong, Erica.
What do women want? : essays / by Erica Jong —1st Jeremy P. Tarcher/Penguin ed.
p. cm.
Originally published: New York : HarperCollins Publishers, c1998.
ISBN-13: 978-1-58542-554-9
1. Women. 2. Women—United States. I. Title.
HQ1150.J66   2007   2007008356
305.40973—dc22

Printed in the United States of America
1 3 5 7 9 10 8 6 4 2

BOOK DESIGN BY NICOLE LAROCHE

For Clarice Kestenbaum

ACKNOWLEDGMENTS

I wish to thank some of the editors and friends who provoked me to begin many of these chapters: Marie Arana, Jack Beatty, Glenda Bailey, Rosy Boycott, Gladys Justin Carr, Lisa Chase, Anna Coote, Shelly Fisher Fishkin, Peter Kaplan, Mike Levitas, Robin Morgan, Nancy Novogrod, Rebekah Presson, Jay Parini, and Robert Pack.

CONTENTS

The one way of tolerating existence is to lose oneself in literature as in a perpetual orgy.

—GUSTAVE FLAUBERT

INTRODUCTION

What on earth—or in heaven—do women want? Even Sigmund Freud was puzzled. And yet it seems so obvious, and we have been saying it for centuries—or at least since the eighteenth century. We want bread and roses. We want fair pay (at the time of this writing American women still make seventy-seven cents for every dollar men make)—and we also want roses—tenderness, love, and emotional support. Very few women in the United States—or indeed the world—get either of those things. Women are starving for roses when we are not starving for bread. In fact, it has astonished me to discover how much women all over the world have identified with these needs (and with my books) in wholly diverse cultures.

Why has it taken so long to have these obvious wants met? Why are women still divided into good and bad girls? Why are women still stoned for adultery in the Muslim world, murdered for being widows in India, genitally mutilated in Africa, raped in all wars, and malnourished as children?

Even in our comparatively egalitarian society where women can go to college and earn good, if not great, salaries, the inequities hit hard when children are born and the question of child care arises. Why, after centuries of feminist outrage, have we still done so little to make women equal?

This book doesn't answer these questions. It would take another *Second Sex* (like Simone de Beauvoir's classic text) even to *address* these issues. But it does give a commentary—humorous, I hope— on what it has meant to be an American woman in the late twentieth and early twenty-first centuries.

Yes, we are privileged. But we look around the world from our outpost of privilege and see outrageous suffering. We also see how American women's rights are going backward in the area of reproductive choice, equal pay, and political access. It's bewildering that we have not yet come close to electing a woman president—as have Britain, Ireland, Germany, the Philippines, Liberia, Latvia, Finland, Chile, and twenty-eight other countries. It's also maddening to see feminism become a dirty word to a generation whose freedoms were won by feminism. But never mind. Women become more radical with age. Sometimes it takes maturity to see that it's still a man's world.

We have heard again and again about what women want, and the buzz seems to put both women and men to sleep. So let's ask the question another way: What can women *give?*

We can give perspective sadly lacking in foreign affairs. We can give a sense of balance to those men who think war is a metaphor

for everything. *War on drugs, war on terror, war between the sexes*—
by conceptualizing everything as war, we perpetuate war. What if
we said: reduce drug dependence, eliminate the causes of terror-
ism, promote *goodwill* between the sexes? The language would be
less dramatic and fear inducing, but we are all sick of lurid language and fearmongering anyway. The war metaphor doesn't
work anymore. It's dead. Time for new metaphors. We can promote new metaphors—metaphors that conceptualize change rather
than defeat or annihilate "the enemy."

Whenever I hear George W. Bush speak, I want to edit the war-
mongering out of his language in the hope of editing it out of his
behavior. But he is a lost cause. Perhaps a new generation of men
will stop using terms like "the enemy" or "the war on terror."
These bellicose metaphors have gotten us exactly nowhere. This
morning I turned on the TV and in two minutes saw these headlines: "War on War," "Battlefield Iraq," "War on Weight," and "War
on Wrinkles." Not only is the metaphor tired, but it has also ceased
to register. Fresh language would be welcome. It might even save
us. Dieting is not comparable to people blowing one another up,
but you'd never know it from watching American TV.

The truth is that many of the improvements in our lives have
come from the participation of women in society. Without seventies feminism, men would not have been encouraged to have close
relationships with children. My father was embarrassed to change a
diaper. Today's fathers are proud to. Baby shit doesn't smell better,
but men have a different perception of it. That's a conceptual change,

and conceptual changes eventually change behavior. Women wield great power to change the thinking that changes behavior. Women can give this gift.

We've never needed it more. Our entire planet is threatened. To save our species, we need to start thinking collaboratively rather than competitively.

Neither women nor men are good at collaborative thinking, but at least some women and men see the *need* for change. This is what women can give.

If more women entered politics and won (at present writing, the percentage of women in the Senate is 14 percent and in the House is 15.4 percent), maybe we could quell the warlike, penile thinking that has invaded every aspect of our lives—the need to be hard, erect, stiff, unyielding and the assumption that softness is a humiliation. Men have made the metaphors and the metaphors are leading us over a cliff. We need a world where nurturance counts more than stiffness, and a new version of Viagra will not help us find it.

The world according to Dr. Strangelove is the vision that has led us to a poisoned planet, endlessly in conflict. Women are our only hope. If we don't save the planet for our children, who will?

Most Americans suffer from historical amnesia,* so they have no idea that longer-lived empires than ours have self-destructed and crumbled. Our leaders are blind and stubborn. They have stopped questioning their right to rule the world. The end of questioning is

---

*In Gore Vidal's brilliant phrase, we are "The United States of Amnesia."

the end of civilization. We are almost there. Not because of Islamists who wage jihad for Allah, but because we Crusaders are *almost* their mirror image. Christians have forgotten the message of Christ and Jews have forgotten the words of their prophets.

These essays were first published in 1998, so I've added some new ones and deleted others. Nineteen ninety-eight seems like a halcyon time compared to 2007. We were not at war in Iraq, our economy was thriving under the Clinton administration, and we had a peace surplus rather than a war deficit.

Seven years of George W. Bush have shown us how bad government can be when cronyism and greed rule and adherence to the Constitution is forgotten. Terrorist attacks did nothing to change politics as usual, but fearmongering ran rampant. Senator Hillary Clinton became an excellent leader and front-runner for the Democratic presidential nomination, yet her political future remains unknown. I hope we will have the guts to elect her president, but I am dubious that sexism is dead in American politics. I'm deeply concerned about the voting fraud and gerrymandering that accompanied Republican rule. Conglomerization of the media has drastically narrowed our access to information. We may be beyond democracy, having stumbled into authoritarianism under the guise of free-trade capitalism.

In my personal life things have also changed drastically—and for the better.

I became a grandmother. And discovered I'm a better grandma than I ever was a mom. I vowed to battle my narcissistic tendencies and embrace Saul Bellow's wisdom: "A man should be able to hear and to tolerate the worst that could be said of him." And that goes for women, too—unlike some of the other things Bellow said. I published a writer's memoir, *Seducing the Demon*, in which I shared with my readers the demons that make me write. The response was mostly a delight. Of course, I got zapped by some critics who still see me as the Queen of Erotica, but I'm used to that. I discovered that saying what you need to say is more important than praise (*of course the fantasy is always to have both*). I hope to share that with my daughter, my grandson, and my readers.

—Erica Jong
September 22, 2006

We still think of a powerful man as a born leader and a
powerful woman as an anomaly.

—MARGARET ATWOOD

When Hillary Rodham Clinton first appeared on the national
scene in 1992, I found her a blast—not a breath—of fresh air. Here
was a woman like most American women: a breadwinner, a working mother, outspoken in her opinions, and visibly strong. Unlike
the previous first lady, Nancy Reagan, who secretly manipulated the
White House schedule with her astrologer; or Jacqueline Kennedy,
who softly cooed that husband and children came first; or Barbara
Bush, who claimed she deliberately never tried to influence George
with her sensible views of abortion,* HRC was a woman of the

---

*Laura Bush, an articulate woman who calls herself a feminist, has also not seen fit to influence
her husband on reproductive choice for American women. This bewilders me. She is, after all,
the mother of daughters.

future—unafraid of seeming as powerful as she was. Her very demeanor said: Times have changed; now even women have to watch
their backs. The protection racket of women is over: It's every
amazon for herself.

I admired Hillary Clinton's fuck-you attitude from the start, and
I was initially surprised to find myself in the minority. When she
admitted to not giving a damn about clothes, when she proudly displayed her hillbilly taste in decorating, I was thrilled. I myself *love*
clothes and care about beautiful interiors, but at last, I thought,
someone is publicly acknowledging how much *time* all that fifties
femininity stuff *takes*. In HRC we finally had a first lady who didn't
grovel, didn't kiss up in the fashion press or the food industry, and
proudly renounced her role as National Yenta. The only thing that
surprised me about Hillary was how deeply unready for her America was at first.

Yes, we had a flurry of delight in her feminism. Remember those
buttons that said "Elect Hillary's Husband in '92"? That was Hillary phase one. But soon the backlash set in, and we were doomed
to endure a period in which women as well as men claimed to hate
Hillary.

Here was the amazing part: Even women just *like* her suddenly
didn't seem to like her. Was she giving away some terrible secret
we didn't want to acknowledge even to *ourselves*? Was it a case of
kill the messenger? Did we simply not want to hear that *sleep dep-
rivation* had replaced *I dreamed I went to Paris in my Maidenform bra*
in the American female psyche?

Perhaps the reason Martha Stewart homecraft and La Perla underwear (Victoria's Secret is the mall version) appeal to the career-obsessed American woman is an intractable case of nostalgia: nostalgia for the good old days when women had time to bake bread, shop for silk unmentionables, stencil their floors, strip their furniture, and prance about without their clothes while wafting through the bedroom in marabou—instead of lying comatose in flannel.

The nostalgia for "I'm all yours in buttons and bows" dies hard, and Hillary Clinton was (in the first Clinton term anyway) an unfortunate reminder of lost leisure. Even to her staunchest supporters, she was downright depressing. Although I agreed with everything Hillary Clinton said about raising a child in *It Takes a Village*, I was put off by its schoolmarmish tone. (And how could the tone be *otherwise* in an election year? Every base had to be touched, every hand shaken, every hardworking volunteer thanked.)

But what really astonished me was how many *Democratic* Hillary-haters there were from the start—and how many of them were women. Because of this relentless opposition to Hillary's strength, everything about her was retouched at the dawn of the second Clinton term—the clothes, the demeanor, the photo ops. For a while, Hillary ceased making policy statements and was seen only on foreign junkets with First Daughter Chelsea. This transformation of the first *uppity* first lady into a femme impersonator sent a clear signal to American women: "Back off. The time is not yet ripe."* This was to be phase two in the Hillary saga. And it ushered in the silent Laura Bush.

HRC had initially insisted on her right to be powerful, self-protective, and strong. She didn't buy into female role-playing. She refused to look weak. In short, she broke the rules decreed for political wives—and for her pioneering she was nearly banished from the public eye during the second presidential campaign.

Even as late as two minutes before the last American presidential election of the twentieth century (November 1996), Hillary Rodham Clinton was still the most problematic first lady America had ever known—admired abroad, hated at home, mistrusted by women journalists even though the Clinton administration had actually done *more* for American women than any administration in our history. She was suspected of being a megalomaniac, accused of perjury, document-losing, spy-hiring, and responsible for the suicide of an aide conjectured to be her lover.

Interestingly, none of these charges materialized as fact. Though HRC was pilloried in the press and jeered at in political cartoons, though she was distrusted even by her admirers, she stood up to her detractors as we all must. She put health care, the rights of children, and the rights of women on the national agenda—no small feats.

---

*Actually, we were deep into the backlash against women's rights and we didn't even notice. Periods of high feminism have historically alternated with periods of backlash. But when you're in the cycle it's hard to see.

Back in 1996 (aeons ago where politics is concerned), I had written an article for the *New York Observer* in which I argued that Hillary Rodham Clinton was the latest victim of America's hatred of talented, clever women who do nothing to disguise their talent and cleverness. When William Safire of the *New York Times* called HRC a "congenital liar" surely he was subjecting her to a different standard than the one to which he had held other first ladies. Isn't social white lying one of the *roles* of the first lady? Can anyone in the laser glare of the public eye be expected to be candid all the time? Did anyone ask Pat Nixon what she thought of her husband's destruction of evidence, or Jackie Kennedy what she thought of her husband's affairs? Was Nancy Reagan interrogated about Irangate? But HRC's gene pool was impugned at the drop of a document. Clearly she was being put in an impossible double bind: asked to play Marie Antoinette and Madame Defarge at the same time. Nobody could have succeeded at this—not even the most talented actress. For it is true that when we wish women to fail, we decree for them endless and impossible ordeals, like those devised for witches by their inquisitors. If they drown, they are innocent; if they float, they are guilty. This has pretty much been the way America has always tried to get rid of its cleverest political women, from Victoria Woodhull and Emma Goldman to Eleanor Roosevelt and Hillary Clinton. And there was no doubt that many people wished HRC ill. She represented the new woman of the twenty-first century, the woman our daughters want to be. Before she got dumbed down and blurred pink and blue around the edges for

the 1996 Democratic National Convention (in response to Elizabeth Dole's southern sugar-baby act), she didn't see any reason
to hide her brains; she expected to run for the presidency as her
husband's full and equal partner; she saw no need to prate of cookery and coiffures (no matter how often she nervously changed
her hair).

In the days of "Elect Hillary's Husband in '92," Hillary Rodham
Clinton had adamantly refused the obligatory Stepford wife impersonation, the fake flirtatiousness that makes political wives seem
safe, the willingness to *pretend* to be the power behind the throne.
When America was not ready for her—preferring the duplicitous
southern charms of Mrs. Dole—Hillary temporarily retreated into
pastels and pearls. Duplicity in women still makes America comfortable, straightforwardness does not.

So Hillary Clinton fell victim to America's discomfort with
powerful women—or so I originally argued before I myself had
been handled by Hillary and her handlers. But given my later run-
ins with this unholy alliance, I began to think that HRC's bum rap
had a lot to do with her own flair for shooting herself in the foot.

Not that I expected access to be easy. Even when I started researching Hillary Clinton, I knew that both Clintons were press-
shy after the beatings they had endured at the hands of various
members of the press. But since I was determined to defend HRC
against her detractors, I began to approach various friends of both
Clintons with an eye to getting an audience with Hillary herself—a
full-scale semiprivate interview—with only the requisite spin doc-

tors in attendance. Armed with testimonials to my bona fides from such Clinton pals as Judy Collins and Letty Pogrebin, I wrote to HRC's press people and top personal assistant, enclosing the sympathetic essay I'd already written and mentioning the publication assignment. There followed a merry chase in which I was tested for my sincerity and tenacity, interrogated by telephone by a series of inquisitors—from Lisa Caputo, Hillary's then-press liaison, to Melanne Verveer, her personal factotum, to various young staffers in charge of scheduling. I was asked everything from "What do you plan to write?" to "How much time do you need with the first lady?" to "How do you propose to tell the truth in *that* paper?" (The London *Sunday Times,* I should have known, was one of the first to blow the whistle on Bill Clinton's panty raids.) My assignment caused no little consternation among Hillary's handlers, who wanted to know early on how I could possibly write "an honest article" for that appalling outlet.* It was not exactly true that the U.S. media failed in their duty to question Clinton's "character," but the *Sunday Times* got there first. This hardly made my job easier. When I explained to Lisa Caputo that I had already thoroughly researched the first lady and only needed some time to talk to her woman-to-woman and get a *feel* for her personality, red flags went up all around. I had the sense I couldn't have said anything worse.

"I don't usually do this," I told Lisa Caputo. "I'm not a member of 'the press,' but a novelist and a poet."

---

*Now (2006), Hillary and Murdoch are chums and even the *New York Post* no longer trashes her.

"We *know* who you are," said Caputo ominously.

"Have you read my piece in the *New York Observer*? I'm *very* sympathetic to the first lady. I think she's taking the heat for all of us, for all strong women. . . . I want to show her as a worthy successor to Eleanor Roosevelt." Something must have clicked in Caputo's head with the magic words "Eleanor Roosevelt," because it was then that I was scheduled for a brief "rope line" interview with the first lady.

Even this mini-interview took more than a month of planning. Lisa Caputo and I spoke not less than five times to discuss whether I should see Hillary when she received an honorary degree at a college in New Jersey or I should attend a Democratic fund-raiser in New York "with other prominent women." After much discussion, it became clear that the latter was the preferred venue. So Caputo arranged for me to attend one of Hillary Clinton's campaign appearances before the New York Women's Democratic Leadership Conference.

I arrived at Madison Square Garden early, was checked out by the gatekeepers, found to be kosher, and handed over to another Hillary handler. There ensued a half hour of confusion about where I should await the first lady and her minions, which elevator or stairs I should take upstairs, and who would escort me. I crossed and recrossed the arena at aerobic speed, dutifully following my bustling and officious guides. Finally I was hand delivered to an upstairs confab room, complete with central bar, to await, with those "other prominent women," the arrival of the first and second ladies.

Rumors of "the coming" floated across the foot-weary crowd. The so-called prominent women had been drinking for an hour or more and were afraid to detour to the toilet for fear of missing the annunciation. Eventually there was a palpable stir in the room. "The first lady is coming!" someone said—and the words were echoed on all sides of the now sardinized space. Would she come from the east or the west? (The room had two entrances, and the faithful were gathered around both.) Rumors flew.

"She'll be coming in *there*!" said a source. "No—*there*!" said another. And finally Hillary and Tipper were glimpsed, surrounded by ladies-in-waiting. And there we all were—ladies-in-waiting ourselves. But our waiting appeared to be over at last. We jostled forward for a better view.

Cheers, whistles, catcalls. Tipper Gore and Hillary Rodham Clinton climbed the raised speakers' platform, while a factotum checked the mike. Tipper Gore was fulsomely introduced over the roar of the crowd. She seemed as warm and fuzzy as Hillary Clinton seemed tense and chilly. With her plump blond, American good looks, Tipper is everyone's Girl Scout den mother, everyone's first-grade teacher, everyone's favorite sister-in-law. She is so normal-as-blueberry-pie and corny-as-Kansas-in-August that she's a hard act to follow. After a short Tipperish speech, full of thanks for the organizers and praise for the first lady, Hillary came on.

It's impossible to watch Hillary Clinton work an audience without being aware of the sheer effort she puts into everything she does. I admire effort. But in politics, effortlessness, a sense of *sprezzatura* (that charming Italian word for the art of making the difficult look easy) is *more* valuable. Hillary spoke well; she always speaks well. She always says things I thoroughly agree with. But in those days she had trouble seeming warm. She was to become warmer and warmer as she grew more powerful—an understandable transformation. Even then, she turned the audience on with references to all their political heroines—the suffragists and Eleanor Roosevelt, in particular—and she convinced us of her erudition and her staunch feminism. But she did not *then* convince us of her everydayness, which was the gift Tipper Gore so abundantly possessed. Hillary Rodham Clinton was always in control.

After her speech, Hillary was led to meet her adoring acolytes, of whom I was one. The Hillary handlers hustled us all into a receiving line behind a rope, and those who had prearranged audiences were told exactly where in line to wait. Secret Service men briskly patrolled the rope lest one of the pilgrims get too close. Hillary went along the "rope line" briefed by her personal assistant and her press secretary about the identity of each of the faithful. Waiting for her, I felt like an idiot. In my time I have hung out with plenty of contemporary icons: Nobel laureates, rock stars more famous than Jesus, movie idols who can't walk unmolested in the streets, politicians in and out of high office. But waiting for Hillary,

I felt diminished. What I had wanted was to know the woman be-hind the mask. That, after all, is my specialty. And here I was being given only a brief glance at the mask—gleaming with many coats of lacquer. I was determined to use even this brief audience as best I could, but the glazed eyes, the fixed smile, the rather too firm handshake, could only remind me of myself in zombie mode in the midst of a twenty-five-city book tour.

What could I say? I admire you so? I need more time with you? I empathize with all the shit you're taking? I said all that and more as we clasped hands and I used the trick so often used on me by fans: I would not let her hand go.

"Call the White House to set up more time," she said, turning to her drudge, who most certainly *heard*. And then she was gone, shaking the tiny hand of a small African-American girl, greeting a fund-raiser here, a prominent woman there—down the line toward her destiny, beginning with the big speech she was to give for the Democratic hoi polloi in the downstairs arena.

It was over. In desperation, I cornered Caputo.

"The first lady has agreed to more time," I told her. Caputo looked incredulous. Then she looked at Hillary and back at me.

"Call me next week. We're off to three more states tomorrow."

"Lisa," I said, "I need to *travel* with the first lady, hang with her. I know her *policies* by heart. I've read her book. I'll go with you starting tonight. Find room for me." I must have been pathetic.

"The plane's too small. The president gets the big planes. There's no room."

Does it comfort me that Caputo "resigned" two months later? Not much. The problem, of course, was mine not Hillary's. I had spent my life in a room writing. I didn't know the rules of political stalking. And I was green about journalism and access. I was also stupidly vain about my possible use to Hillary. She didn't *need* me—especially when I was writing for a U.K. publication. I was terribly naïve.

Downstairs in the main arena, thousands of women had assembled to hear the first lady's official speech. Many had been brought in buses hired by labor unions and New York City and State Democratic clubs. A rainbow of races—working-class women in their Sunday best. I was shepherded to the VIP section and settled in among the prominent, the press, the Big Donors—all the while thinking how hypocritical it was to have this separation between plebes and aristos. In a democracy, such division rankles even if one is the supposed beneficiary of it.

The glorious Jessye Norman sailed onto the stage in a silk caftan. Was she going to sing with Judy Collins? What a sensory experience that would be! Not unaccountably, Jessye Norman was there only to *introduce* Judy Collins, who graciously said that she would go anywhere to be introduced by the opera diva. Judy, who is my dear friend, spoke about the history of the song "Bread and Roses." Then she sang it. The audience cheered.

By the time HRC spoke, we had all been there—mostly waiting—for at least two hours. And her speech was worth the wait. She made frequent references to the history of the women's suffrage

movement and predicted that we would see its ultimate fulfillment
in the next presidential election (that prophecy proved wrong even
in 1996). It was a speech designed to please both the rank and file
and the intellectual elite. There was something for everyone—
union members, academic feminists, fund-raisers. And indeed,
with Hillary's help, Bill Clinton was, at first, the major beneficiary
of the gender gap in American politics. He was also, of course,
aided by the Republican Party, which continued to tailor its party
platform to please the powerful Christian Coalition on the issue of
reproductive rights. It was entirely clear from Hillary's speech that
the Democrats were going all out to woo women voters. And they
succeeded—at least in the 1996 presidential election. The backlash
of 2000 (not to mention the vote-stealing) changed everything.

I went home from the Women's Democratic Leadership Conference having been promised more "quality time" with the first
lady and determined to pin down the promised opportunity. I
called and called and *called* the White House. I spoke to Friends of
the Clintons and Friends of Friends of the Clintons. I did everything but contribute $650,000 to the presidential campaign, which
I guess was then the price of sleeping in the Lincoln Bedroom.

After that I was to endure another month of delays by sched-
ulers, another month of being told to call next week and the week
after and the week after. In the process, I heard repeatedly, from
Clinton supporters and strategists whom I interviewed, that Hillary
Rodham Clinton's people had a deadly knack for turning acolytes
into enemies. At that time, they truly could not distinguish friend

from foe. Was the first lady so rattled by criticism that she hid when she should have been frank, and locked herself up when she should have been candid? Was she a control freak who feared her admirers as much as her detractors?

Whatever the answer to these questions, she is now, as New York's senator and the leading Democratic candidate, a totally different politician. Relaxed, funny, sincere, caring, competent—she is a charming and warm speaker. Experience does help. And now she has experience. Few women leaders get the opportunity to evolve as she has. Her spectacular growth is impressive. It also shows us how important it is that women be allowed to get political experience.

Rereading my Hillary Rodham Clinton file before writing about her in the past, I was struck by the great number of times she had gone public with her desire to know why she was failing to get through the barrage of hostility put up by the press. Several times she convened important editors and columnists and asked them why she was so badly treated in print and what she could do to remedy it. Either they were not candid with her or she did not listen. Or she may have lacked the born diplomat's talent for making other people feel important. People used to come away from encounters convinced their noses have been rubbed in the mud. I certainly did. Now Hillary is much better at having her audience love her.

Was her past awkwardness because, on some level, Hillary Rodham Clinton didn't realize *how* important she was politically and historically, and thus left the management of access to amateurs? I came to think so after months and months of dealing with "her people." Chaos and contradiction were rife. One hand didn't seem to know what the other hand was doing. After being promised more time by Hillary *herself,* I was cut off at the knees by her staff. Apparently they had been so scarred (and scared) by the attacks on the first lady that they could not distinguish honest enthusiasm from journalistic seduction. None of which would even be worth remarking on if Hillary Clinton had not always beaten her breast publicly about her puzzlement regarding the hostility of the press.

Why didn't somebody from the State Department give her a quick course in diplomacy? Why did the people whose job it was to present her to the public do such a lackluster job? And why did the Clinton campaign decide to "disappear Hillary" (as Russell Baker pointed out in the *New York Times*) for most of the summer of the second presidential campaign? When she returned, she was a softer, newer Hillary, wearing nursery colors and saying "my husband" every thirty seconds, but we found it just as hard to believe this incarnation. The trouble was, she had reinvented herself too many times—and what works for rock stars (Madonna, for example) doesn't work for first ladies. We want our rock stars bizarre and our first ladies ordinary. HRC will never be ordinary if she lives to be 127.

This kaleidoscope of Hillary images and the frequently self-destructive behavior of the first lady are particularly regrettable because the Clinton administrations and the Clinton marriage are both historic. As a couple, the Clintons raise major issues about political and sexual politics. They are the first couple to have been elected president of the United States jointly. It is clear that without HRC's participation, Bill Clinton would have gone right down the Gary Hart sewer. Because his wife stood by him on that first Barbara Walters interview in 1992, because he did not exactly deny "causing pain in the marriage," while Hillary held his hand supportively, the first Clinton campaign was able to weather and rise above what had been killing sexual crises for other presidential candidates. The Clintons have been sailing above one sexual crisis after another ever since. Their marriage only appears to be stronger while America appears ever more blasé about sexual scandals.

In fact, this became the pattern in the second administration. Hillary emerged as Bill's protector and crisis manager. Phase-three Hillary was the twenty-first-century wife who finally silences her detractors.

Before Monica Lewinsky, public adulterers were doomed forever. Even the "little woman" could not save them. Without Hillary Clinton's forgiveness, Bill Clinton's sex addiction would surely have sunk him. But because of her fierce protectiveness, his postpresidency even triumphed. Hillary single-handedly revolutionized the political marriage. America has even seemed to grow up sexually because of Hillary.

Two for the price of one. Elect one, get one free. Hillary was originally the freebie. Never before in American politics had any couple campaigned this way—or served this way. The very American ideal of a "power couple" that add up to more than the sum of their parts was perfected during the Clinton presidency. After the unveiling of Monica Lewinsky and Kathleen Willey, Hillary

Clinton claimed even more power in the marriage. She became Bill Clinton's indispensable character witness. And even though nobody believed his character was any good (sexually anyway), Hillary loomed larger than ever. During the spring 1998 African junket, she loomed like an ancient mother goddess.

In all three phases of her public incarnation, Bill Clinton had the best of Hillary: She validated his feminist credentials with the electorate while he remained free to go on being a Dogpatch Bob Packwood—supporting womankind in public, groping individual women in private.

The deal of the Clinton marriage fascinates me, and I know it fascinates many. It is a marriage that reflects our time better than any political marriage I can think of. Clearly Hillary Rodham Clinton figured out in law school that if the time was not yet ripe for a woman president, it was likely to be ripe for a guy as driven and smart and personable as Bill Clinton. And she could be his chief adviser, patron (she made the money—with no small help from his political position), cheering and booing sections, and disciplinarian.

However much she may have warmed to his southern charm, no matter how much she may have loved him, his political ambition turned her on just as much. Not that there is anything wrong with a marital deal. You might even say that the more things bind a couple together, the better their chance of staying together. But theirs is a radical deal for an American political marriage. Hillary has never staked out highway beautification as her bailiwick (as did Lyndon Baines Johnson's wife, Lady Bird) or crusaded to put warning stickers on rock albums (once the one-woman campaign of Second Lady Tipper Gore). Hillary Clinton claimed the stage with top *policy* issues. This audacity dazzled at first. But then, why *should* a first lady stick to so-called women's issues? Hillary was always policy-minded, always loath to be ghettoized ideologically. She was always far more serious than Bill, even in college and law school.

He was a people pleaser. She was a woman who put intellect first, which meant automatically that many men—and women—would not be pleased by her. Probably one of the reasons she hooked up with Bill Clinton was because he was the first man who seemed to not be afraid of her brains, but rather challenged and attracted by them. He was determined "to marry the smartest girl in the class," as an old Arkansas buddy of his told Roger Morris, the author of *Partners in Power.* He was sick of beauty queens. "It was Hillary or nobody," he informed his mother, cautioning her to be nice to Hillary when he brought her home to meet the family in 1972. Though Bill apparently had nostalgia—and a use—for those beauty queens after he and Hillary were married, Hillary's cleverness turned him on more. She excited him intellectually. I'm sure she still does.

One of the difficulties of being a smart, driven woman is finding men who are turned on by brains. Hillary's initial attachment to Bill probably had a lot to do with the excitement of finding such a fearless man. Later, it seems, she had invested so much of herself in the marriage that she wasn't willing to throw it all away, even in the face of his compulsive, repeated infidelities.

Here is the strangeness of the public image put forward by this revolutionary presidential couple. They were elected as a team, deliberately stressing their teammate spirit in the first campaign, but they have absolutely refused to make the *terms* of their marriage public, except to admit early and later that "he caused pain." It is the inconsistency of this position that accounts for a great deal of the confusion. If you vote for a couple, you feel entitled to know about the bonds that hold them together. But Hillary and Bill insist those bonds are private. People resent their determination to have it both ways. But how on earth can the Clintons own up to the details of Bill Clinton's sex life?

The more you read about Bill Clinton, the more it becomes clear that he *did* use his position to facilitate affairs and that women were not as unwilling as they protested they were. Women love players and then we love to denounce them. Let's admit it. Men like Bill Clinton turn us on—but knowing we can't really possess them, we have to attack them verbally. They make us feel utterly powerless. Nobody likes that.

Bill Clinton was a player long before Monica Lewinsky came along and forced the nation to look at his philandering. But can we really scream sexual harassment when it seems clear that Bill Clinton, like Jack Kennedy, was always surrounded by adoring females? Isn't sex one of the perks of power for men? Isn't this why the role of alpha male is so appealing? I find Bill Clinton sexy myself, not that I would ever act out my fantasies with him. His combination of boyishness and lasciviousness can be adorable. We all have fantasies of saving him from himself—getting him to treat his sex addiction and grow up—like Warren Beatty with Annette Bening, or Mr. Rochester with Jane Eyre. In the eighteenth century they used to say a reformed rake makes the best husband. I doubt we have progressed much beyond that. Look at Jack Nicholson's character in *Something's Gotta Give*. (I myself would have taken the young, adoring doctor, but Hollywood is still behind the times where women's evolution is concerned.)

I assume that Bill Clinton's erotic life is no better and no worse than any other male politician's. At least his legislative and executive initiatives are consistently pro-woman and pro-choice. Like all of us, he's a mixed bag. I appreciate his humanity, with all its contradictions—contradictions are, after all, the soul of humanity. Of course, I don't approve of Bill Clinton's piggish behavior with women, but since I assume the piggishness is merely the norm among male politicians, I'm glad his political agenda is feminist. If that seems like a copy of his own wife's take on him, it tells you why I feel enormous empathy for Hillary Clinton. She is in the same bind as many strong, intelligent women. She has made her deal with the devil, and now she must live with it.

Hillary Clinton's history is full of paradoxes. A baby boomer who grew up in a straight-arrow Methodist Republican family in an all-white, upwardly mobile suburb of Chicago, she became a left-leaning Democrat at Wellesley. At Yale Law, she was studious, solitary, solemn, given to wearing flannel shirts and thick glasses, noted for her brilliance and hard work. (Remember, this was the seventies—that halcyon and *brief* feminist period.) Her mother had compromised with life and did not want Hillary to do the same—a familiar mother-daughter story (it is also mine). Her father was stern, tight with money, and difficult to please.

Imagine a girl like that winning the good ol' boy who has been dating beauty queens! It gives you an idea of how much his "locking in on her" (as one old friend put it) must have meant to her. Hillary Rodham Clinton remains an appealing figure to me because her life shows the strange compromises gifted women make. She has already changed her politics, drifted away from her parents' reactionary Methodist attitudes. What lay ahead were other complete makeovers. Looks, name, ideals—everything would have to change for the greater glory of Bill Clinton and the pillow power he bestowed.

If Hillary Clinton used to come across as angry and unsettled, as constantly remaking her image, it was probably the case. How could she *not* be angry in Arkansas? Like an ancient Chinese noblewoman with bound feet, she had to deform even her anatomy to get where she needed to go. She hobbled her own fierce ambitions to transplant herself to Arkansas and defend his ambitions. She temporarily gave up her maiden name, reneged on her end-of-the-sixties indifference to female fashion, and compromised her passion for social justice and her native disgust with hypocrisy. Then, while he used her feminism as a shield to cover himself and his philandering, he proceeded to make a mockery of everything she believed in. Since he had always been clear about his ambition to be a top

Arkansas politician and then president, his path never changed. Hers changed constantly—and with it her hair, her eyes, her name. At some point she must have had to decide that all these changes were worth it. How else can a smart woman justify such metamorphoses? Hillary had to recommit herself over and over again to life with Bill. No wonder she demanded certain paybacks—like running health care reform and his public life. She would have felt demolished otherwise. One sympathizes with her strength to *make* demands. But the power struggle of the marriage inevitably impacted the power politics of the nation, and that is what was so radically new about the Clinton presidency.

Now, as senator, Hillary is far more relaxed and affable. She's grown and so has her husband. Good for them. I admire people who can change, who refuse to be stuck in old patterns. Nothing transforms a couple like the deaths of parents, and nothing makes a couple evolve like surviving infidelities. Not to mention having a daughter and watching her grow to womanhood. I like the Clintons more for having changed with all these changes.

George Bush the First used his first day in the presidency to publicly congratulate antiabortion marchers—even while intimating that First Lady Barbara Bush did not agree with him. George Bush the Second went further. He hobbled our choices at home while prating hypocritically of the rights of women in Afghanistan and Iraq.

No such stand for Bill Clinton. He and Hillary were joined at the hip intellectually, however much stress their marriage might be under. Their presidency redefined public and private. That is why it is so important historically. Both Clintons' policies are in lock-step, even though their marriage may have been chronically on the rocks. And as for Dubya and Laura, you cannot but think that she thinks he's a dunce but shuts up about it. She has her own friends, her daughters, and her own life. She probably tells him to pretend he reads. And he's smart enough to listen to her.

"We cared deeply about a lot of the same things," Hillary told an interviewer for the campaign film *The Man From Hope* in 1992. This revealing quote, edited out of the final film, makes the deal of the marriage clear. "Bill and I are really bound together in part be-cause we believe we have an obligation to give something back and to be a part of making life better for other people," Hillary went on (as quoted by Bob Woodward in *The Choice*). The tragedy of their story is that such idealism *had* to be replaced by a ruthless commit-ment to politics, and this deformation of principle clearly came much harder to her than to him.

Hillary Clinton's image problem always had several root causes. One was undoubtedly the awkwardness of her early staff. Another was the undeniable factor that there is no way for a smart woman to *be* public without being seen as a treacherous Lady Macbeth figure or a bitch goddess (our failing more than Hillary's). But the deepest problem was that Hillary at first came across on television as cold and controlled. She rejiggered her image so often, retailored it so much to please the spin doctors, that it came to seem inauthentic.

Television is an essentially crude medium. It is not much good for presenting ideas well; it tends to oversimplify and to turn subtle

issues into either corn mush or screaming tabloid headlines. But it
is a usually reliable litmus paper for personalities: Warm personalities like Bill Clinton's come across as warm; cool personalities like
Hillary Clinton's public persona sometimes come across as cold.

The truth is that Bill Clinton *is* what he is—warm, tear-jerkingly
populist, dying to please, woo, and pander. He's a born salesman,
"riding on a smile," in the immortal words of Arthur Miller.
Hillary Clinton, meanwhile, is a brainy girl trying to look feminine; a law school grind trying to look like the happy housewife, a
fierce feminist who at first submerged her identity in her husband's
ambitions. It didn't add up—too many contradictions—which is
why we never quite believed it, at least at first. We kept expecting
Lady Macbeth to reappear, rubbing the blood from her hands. I
love the way Hillary has grown as senator. It shows us the way.
Experience *does* count. And as long as women can't get political experience, we can't evolve.

We should empathize with Hillary Clinton rather than criticize
her. She is a perfect example of why life is so tough for brainy
women. The rapid transformations of her public image revealed
the terrible contortions expected of all bright women. Look pretty
but be (secretly) smart. Conform in public; cry in private. Make the
money, but don't seem to be aggressive. Swallow everything your
husband asks you to swallow but *somehow* keep your own identity.
Hillary Clinton demonstrated just how impossible all these conflicting demands were to fulfill. And the television camera acted

like a lie detector, showing her original deep discomfort with all her forced metamorphoses.

For Hillary and my generation, "no single act came to symbolize so vividly her role and sacrifice as the surrender of her maiden name," as Roger Morris pointed out in *Partners in Power*.

Morris told the story in which Clinton aide Jim Blair suggested that the only way to make peace with Arkansas's voting hillbillies and white trash was to "have a ceremony on the steps of the Capitol where Bill puts his booted foot firmly on [Hillary's] throat, yanks her up by the hair, and says, 'Woman, you're going to go by my last name and that's that.' . . . Then wave the flag, sing a few hymns and be done with it."

A humorous story, but not so humorous if you are Hillary Rodham Clinton. Refusing to be submerged in the identity of wife is a burning issue for our generation. A woman can give up on this outwardly and continue to fume inwardly. Emma Goldman once said that in politics you have to be either "a dunce or a rogue." Hillary is certainly no dunce, and her early discomfort with her public persona showed that she was, admirably enough, a reluctant rogue. The trail of wrecked lives she and Bill Clinton left behind them— from Lani Guinier's to Vince Foster's to Monica Lewinsky's— cannot be lost on her.

Hillary used to be a seething mass of contradictions, so perhaps that was why she dared let none of her feelings show. She gave off an aura of discipline and ferocious tenacity in which it was impossible to glimpse the human being beneath the mask. All those stories of Hillary's breaking into tears or having fits of rage in private after perfect composure in public seem wholly believable. But the Hillary of today has earned her poise and is comfortable in her skin. She has earned it many times over.

What is familiar about this picture? A woman is sacrificed to her husband's ambitions. Her personality is deformed. She takes almost all the flak in the press while he gets away with murder. You might almost say that she is taking the punishment for him—and for all women who step outside the lines prescribed for paper-doll political wives. Hillary Rodham Clinton looks more to me like Joan of Arc every day. She accepted being burned as a witch week in, week out, so her husband could rise in the polls. She often played the role of the scapegoat half of the Clinton duo, the rear end that got whipped so the smiling Clinton head could triumph. She was Iphigenia sacrificed for a propitious wind, Alcestis going across the Styx instead of her husband. She was the woman who endured humiliation and saved the marriage so that Bill Clinton could flourish. Bill Clinton owes Hillary. Big. *The only difference between him and other guys is that he seems to know it.*

During the ongoing sexual scandal of the second term, Hillary Clinton grew to her full potential. Instead of looking foolish for defending Bill against charges of philandering, she looked like the only one in power who had a sense of proportion. It was as if *she* were president and he first husband. The strength and tenacity were clearly hers. She appeared to be supplying his backbone. And it was at that moment that Hillary's fortunes definitively turned.

As the president appeared less and less capable of impulse control, the first lady rose in our estimation. We still didn't fully understand the terms of the marriage, but it was clear she was the one who held it all together. The strength of one woman had never impacted on our country more. Now, as senator, she has triumphed. Her hard work and wisdom have never been clearer. Yet she carries them off with humor and rare serenity. She has walked through the fire and emerged untouchable.

I predict that Hillary Rodham Clinton is eventually going to make as much of a difference as her role model, Eleanor Roosevelt. By acting as a lightning rod for all of us, she has fully expanded the possible roles for American women. Perhaps her position remains controversial, but it may end up changing the course of women's history. If America eventually has a woman president, the credit will be, in large part, Hillary's. She is getting us ready to accept female leaders who don't hide their brains. She has gotten us ready to accept women who talk back in public. She has single-handedly revolutionized the political marriage.

I want to say, *Bravo, Hillary; you're the latest incarnation of Ms. Liberty.* Thank you for enduring the slings and arrows of your outrageous fortune. Because of you, someday—as in Britain, Ireland, India, and Israel—even backward America will be able to elect a woman chief of state. It may even (Goddess willing) be you!

A NOTE FROM THE AUTHOR

This essay has gone through many incarnations. Originally, I wrote about Hillary for the New York Observer, *then for* The Sunday Times, *then again for the* New York Observer, *then for* What Do Women Want, *my book of essays, and now for a new edition of my essay book.*

During that time, Hillary evolved from a controversial first lady into a popular and productive senator from New York, then a presidential candidate.

The vicious criticism of her, however, has never stopped. It has only taken new forms—often from women.

In the beginning she was trashed by the predictable female journalists who rose to power by attacking other women—a time-honored strategy. What gives with these dames? (I will not name them. They know who they are.) Don't they know how hard it is to be a public woman? Is it the Queen Bee syndrome made famous by Claire Booth Luce? "I got up here. Now watch me kick any climber who tries to get to the top with me"? This is an old-fashioned shtick. Today's young feminists know that collaboration, not *competition, is the name of the game. Women need to support other women and criticize only with affection and concern. Of course we can disagree, but we must disagree with respect, not slander. There's room for all of us at the top—not just the Queen Bee.*

But in the years since I started observing HRC and researching her, I have come to understand that she and her partner in power, Bill, are brilliant at controlling access. You don't get to say hi without meeting them at fund-raisers. So far I have met Hillary at several fund-raisers and she has always been most cordial since I parted with my money. My childhood pal, Alan Patricof, chair of her finance committee, must see a lot more of her. The Clintons, like all politicians, need money. And they weren't born with it. So they must court the rich—one of the major flaws of our political system.

Sadly, our political system favors those born with money. Look where it got us with George W. Bush! And his father! And his grandfather! (See Kitty Kelley's The Family for the complete history of those hypocrites.) But Dick Cheney, who was born middle class, may be even worse. So money is not alone the problem.

The last fund-raiser I attended was Hillary's birthday party at Tavern on the Green on October 26, 2006. I'm sure I'll attend many more before 2008.

Hillary greeted me warmly, but I'm sure I'll have to give far more generously if I want more time. And why not? She has no leisure. She must plan what time she has carefully. What does she need with me? If her political fortunes rise even further, she'll get glowing press. If they fall, people will attack. It's human nature. We love winners and have contempt for losers.

The Hillary birthday was part of a weeklong Clinton Cashonalia. Even the faithful claimed to the New York Times that they were "Clinton-ed out."

And I was a pisher with my two-thousand-dollar contribution. I tried to get my writer friends to come and make a writers' table, but not one of them had the requisite dough. Cultivating the rich has never been *my forte, but then, I'm not a politician. My tendency is to love those who are richer in words than money. I've always been out of step in America in loving poets more than politicians.*

Still, the birthday was really interesting. My husband and I sat at a table with accomplished women—doctors, lawyers, and political fund-raisers.

We had fun. We knew lots of people. And the sheer numbers were astounding. Bill Clinton looked sort of dazed when I said hello to him. And Hillary was warm as toast. She has really grown in office. And I . . . I knew I wasn't there for truth, justice, and the American way. Still, I wish Hillary well. And I plan to work for her presidential campaign. All the smart women I know say she can't possibly win. But she has surprised us before and I know she will again. Her capacity for growth is what I admire most about her.

Writing an autobiography and making a spiritual will are almost the same.

—SHOLEM ALEICHEM

All we know of love comes from our mothers. Yet we have buried that love so deep that we may not even know where it comes from. If we have been wounded and have grown scar tissue over our hearts, we confuse the scar tissue with the heart itself, forgetting the wound that caused it.

My first memories of my mother come from the year my younger sister was born. I do not remember *ever* being the center of the universe, because when I came into the family, my older sister—four and a half to my zero—was already there.

I am four and a half when my younger sister is born, and my mother lies in bed like a queen receiving guests, children, parents, friends. She is beautiful and brown-eyed, with reddish-brown hair, and she wears a padded silk bed jacket over a silk nightgown. The women in my family wear bed jackets only in times of great ceremony—childbirth, illness, death—and we rarely spend daylight hours in bed. We are all so energetic that we clean up after our housekeepers, word-process for our secretaries, and instruct caterers in how to cook—though cooking is not exactly a family talent. So if my mother is in bed wearing a bed jacket, it *must* be important. And it is: Daughter number three has just been born.

The baby has a cold caught in the hospital, and four-and-a-half-year-old Erica has ringworm caught from her best friend's cat. She is forbidden to touch the baby—who is guarded by a dragonlike baby nurse. Erica feels contagious to the point of leprosy, so superfluous, she thinks no one will even *care* if she runs away. At four and a half, she can only conceive of running away to her best friend's house, on the floor below—but that is where she *caught* the ringworm in the first place. (In later days she might have run around the corner to the candy store—though every time she did *that* she ended up using one of her sweaty nickels to call home from the musty, cigarette-smelling phone booth. Invariably the adults wheedled her into saying where she was. She wanted to be found so badly she always *told*. She let them convince her to come home, though it meant crossing the street like a big girl.)

So she stays in the apartment, a rambling dilapidated West Side palace whose double-height front windows give north light—many of the people in the family are painters.

Erica's mother will not remain in bed wearing that quilted bed jacket for long. Pretty soon she will be up and running around, doing a "quick sketch" of the infant in her crib, telling the nurse how to care for the baby, stuffing the chicken to be roasted, and cutting together the butter and flour for the crust to enclose the apple pie she has told the housekeeper to make. Then she will dash to ballet school or the park or the ice-skating rink at Rockefeller Center with her two "big girls."

But the time—a day? two days? a week?—her mother stays in bed seems endless to four-and-a-half-year-old Erica. Especially after the dragon screams at her: *"Don't you* dare *touch the baby with that hand!!!"*

Baby Erica has never forgiven her mother for this abandonment. Pointless to explain that the obliviousness of the baby nurse to the teachings of Freud was hardly her mother's fault. Useless to say that the baby nurse was probably a poor soul who earned her meager living going from household to household, from baby to baby, without hope of a household or a baby of her own. It was an abandonment, and abandonments are, by definition, always your mother's fault. In my grown-up mind, I am strong and successful. In my baby mind, I am an abandoned child.

These are merely some of *my* memories of my younger sister's entrance into the world. Surely my mother's are entirely different. My older sister's are surely different, too. And as for the baby, what does she remember of those days except what we tell her? But somewhere in the most primitive part of my brain lies the fierce sense of betrayal my baby sister's birth must have provoked. I have never quite forgiven my mother for it. Even after years of lying-down analysis and sitting-up therapy, I still, at times, feel like that abandoned four-and-a-half-year-old with ringworm all over her arms and torso.

My mother and I have long since reached a truce. She turned eighty-six this year, and I have endured and surpassed my fear of fifty, so we are very tender with each other, like glass unicorns who might break each other's horns by kissing too passionately.

Now that I have a nineteen-year-old daughter myself, I understand all my mother's difficulties raising us. I have even been moved to fall to my knees before my mother and say: "You are my heroine simply for *surviving* three daughters!"

My daughter now rails at me as I once railed at my mother. When Molly monologues, sparing no one with her barbed wit, my mother and I look at each other and smile.

"Tell her you're sorry you were such a *dreadful* mother," my mother says, her voice dripping with irony. "And *apologize*." I even *listen* to my mother now.

"Molly," I say, "I only did the best I could. I'm sure I made plenty of mistakes. I *apologize*."

"Yeah, yeah, yeah," says Molly, impatient. She looks at me with the sheer contempt that is grounded in excessive love. To myself I may sometimes be a four-and-a-half-year-old with ringworm, but to her I am Kali with a necklace of skulls, or the giant statue of

Athena that once stood in the Parthenon, or snake-headed Medusa guarding the Golden Fleece. Just wait till *you* have a daughter, I think. But I am too wise to say it. And my mother and I grin at each other like co-conspirators. Raising a daughter requires superhuman patience. Raising a daughter is definitely tougher than writing.

I recently published a novel about mothers and daughters. In *Inventing Memory,* I traced the mother-daughter daisy chain through four generations, showing how we are shaped by both our mothers' yearnings and our own desperate need to break free of them. The dynamic between these two powerful forces is largely what molds our lives as women. Yes, our fathers and grandfathers matter, but what we learn from our mothers and grandmothers stays in the bone marrow. It surfaces as soon as you become a mother yourself. And what you sow as a daughter, you will inevitably reap as a mother.

My mother was brilliant in setting me free. Or maybe I was tenacious in demanding my freedom. With mothers and daughters you never really know *whose* is the initiative. We are so interwoven, so symbiotic, that you cannot always tell the mother from the daughter, the dancer from the dance.

Of course, I barely understood any of this about my mother and me in my teens or twenties or even thirties. I was locked in mortal combat with her, denouncing her to her face and behind her back, pillorying her in my novels—even as they betrayed my passionate love for her. Of course, I thought I was the first daughter in history to have these tumultuous feelings. Of course, I thought my mother was oblivious of my needs, hypocritical in her life and in her art, and desperately in need of enlightenment by me. I must have been insufferable. But she greeted most of my excesses with love. And it was her love that set me free.

For how is the gift of freedom bestowed *except* by love? By never letting me doubt that I was loved, my mother fueled my books, my life, even my own parenting. Though I was fiercely independent and refused to take financial support from my parents after college graduation, I always knew I *could* go home again. When I wrote painful things about my mother in my novels, she simply said: "I never *read* your novels, because I consider you a poet first." I knew I could write whatever I had to write and still be loved.

My mother had a benign relationship with her mother but a tortured one with her father. He was a brilliant artist, who was a relentless taskmaster to his two painter daughters. And because he considered my mother the more talented of them, he drove her mercilessly. He pushed her so hard that after she married my father, she escaped into the primal pleasure of having babies. By the time her art surfaced again, in middle age, she had three amazons— us—to distract her. It cannot have been easy to go on painting and also mother us all. But she did it. She still paints nearly every day of her life.

In our house, draftsmanship was held to my grandfather's relentless standards. You had to draw from life before venturing into the world of the imagination. You had to master charcoal and conté crayon before indulging in color. You had to do hundreds of still lifes before you could draw "the model." And you had to be able to draw a creditable nude before you dared paint people with clothes on. I found all this regimentation so daunting that I gave up painting. From the age of eleven, I had spent every Saturday at the Art Students League in New York, drawing alongside professional artists and holding myself to such impossible standards that I always felt like an abject failure. Though I painted all through high school and much of college, I relinquished painting with great relief when, in my teens, I discovered the obsession to write. Being an artist was too fraught with conflicting feelings for me.

I needed something to call my own. Writing belonged to me alone, as painting never could.

So I empathize with my mother's struggle to enter her father's profession. She never stopped painting, but she expressed her deep ambivalence by not promoting her work publicly. She was afraid to compete, afraid that she might in fact succeed and "kill" her father. As with so many women, her courtship of failure had a purpose: to please a man.

My daughter, Molly, may well be the bravest of our amazon clan. At nineteen, she is already writing her first novel. She reads me chapters every few nights, and in her fledgling book my role is clear: I am the mommy monster.

"Mommy, I hope you don't mind," my daughter mischievously says, "but I've made you a total narcissist and a hopeless alcoholic in my novel. . . ." She laughs provocatively, hoping to get me mad. I think for a minute, remembering what my friend Fay Weldon, the

British novelist, says about teenagers: Never react to *anything* they say except with a neutral "I see" or "Hmm." Teenagers exist to provoke their parents. Your only defense against them is not to be provoked.

It's true that I don't *recognize* myself in the character Molly calls "my mother" in her blisteringly funny first fiction. But who am I to censor her? If *I* don't understand that fiction is not fact, who the hell will? I've been using *my* family as comic material for twenty-five years—how can I deny that basic right to my daughter?

"You're sure you're not insulted, Mommy?" Molly asks, hoping I am.

"I'll laugh all the way to the bank with you," I say, hugging her.

In a family of artists, you come to understand early that what you have at home is what you paint. That pumpkin may be intended for pie—but it's fated first to pose for a painting. The tiny baby in the crib is simply the family's newest model. My mother and grandfather both stand over the crib sketching, sketching, sketching. My sister is born with a golden frame around her face. In truth, we all were. And if your family is unavailable to pose? Well, then, you paint *yourself*. My grandfather kept a mirror opposite his easel so when he had no other model, he could always paint himself. He painted himself in every stage of life, and he did the same for us. There are dozens of portraits of me at all ages, in various costumes. In one portrait at age five, I wear a black velvet dress with an ivory lace collar and a floppy black velvet hat with black marabou pom-poms. I look as if I were sitting for Rembrandt—

my grandfather's favorite painter. In another portrait—done by my mother—I am seventeen and wearing a Japanese wedding kimono with an antique obi. My hair is rolled in stiff pompadours held with lacquer combs as if I were a blond geisha. My face is powdered white with rice powder. A crimson dot of lipstick makes a bull's-eye of my lower lip. Whenever I look at the portrait I remember the summer of my seventeenth year, which we spent in Japan.

All these portraits have empowered me in various ways. Some may not be to my taste and some are hardly flattering, but I am certainly glad they *exist*. I exist more richly because they exist. My memories are captured by a wall of portraits in my mother's dining room.

So throughout my childhood, I was the subject of works of art. I came to feel that making art was as natural a process as breathing.

But the process of art is also the process of metamorphosis. I may be an ogre in Molly's first novel, but I am likely to be an angel in her last. My mother may have sharp edges in *Fear of Flying;* in *Fear of Fifty,* those edges are as soft as a scarf woven of cashmere and silk. I have many more mothers than one. And each of those mothers parallels a particular phase in my life. Each represents a change in *me* more than it represents a change in my mother. As I grow more confident of my identity, I fault my mother less and less. As I grow older, my mother grows mellower along with me.

There is no end to this story. As long as I live I will be redefining my daughterhood in the light of my motherhood. Because I am a writer, I will process these changes in words. Since writing is my principal way of staying sane, I need to write to know what I think. But there will never be a final incarnation of my mother, of my daughter, of me. We are all works in progress.

What is constant is the metamorphosis itself. Kurt Vonnegut said in one of his novels that people are like centipedes wearing different faces as they make the trek from infancy to old age. I have always loved that image: each of us as a centipede, marching through time.

My mother is a centipede, and so is my daughter. Sometimes our paths intersect as we trudge along on our three hundred feet. But we have already marked each other in millions of ways. We share the same DNA, the same dreams, the same daring. If Molly is destined to be the most daring of all, it's no less than I expect. So many generations of women have empowered her. So many mothers and grandmothers have gone into her making. May she dare to follow her dreams *wherever* they lead! Without daring, what use are dreams? Without daring, what use are all the struggles of your mother, your grandmother, your great-grandmother? Make no mistake, these ancestors are watching you. If you disappoint them, you disappoint yourself.

"We think back through our mothers if we are women," Virginia Woolf said. And through us, our mothers think forward into the future.

What is home without a mother?

—ALICE HAWTHORNE

Mommy guiltiest? So reads the headline in the New York *Daily News*'s rehash of the "Nanny Case," which has riveted the media's public since everybody overdosed on treacly elegies to Diana, Princess of Wales. The *Daily News* has proved once again the old saying "Vox populi is, in the main, a grunt." The *News* is supposed to cater to the downmarket crowd that doesn't read the *New York Times* or the *Wall Street Journal,* but in truth most people in the word biz read *all three,* as well as the *New York Post* and the *New York Observer.* But without the *News,* you can't possibly know all that's *not* fit to print. And, of course, that's what tells you about the vacillations of the zeitgeist. And the zeitgeist is currently into blaming mommies for the deaths of their kids.

For *this* is the lesson of the nanny trial: Louise Woodward may have been nineteen, inexperienced, drowsy in the mornings and moonfaced at night, but Dr. Deborah Eappen was *really the one at fault,* because she worked three days a week as an ophthalmologist rather than staying at home full-time with her baby. Never mind that she came home at lunch to breast-feed on the days she worked. Never mind that she pumped out breast milk on the *other* days. Never mind that she was an M.D. working a drastically reduced schedule—a schedule no intern or resident would be *permitted* to work. *She* is the one to blame for the heinous crime of baby murder.

In an age when most mothers work because they *have* to, it is nothing short of astounding that this case resulted in raving callers to talk shows who scream that Dr. Deborah Eappen *deserved* to have her baby die because she left him with a nineteen-year-old nanny.

So much for twenty-five years of feminism. So much for smug commentators who say we live in a "post-feminist age." The primitive cry is still "Kill the mommy!" She deserves to be stoned to death for hiring a nanny.

Of course, we Americans already knew that *welfare* mothers were monsters. Dear Bill Clinton, champion of women and children, signed the most disgusting welfare bill in American history—a bill more appropriate to Dickensian England, a bill basically reinstating the workhouse in millennial America. But, of course, we *know* the American poor deserve nothing. Poverty is, after all, un-American.

America has abolished any definition of the worthy poor (children, mothers, the blind, the lame) and decided that *they* alone shall pay for the budget deficit run up by male politicians. After all, children have no votes—unlike savings-and-loan officers. Besides, the latter have lobbyists, and poor children naturally can't afford them. So we have no worthy poor in the country I so lavishly fund with my taxes, but neither have we any child-care initiatives—let alone child care.

Even some *reactionary* countries—La Belle France, for example—have mother care, crèches, kindergartens, but in America we rely on nature red in tooth and claw, so crèches are seen as "creeping socialism," and nobody's allowed to have creeping socialism except the army and the nontaxpaying superrich.

Okay—welfare mommies are monsters, but what about *entrepreneurial M.D.* mommies? What about women who *delayed* childbearing to finish school, had babies in their thirties and forties, and work part-time? Well, now we learn that they, also, are monsters. Why? Because they don't *stay home* full-time. Apparently *all* mommies are monsters—the indigent *and* the highly educated both deserve to watch their babies die.

Wait a minute. What happened here? Is this 1898 or 1998? It doesn't seem to matter. Where motherhood is concerned we might as well be in Dickens's England or Ibsen's Norway or Hammurabi's Persia. Mothers are, by definition, monsters. They're either monsters because they're poor or monsters because they're rich. Where mothers are concerned, *everything* is a no-win situation.

Poor Louise was nice but somewhat incompetent. Maybe she *did* shake poor little Matty—the medical evidence is inconclusive. After all, she was a Brit, and Brits *love* caning kids; shaking is *nothing* to them. But Deborah was even *worse* than Louise. She was a doctor's wife (and a doctor, but who cares?) who chose to work.

Both women have been thoroughly trashed. Nobody inveighs against the *other* Dr. Eappen—the one with a penis—and nobody screams that *his* baby deserves to die. Nobody talks about Matty, either. He's just a dead baby. Dead babies have no votes and no lobbyists. No—what everyone carries on about is which *woman* is at fault.

The mommy or the nanny? The lady or the tiger? Women, by definition, are *always* guilty. Either they're guilty of neglect or they're guilty of abuse. Nobody asks about the father's role or the grandparents' role. If it takes a village to raise a child, as Hillary Clinton's bestseller alleges, then that village consists of only *two* people: monster mother and monster au pair. Everyone else is off the hook. (Including a government that penalizes working moms in its tax policies, its immigration policies, and its lack of day care.)

How must Dr. Deborah Eappen feel, first losing her son and then facing this chorus of harpies (for the women-haters are often women)? Imagine the trauma of losing your baby, the trauma of reliving the pain at the trial, only to face the further trauma of trial by tabloid. Dr. Deborah *chose* her job because it allowed flexible hours. So did her husband, Dr. Sunil Eappen. But nobody's blaming *him*. If we have come so far toward the ideal egalitarian marriage, then why does nobody discuss the *couple*? Only the women are implicated. Both nanny and mommy face death by tabloid firing squad.

If the nanny trial is used as a litmus test for social change, then we must conclude that very little change has occurred. No wonder generation Y is full of young women who want to stay home with their babies! They saw what happened to their weary boomer mothers, and they don't *like* what they saw. If all feminist progress is dependent on the mother-daughter dialectic (as I believe it is), then we are in for a new generation of stay-at-home moms, whose problems will be closer to our grandmothers' than our own. Betty Friedan's *Feminine Mystique* will be as relevant in 2013 as it was in 1963—and our granddaughters will have to regroup and start feminist reforms all over again.

No wonder feminism has been ebbing and flowing ever since Mary Wollstonecraft's day. We *have never* solved the basic problem that afflicts us all—who will help to raise the children?

> *Women have been burnt as witches simply because they*
> *were beautiful.*
>
> —SIMONE DE BEAUVOIR

When I was researching my book *Witches,* fifteen years ago, it was considered rather kinky to talk about female aspects of divinity or to attempt to rehabilitate witches from the libels perpetrated on them by their inquisitors. Witchcraft was a bog of myth, misinformation, and Halloween gear. There were people who called themselves contemporary witches, or Wiccans—and I met plenty of them— but they seemed as confused about their origins as anyone else. Some called themselves goddess-worshipers or contemporary pagans. Some were feminists rediscovering the female roots of divinity, and their rituals were as muddled as they were sincere. Nobody could quite decide whether to be a white witch and do good with herbs or— more exciting—to be a bad witch and go to bed with devils.

The popular image of the witch reflected this confusion. There were both good and bad witches in picaresque movies like *The Wizard of Oz*, and only bad witches in scary movies like *Rosemary's Baby*. Did witches worship Satan, or did they worship a benevolent mother goddess? Hardly anyone would have posed the question that way. It fell to my book on witches to put the question to a popular readership for the first time—and that has been a large part of its appeal.

The truth is that the witch is a descendant of ancient goddesses who embodied both birth and death, nurturing and destruction, so it is not surprising that she possesses both aspects. But when religions decay and gods are replaced, there is a consistent dynamic: The gods of the old religion inevitably become the devils of the new. If serpents were once worshiped as symbols of magic power, they will later be despised as symbols of evil. If women were once seen as all-powerful, they will be relegated to pain in childbirth and obedience to men. The symbols remain, but their values are reversed. The snake sacred to the goddesses of ancient Crete becomes the incarnation of the devil in Genesis. The first female, Eve, goes from being a life-giver to a death-bringer. Good and evil are reversed. This is the way the politics of religion works.

The contemporary image of the witch incorporates detritus from many religious sects over many millennia. Like the wall of a Crusader castle in the Middle East, it rests upon a foundation of remnants from a variety of periods. Like Hecate and Diana, the witch is associated with the moon and lunar power. Like Aphrodite and

Venus, she can make love potions and fly through the air. Each attribute of the witch once belonged to a goddess.

All over the ancient world goddesses were worshiped. These goddesses represented womanhood distilled to its ultimate essence. Ishtar, Astoreth, Aphrodite (as she was eventually known), held sway over love, procreation, fecundity—and most of the gods obeyed her urgings. Many-breasted, in charge of flowers, wheat, all blossoming, she echoed something primal in the human heart. Born of woman ourselves, we find godhead natural in womanhood. Any faith that renounces the mother is bound to see her creep back in another form—as Mary perhaps, the mother of the sacrificed god.

Witchcraft in Europe and America is essentially this harking back to female divinity within a patriarchal culture. If you insist long enough that God is the father, a nostalgia for the mother goddess will be born. If you exclude women from church rites, they will practice their magic in the fields, in forests, in their kitchens. The point is, female power cannot be suppressed; it can only be driven underground.

Take a little honey in a jar. Write your deepest wish on a bit of brown paper and hide it in the honey. Focus all your energy on your intention (which must be sweet), and eventually your wish will be granted. Intention counts for everything. It must be positive. And the more witches there are sitting in a circle practicing communal intention, the more potency the magic will have. The desire for magic cannot be eradicated. Even the most supposedly rational

people attempt to practice magic in love and war. We simultaneously possess the most primitive of brain stems and the most so-
phisticated of cortices. The imperatives of each coexist uneasily.

We may even prefer to see the witch as an outsider, a practi-
tioner of the forbidden arts, because that makes her even more
powerful. Perhaps we are ashamed of our wish to control others
and would rather pay a maker of magic than confess to these wishes
ourselves. Perhaps we would rather not be in charge of magic that
might backfire.

Since we believe witches can make wishes real, we both need
and fear them. If they have the power to kill our enemies, couldn't
they also kill us? If they have the power to grant love, couldn't they
also snatch it away? Witches remind us of the darkness of human
wishes. That is why we periodically find reasons to burn them.

In *The White Goddess*, Robert Graves asserts that all real poetry
is an invocation of the triple goddess of antiquity—she who con-
trols birth, death, procreation—and that it is the poet's fealty to her
that determines the authenticity of his work. "The main theme of
poetry," Graves says, "is the relations of man and woman, rather
than those of man and man, as the Apollonian classicists would
have it." The male poet woos the goddess with words in order to
partake of her magic. He is at once her supplicant and her priest.
Where does this leave the female poet? She must become an incarnation of the triple goddess herself, incorporating all her aspects,
creative and destructive. This is why it is so dangerous to be a female poet. It is a little like being a witch.

Adelaide Crapsey's* poem "The Witch" evokes this well:

When I was a girl by Nilus stream
I watched the desert stars arise;
My lover, he who dreamed the Sphinx,
learned all his dreaming from my eyes.

I bore in Greece a burning name,
And I have been in Italy
Madonna to a painter-lad,
And mistress to a Medici.

And have you heard (and I have heard)
Of puzzled men with decorous mien.
Who judged—the wench knows far too much—
And hanged her on the Salem green.

Adolescence is a time when witchcraft exercises a great fascination. Disempowered by society and overwhelmed with physical
changes, teenage girls fall in love with the idea of forming covens.
Whatever bric-a-brac of magic is around they will pick up and
shape to their own uses.

Writing a book about witches made me a heroine to my friends'
daughters. It also became the most banned of all my books—
probably because the idea of female godhead is still anathema to

*Adelaide Crapsey (1878–1914), a much-neglected poet of the late nineteenth and early twenti-
eth century, often probed women's issues.

many people. Once, I received a Polaroid picture of *Witches* that showed it burned around the edges. The letter accompanying it said: "My father burned your book. Could you send me another copy?" So much for the efficacy of censorship.

The more disempowered people are, the more they long for magic, which explains why magic becomes the province of women in a sexist society. And what are most spells about? Procuring love, with usually, the hexing of enemies running a close second. When men turn to magic, they are more likely to seek infinite power (think of Dr. Faustus) or infinite immortality (think of the pharaohs of ancient Egypt). Contemporary moguls who spend fortunes to assure that their corpses will be frozen are not likely to be attracted to love spells. Their love is self-love. They want their DNA to endure singly, not to commingle with a lover's.

So witchcraft remains a woman's obsession.

John Updike captured the essence of women's urge to practice witchcraft in his novel *The Witches of Eastwick*. Disempowered women use their coven to become the secret legislators of their little town. Their magic cannot be separated from their sexuality. That is, of course, the point.

I would love to be a witch. I would love to learn to control the uncontrollable by making secret spells. (Who wouldn't?) I believe I was really motivated to write *Witches* because I hoped I would learn to master my own fate through *magick*. In that I was like Fanny, the heroine of my third novel, who was also drawn into the study of witchcraft as a means of mastery. In *Fanny, Being the True*

History of the Adventures of Fanny Hackabout-Jones, my eighteenth-century heroine is a powerless orphan, raped by her guardian, who turns to witchcraft in the hope that it will equalize her power with men. I imagined a coven of proto-feminist witches who attempted to compensate for the female's lack of power in society by making spells and riding through the air. They initiated Fanny into the craft, and her newfound power stayed with her the rest of her life, helping her in different ways than she first expected. Witchcraft in *Fanny* proves to be the magic with which mothers inspire daughters and vice versa. It proves to be women's wisdom—ancient and life-giving.

We have come a long way since the days when it was impossible to imagine a female deity. Now the idea of an inspiring goddess has almost become commonplace. Yet women are still not equal to men politically or economically. Will we ever be? Is our ultimate power still the power to give life? And if so, will we never be forgiven for it?

Since the goddess of birth is also the goddess of death, women are accused of bringing death into the world as well as life. This is why the witch is depicted as young, beautiful, and bedecked with flowers, and also as a frightening crone covered with cobwebs. She represents all the cycles of life, and if she is terrifying, it is because the cycles of life terrify. They are inexorable. They remind us of the mutability of all living things.

In certain periods it seemed less disturbing to worship beautiful young males—Michelangelo's David, the perfect boys of Platonic discourse—because they could be more easily seen as detached from change and decay. Periodically, our belief systems go through this cataclysm, from the worship of the female cycles of birth and decline to the isolated perfection of young maleness. The Socratic notion that true love was possible only between males represents both the denial of woman and the denial of death. The rejection of females' bloody cycles, mewling infants, and chthonic vendettas reasserts itself in many cultures. Woman is made the scapegoat for mortality itself. Then she is punished as if she were responsible for all nature's capriciousness, as if she were Mother Nature incarnate—which of course is true.

Since we inherit a worldview that sees man as reason and woman as nature, we are still in the grip of the beliefs that fostered witch burning. We must understand the witch to understand misogyny in our culture. We must understand the witch to know why women have been denigrated for centuries. The witch is a projection of our worst fears of women. Whether fattening children for food in "Hansel and Gretel" or disappearing into a puddle of ooze in *The Wizard of Oz*, the witch inhabits a dimension where the primitive fears of children become the wishes of reality.

Love is only a magic poppet away. Mountains of gold glimmer beneath the earth. Enemies disappear with one magic formula, while blossoms spring up with another. The witch can vaporize people at will, keep spring on earth all year long, make the lion lie down with the lamb. She can fly and enable others to fly. She can abolish death.

Surely we would like to be like her, and a book about witchcraft can only be a beginning. Like all secret arts, witchcraft is learned by apprenticeship. Its deepest secrets are printed nowhere. One witch hands down her *grimoire* to her successor, who alone can decipher its coded spells and recipes. If a true witch were to publish her secrets for all to see, she would immediately lose her powers.

"Power shared is power lost," say the witches. Legend has it that true books on witchcraft have at times been published, but the pages spontaneously burned to cinders before they could be bound. So I had to be very careful when I published *Witches*. Like the weaver of a great rug who does not wish to arouse the wrath of Allah, I had to introduce small errors. I had to code certain messages and print my recipes and spells with missing ingredients or missing steps. Otherwise the book would go up in smoke before it could be read. But the clever reader, the witch-to-be, the natural adept of *magick,* will read about witchcraft holding in her hand a pen dipped in invisible ink. Guided by the unseen force, that hand will supply whatever is missing from my imperfect text. With practice, with deep concentration, the hand of the adept will fill in the missing formulae. Just as the Delphic oracle uttered words whose import she could not divine, the hand of the true witch-in-training will scribble the truth. Watch for those words. They are all the *magick* you will need to know.

It was better to be in a jail where you could bang the walls
than in a jail you could not see.

—CARSON MCCULLERS

In Cynthia Ozick's short story "Virility," a talentless male poet gains fame by publishing the verses of his talented aunt under his own name. The book is entitled *Virility* and is accordingly praised for its "masculine" virtues: strength, power, mastery. The poet wins the homage of critics and the love of women, collects large lecture fees, and for a little while enjoys the kind of unambivalent success that is possible for men in a man's world. When the aunt dies, the poet breaks down. In a fit of remorse, he publishes her last poems under her own name and confesses his imposture. Do critics thereby conclude that genius has no gender? Do they praise her work at last on its own merits? Of course not. "Lovely girlish verses," the critics say; "thin, womanish perceptions." A rose by any other name does not smell as sweet. A poem under a man's name smells *virile*. Under a woman's name, the same poem smells thin.

One of the most notable and faintly horrifying memories from my college years is of the time a distinguished critic came to my creative writing class and delivered himself of this thundering judgment: "Women can't be writers. They don't know blood and guts, and puking in the streets, and fucking whores, and swaggering through Pigalle at five A.M. . . ." But the most amazing thing was the response—or lack of it. It was 1961 or '62, and we all sat there, aspiring women writers that we were, and listened to this claptrap without a word of protest. Our hands folded on our laps, our eyes modestly downcast, our hearts cast even lower than our eyes, we listened meekly—while the male voice of authority told us what women could or couldn't write.

Things have changed since then. When I went to college (from 1959 to 1963), there were no women's studies courses, no anthologies that stressed a female heritage, no public women's movement. Poetry meant William Butler Yeats, James Dickey, Robert Lowell. Without even realizing it, I assumed that the voice of the poet had to be male. Not that I didn't get a good literary education. I did. Barnard was a miraculous place where they actually gave you a degree for losing yourself in a library with volumes of Chaucer and Shakespeare, Byron and Keats, but the whole female side of the literary heritage was something I would have to discover for myself years later, propelled by the steam generated by the women's movement.

No critic, however distinguished, would dare say such things to a college class today, however much he might privately think them. Sexism is somewhat better hidden now, though far from eradicated. And no college class would sit listening meekly to such rubbish. That is one of the things that have happened in the years since I graduated from college, and I am proud to have been part of the process. Now, when I go to read my work at colleges, I find the students reading and discussing contemporary writing by women as if there had never been a time when a critic could say "Women can't be writers"—even in jest. I am grateful for that change, but it has not been won without pain. Nor is it necessarily a lasting change. Like the feminists of the twenties, we could easily see the interest in female accomplishments eclipsed once again by reactionary sexism, only to have to be passionately rediscovered yet again, several decades later.

It's ironic that the critic—the late Anatole Broyard—should have identified "blood and guts" as the quality that women writers supposedly lacked, since clearly women are the sex most in tune with the entrails of life. But we can better understand the critic's condemnation if we remember that in the nineteenth century, women writers were denigrated for their delicacy, their excessive propriety (which supposedly precluded greatness), while in the past couple of decades they have been condemned by male critics for their impropriety—which also supposedly precludes greatness. Whatever women do or don't do precludes greatness, in the mind of the chauvinist. We must see this sort of reasoning for what it is: prejudice.

In the beginning of the "second wave" of the women's movement (late sixties, early seventies), there was so *much* blood and
guts in women's writing that one wondered if women writers ever
did anything but menstruate and rage. Released from the prison of
propriety, blessedly released from having to pretend meekness,
gratefully in touch with our own cleansing anger, we raged and
mocked and menstruated our way through whole volumes of prose
and poetry. This was fine for writers who had a saving sense of
irony, but in many cases the rage tended to eclipse the writing.
Also, as years went by, literary feminism tended to ossify into convention. Rage became almost as compulsory to the generation of
writers who came of age in the late sixties and early seventies as
niceness and meekness had been to an earlier generation. Feminists
proved with a vengeance that they could be as rigidly dogmatic as
any other group. They did not hesitate to criticize works of art on
political grounds, or to reject poems and novels for dealing with
supposedly counterrevolutionary subjects.

This was unfortunate. It was also, I suppose, inevitable. Anger
against the patriarchal stifling of talent had been so proscribed for
so many centuries that in letting it loose, many women writers
completely lost their sense of humor. Nor could anyone maintain
that getting in touch with anger was unimportant. It was, in fact,
a vitally important phase of women's writing. Nothing is more destructive of the spirit and ultimately of creativity than false meekness and anger that does not know its own name. Nothing is more
freeing for a woman or for a woman writer than giving up the

pleasures of masochism and beginning to fight. But we must always remember that fighting is only a first step. As Virginia Woolf points out in *A Room of One's Own,* many women's books have been destroyed by the rage and bitterness at their own centers. Rage opens the doors into the spirit, but the spirit must then be nurtured. This is hardly easy—because women writers tend to be damned no matter what they do. If we are sweet and tender, we are damned for not being "powerful" enough (not having blood and guts), and if we rage, we are said to be "castrating," amazonian, lacking in tenderness. It is a real dilemma. What is the authentic voice of the woman writer? Does anyone know? Does anyone know what the authentic voice of *woman* is? Is it sweet and low like the voice of Shakespeare's Cordelia, or is it raging and powerful like the voice of Lady Macbeth?

The problem is, I suppose, that women have never been left alone to *be* themselves and to find out for themselves. Men need us so badly and are so terrified of losing us that they have used their power to imprison us—in castles of stone as long as that was possible, and in castles of myth thereafter. The myths, most of them ways of keeping us out of touch with our own strength, confused many generations of women. We were told we were weak; yet as we grew older, we increasingly knew that we were strong. We were told that men loved us for our dependency; yet as we grew older, we observed that, despite themselves, they loved us for our independence—and if they didn't, we found we didn't always care. We discovered that we could grow only by loving ourselves a little, and loving our strengths, and so, paradoxically, we found we could grow up only by doing the opposite of all the things our culture told us to do. We were told our charm lay in weakness, yet in order to survive, we had to be strong. We were told we were by nature indecisive, yet our survival often seemed to depend on our own decisions. We were told that certain mythic definitions of women were immutable natural laws, biological "facts," but often our very endurance depended upon changing those supposedly unchangeable things, even upon embracing a life credo of change.

In fact, when I look back on the years since I left college and try to sum up what I have learned, it is precisely that: not to fear change, not to expect my life to be immutable. All the good things that have happened to me in the last several years have come, without exception, from a willingness to change, to risk the unknown, to do the very things I feared most. Every poem, every page of fiction I have written has been written with anxiety, occasionally panic, and always with uncertainty about its reception. Every life decision I have made—from changing jobs to changing partners to changing homes—has been taken with trepidation. I have not ceased being fearful, but I have ceased to let fear control me. I have accepted fear as a part of life, specifically the fear of change, the fear of the unknown. I have gone ahead despite the pounding in the heart that says: Turn back, turn back; you'll die if you venture too far.

I regard myself as a fairly typical member of the female sex. In my fears and feelings, I am just like my readers. Writing may propel me into places and situations where I wouldn't otherwise find myself, but in the dark of night, insomniac, I think the thoughts any woman thinks. I am impatient with successful women who feel that their success has lifted them out of the ordinary stream of women's lives. I cringe when I hear them say to their fearful, un-fledged sisters: *I did it against the odds. You can, too.* As a writer, I feel that the very source of my inspiration lies in my never forget-ting how much I have in common with other women, how many ways in which we all are similarly shackled. I do not write about superwomen who have transcended all conflict. I write about women who are torn, as most of us are torn, between the past and the fu-ture, between our mothers' frustrations and the extravagant hopes we have for our daughters. I do not *know* what a writer would write about if all her characters were superwomen, cleansed of conflict. Conflict is the soul of literature.

I know I would not mind a world in which my daughter were free *not* to be a feminist, were free (if she chose to be a writer) not to write about women's conflicts, not to assume that the accident of her gender compelled her work to have a specific creative bias. I would welcome a world in which feminism were obsolete. But I would also like to see a world in which male writers wrote without masculine bias, in which phallocentric mythologies were perceived to be as bizarre as the most absurd excesses of militant feminist rhetoric, and in which consciousness had become so truly androg-ynous that the adjective "feminist" itself would be puzzlingly ob-solete. I wish I thought our culture was heading in this direction.

But it is not. After a brief flirtation with egalitarianism brought about by what has been termed the "second wave" of the women's movement, the culture is sliding back into its habitual sexism— with, of course, some trendy new terminology.

Some radical feminists have abetted this process of backsliding by becoming quite as simplemindedly dogmatic as the most dogmatic male chauvinists, by disassociating themselves from the anchors of most women's lives: children they love and men they learn to live with. It is unrealistic to assume that after living in families and tribes for millions of years of human evolution, women will suddenly cease being gregarious animals and become either reclusives or feminist communards. The human need for companionship and sexuality is far stronger than any intellectual theory. So the point should be not to keep women from establishing families but rather to make their *position* in families less that of semislaves and more that of autonomous individuals.

Where does all this leave the woman writer of our age? Usually in a quandary. As a sharp observer of her society, she cannot fail to see that it still discriminates against women (often in emotionally crippling and physically murderous ways), but as an artist she cannot allow her vision to be polluted by the ephemeral dogmas of political movements. It is simply not possible to write a good book that "proves" the essential righteousness of either lesbianism or heterosexuality, childbearing or its avoidance, man-loving or man-hating. Righteousness has, in fact, no place in literature. Of course, the keen observer of her culture will feel deeply about the oppression she sees around her, the inhumanity of man to man, of man to woman, of woman to woman, but her vision must be essentially personal, not abstractly political. Books are not written by committees—at least not good books. And the woman writer has as much right as any other artist to an essentially individual and idiosyncratic vision. If we judge her books according to their political "correctness," we are doing her as great a disservice as if we judged them according to her looks or her behavior in the voting booth. Certainly human history is full of such judgmentalism—most of it not coming from women—but always it is antithetical to the creation of works of art.

After saying this, I must also gratefully acknowledge that the second wave of the feminist movement liberated my writing and my life. Not by supplying me with dogma, but by making it easier for me to assume that what I felt was shared by others. Literature, as we previously knew it, was the literature of the white, the affluent, the male. Female experience had been almost completely omitted. Because of the second wave, I learned to assume that my thoughts, nightmares, and daydreams were the same as my readers'. I discovered whenever I wrote about a fantasy I thought wholly private, bizarre, kinky, that thousands of other people had experienced the same private, bizarre fantasy. I have learned, in short, to trust myself.

It seems to me that having now created an entire literature of female rage, an entire literature of female introspection, women writers are beginning to enter the next phase: the phase of empathy. Without forgetting our hard-won rage, without forgetting how many puritanical voices would still like to censor our sexuality, we are starting to be free to explore the whole world of feeling in our writings—and not to be trapped forever in the phase of discovering buried anger. Anger is a strong propellant to creation, but it is hardly the only propellant. Stronger even than anger is emotional curiosity, the vehicle through which we enter into other states of being, other lives, other historical periods, other galaxies.

Curiosity is braver than rage. Exploration is a nobler calling than combat. The unknown beckons to us, singing its siren song and making our hearts pound with fear and desire. I see us entering a world where women writers no longer censor themselves for fear of criticism, but I rarely see the critics catching up. Sometimes I think the response to women's books is still back in the age of *Virility*, even while a new generation of young women writers forges ahead without restraints. Literature as well as life is in the midst of an unfinished revolution. The explorers have set out to sea without life preservers. But pirates are still coming after them to board their decks and try to sink their ships. And some of these pirates, I must sadly say, are other women.

*Altogether the autobiography of Jane Eyre is pre-eminently
an anti-Christian composition.*

—ELIZABETH RIGBY

When a book is beloved by readers and hated by contemporary critics, we should suspect that a revolution in consciousness is in progress. This was certainly the case with *Jane Eyre*. The pseudonymous author, Currer Bell, was blamed for committing the "highest moral offence a novel writer can commit, that of making an unworthy character interesting in the eyes of a reader." The book was said to be mischievous and vulgar, pandering to the public's taste for "illegitimate romance." As for the character of the heroine, "Jane Eyre is throughout the personification of an unregenerate and undisciplined spirit . . . she has inherited in fullest measure the worst sin of our fallen nature—the sin of pride."

These criticisms were put forth by a woman reviewer, Elizabeth Rigby, in the *Quarterly Review* in 1848, the year after the novel was published, when it was already a roaring success. The same critic took pains to dispute the rumor that "Currer Bell" was a woman, explaining that the descriptions of cookery and fashion could not have come from a female pen. She also argued that the book would do more harm than good to governesses, and for good measure, she condemned Jane Eyre as one "whom we should not care for as an acquaintance, whom we should not seek as a friend, whom we should not desire for a relation, and whom we should scrupulously avoid for a governess."

Such character assassinations would be too absurd to quote if they did not foreshadow the charges against every important novel of the nineteenth and twentieth centuries that depicted a woman as a complex human being rather than a stereotype. More than that, they foreshadow contemporary assaults on women's anger, rebellion, and nonconformity—whether exemplified in fiction or in life. For Jane is nothing if not a rebel. She will not lie even if lies would smooth her progress. From the moment we meet her, she is struggling against the injustice of her lot and she refuses to be convinced that humility is her only option. In many ways, she is the first modern heroine in fiction.

The perennial popularity of *Jane Eyre* with readers is surely based on Jane's indomitable spirit. Given every reason to feel crushed, discouraged, beaten, Jane's will remains unbroken. Neither beautiful nor rich nor supplied with a cosseting family, Jane seems to be possessed of the greatest treasure a woman can have: self-respect. That alone makes her an inspiring heroine. No one can take away her inner esteem. It is apparent from the very start of the book, when ten-year-old Jane tells her supposed "benefactress," Mrs. Reed (who has unjustly punished her by secluding her from her cousins): "They are not fit to associate with me." We love Jane because she seems to know her own worth—an unforgivable thing in girls and women.

It is her grittiness that saves her at Lowood school, where punishments are meted out unfairly and girls are sent to starve and sicken. Helen, who meekly accepts unjust punishments, dies. Jane survives because she does not accept them. In fact, it is remarkable how often Jane says the thing she knows she should not, as if overcome by an irresistible force. She is active where all her training tells her to be passive. She speaks the truth when she is supposed to flatter. She longs for the wide world when she is supposed to be content with her narrow lot. "I could not help it; the restlessness was in my nature," she says, pacing "backwards and forwards" on the third story of Thornfield Hall. "Women feel just as men feel," Jane says. "They need exercise for their faculties and a field for their efforts."

When a book has been copied as much as *Jane Eyre,* has spawned as many bad imitations, as many movies and adaptations, it's necessary to go back to the text and try to see it as if for the first time. What has usually been imitated about this novel is not the spirit of the heroine but the gloomy house with its dark secret, its glowering hero, and the star-crossed romance of its two principal characters. These strike me as the *least* important elements of the story. If Jane were a passive heroine, neither the romantic battlements of gloomy Thornfield nor the curmudgeonly charms of Mr. Rochester would capture us. But Jane's bluntness, the modernity of her strivings for independence, invite us into the tale. From the first instant we meet Jane Eyre, we know she is a different breed.

As a novelist, what interests me most about *Jane Eyre* is the way Charlotte Brontë transformed autobiographical materials to create a myth that is larger and more powerful than any of its parts. Apparently Charlotte and her siblings *did* have a forbidding aunt who attempted without success to replace their dead mother. Apparently they *were* sent away to a harsh charity school not unlike Lowood. Apparently Charlotte *did* fall in love with a married man—M. Heger, the headmaster of the school in Brussels where Charlotte, for a time, taught. But the way Charlotte *changed* these materials is far more interesting than the way they agree with her autobiography. She sets the struggle not in a school in Brussels but in a foreboding North of England country house, where the restless master comes and goes. The house represents the fate of woman in the nineteenth century: enclosure, entrapment, no hope of escape. Not only Jane is captive there, but so is Jane's alter ego, Bertha Mason, the mad wife in the attic. And the mystery revolves around the discovery of the mad wife whose existence is denied even when her rages threaten the lives of those in the house.

It was Charlotte Brontë's genius to find a threefold representation of nineteenth-century woman: the feisty Jane, the animalistic

Bertha, the mansion that is destined to burn down because of its incendiary contents. If Bertha is sexuality denied, then Jane is freedom denied, but they are both aspects of entrapped womanhood. Thornfield Hall itself represents the outdated rules imposed on women—which cannot endure any more than a house with a trapped madwoman can.

Surely all these symbols were unconscious with the author. Otherwise she could not have made them so convincing. But the unconscious of an artist is her greatest treasure. It is what transmutes the dross of autobiography into the gold of myth.

Jane Eyre takes the form of a pilgrimage in which a little girl who is old before her time, from being reared in the most constricted of circumstances, gradually finds a way to blossom. But first she must submit to many tests. She must reject a variety of hypocritical masculine figures who feel it is their right to rule her. She must reject the fate of being a female victim—the only model presented to her by other women. She must reject the entreaties of her potential lover until he has been transformed by his own purifying odyssey.

To be the equal of Jane Eyre, Rochester must renounce all other women, see his patrimony go up in flames, lose an eye and a hand, and become grateful where he once was arrogant. Only when he has been thus transformed can he and Jane have a happily-ever-after.

Charlotte Brontë's brilliance was to create a myth that is the embodiment of female wish fulfillment. The universe of *Jane Eyre* operates according to female laws. Jane's success as a heroine depends on her breaking all the rules decreed for nineteenth-century women. Outspoken where she should be submissive, bold where she should be grateful, Jane Eyre has apparently never been told that she is plainer than Cinderella's stepsisters and has no business turning down a rich suitor before she knows she is an heiress herself. This is a fairy tale that reverses all the rules of fairy tales. No wonder it strikes readers as a burst of light into the heart of darkness.

To a remarkable extent, the novel relies on the heroine's sensitivity to dreams and visions—as if the author were saying that only a woman in touch with her deepest dreams can be a strong survivor in a world so toxic to women. Dreams are crucial in *Jane Eyre*. The night before Jane is to marry the already married Rochester, she prophetically dreams "that Thornfield Hall was a dreary ruin, the retreat of bats and owls." The house is reduced to "a shell-like wall, very high, and very fragile-looking," and Jane wanders there with an unknown child in her arms.

Perhaps the child in the dream represents the innocence that she is soon to lose. At church the next day, the wedding is canceled when Rochester's bigamy is revealed. Because he thinks of Bertha Mason as a "clothed hyena," whom he was entrapped into marrying, Rochester has no qualms about betraying his mad wife. But Jane, though she loves him, refuses to be drawn into his error. He married Bertha for her money, and that falsehood is not so easily cured. In this female universe, a man is not forgiven for a cynical marriage even if it is the rule in his society. So Jane, though heartbroken, leaves Thornfield Hall. She wanders in the dark woods of her destiny, finds she is an heiress herself, is commandeered in marriage by another man (the dour parson St. John), while Rochester's soul is being shriven.

Rochester may be arrogant and full of male entitlement, but he is not cold and calculating like St. John. In fact, it is St. John who evokes in Jane the certainty that she can marry only for love. He wants Jane because she will make a good missionary in India, not because he loves her. This Jane feels as an "iron shroud contracted round me." She can't allow herself to be with a man whose brow is "commanding but not open," whose eyes are "never soft." By refusing to marry him, "I should still have my unblighted self to turn to: my natural unenslaved feelings with which to communicate in moments of loneliness. There would be recesses in my mind which could be only mine." As his wife she would become "the imprisoned flame" consumed from within.

Jane may be the first heroine in fiction to know that she needs her own identity more than she needs marriage. Her determination not to relinquish selfhood for love could well belong to a contemporary heroine.

Jane can return to Rochester only when she can say: "I am an independent woman now." And she can surrender to him only when *he* says: "All the melody on earth is concentrated in my Jane's tongue to my ear." "The water stood in my eyes to hear this avowal of his dependence," Jane says. And indeed she cannot marry Rochester until he knows he is as dependent on her as she is on him. Their odysseys have equalized them, Jane has become an independent woman, and Rochester has been cured of entitlement.

Only that way can a woman and a man become equals in a patriarchal society.

We are drawn to those myths that speak the truth we know about our inner lives. *Jane Eyre* endures because it tells the truth about what makes a marriage of two minds possible. The shoe fits—far better than Cinderella's glass slipper. Men must be stripped of arrogance and women must become independent for any mutually nurturing alliance to endure between the sexes. Charlotte Brontë's unconscious was ahead of her time.

I have not laughed since I married.

—MRS. INCHBALD

I never knew Diana, Princess of Wales, except as an icon (our new word for a megacelebrity of a wattage surpassing that of the Virgin Mary), but my life and hers ran parallel for almost two decades and I watched her as intently as I ever watched any famous woman.

She appeared on the scene the summer my third marriage was coming apart, and since she represented the delusion of happily-ever-after at just the moment in my life when such a delusion was most painful, I didn't much like her. I was the mother of a three-and-a-half-year-old daughter and had staked my heart and soul on a union that now seemed irretrievable. Diana, meanwhile, was walking down the aisle in Saint Paul's like an advertisement for everything I was losing. I spent the day of her wedding drunk on

champagne and passed out on the guest bed of my English publisher's thatched cottage in Berkshire. It didn't help that I had been
assigned by *Paris Match* to write an article on the royal match and
Paris Match had turned my piece down because I had dared to wonder aloud why Diana's virginity was so much of an issue in 1981.
Virginity? It was a word we hadn't heard since the era of Doris
Day (about whom some wag supposedly said: "I knew her *before*
she was a virgin").

So I was divorcing while Diana was wedding. Still worse, all the
paraphernalia I and my contemporaries had spent our whole adult
lives throwing away was back with a vengeance: ruffles, tiaras,
hoop skirts, leg-o'-mutton sleeves, engagement rocks, and—good
grief!—*virginity*. What the hell was going on? We had been shout-
ing *No more alimony*, and meanwhile a new generation (born while
we were marching against the war in Vietnam) was picking up our
cast-off crinolines and strutting in them! They had discovered
marrying for money as if it were an entirely new thing. We were
hopelessly out of step with the times.

I was single and starting to enjoy it when Diana gave birth in
rapid succession to the heir and the spare. We still didn't know
about the anorexia, the bulimia, or Camilla Parker-Bowles, so the
photo ops of Diana, the Virgin Mum, continued to irritate. She
looked thinner. The hats like flying saucers gave way to the hats
like woks, which in turn gave way to the hats like cachepots, but
still this disgustingly retrograde ideal of femininity was being pa-
raded before us. A marriage like Diana's was everything my gener-

ation had run away from, and now it was being displayed as a platonic ideal. The eighties were in full swing. Limousines were in
style, and so were pouf skirts and masters of the universe. Who
could make sense of it? I decided the world was mad and went on
raising my daughter, writing my books, and paying my mortgage.

But by now the fairy tale seemed frayed around the edges. Diana and Charles were facing in different directions in the tabloids,
if not yet on the tea towels. All was not well in paradise. She had
two adorable boys to my one adorable girl, but she was starving
herself and throwing herself down stairs. Virginity followed by
sapphire rings and marital bliss didn't seem to be working. Hello.
What's this? The Cinderella story is a myth? Do tell! The year was
1989 and I was getting married to my best friend, but Diana seemed
to be on the verge of coming apart.

We were married in the Vermont woods by a female justice of
the peace, and my engagement present was not a rock but a first
edition of *Ulysses*. I read a poem I had written for him, and he said
the Hebrew prayers for a marriage. Astonishingly, I married a man
I never tired of conversing with, while Diana discovered she had
nothing to say to her prince. Or he to her. The fittings and the fits
continued. By the summer of '92, when Andrew Morton published
the beans Diana had been spilling, the fairy tale was revealed for
the myth it was. The prince had a mistress. Under her mattress, the
princess had a pea the size of Camilla's horse. Diana's vaunted virginity had availed her naught. All was wrong in the palace when
the clock struck twelve.

Now began the war of the wedded. Once Shy Di rose to her full height as the woman scorned, Charles seemed utterly clueless about her rage. She had her diamonds and pearls; what the devil *else* did she want? Surely not love! Didn't the silly Sloane Ranger know that love wasn't *part* of the bargain? Apparently not. It seemed she'd *believed* the Cinderella story after all. How very retro of her. Even the queen was alarmed. And Philip, the perfect consort, faultless for photo ops but with a mind of his own when it came to mistresses, couldn't believe it, either. Didn't the girl know *the rules?* She'd made her bed and now must lie in it. What sort of princess complains about the size of her pea?

Diana disillusioned didn't play as well as Shy Di the virgin. The press can deal with virgins and whores—but what about a princess who is neither?

The next period of Diana's life was dicey. Her press got progressively worse as separation and divorce loomed. Diana had to do *something* to save the day. She had played Shy Virgin. Now it was time to assume the role of woman of the world. But that's tougher for any woman to pull off, and Diana's clip file shows its perils. Diana was pilloried for trying to have a love life, hounded both at the health club and at the eating disorders shrink's. Her soul was stolen on film, and with each photo her spiritual center became more damaged. Even her friends the paparazzi tried to show her looking loony. No longer virginal, not willing to shut up and disappear like a good girl, she became a kind of media joke. And this is when, apparently, she took up humanitarian causes.

She looked so healthy and fit holding hands with AIDS patients, so long-limbed and lovely with a one-legged land-mine victim on her lap. These were the photo ops of a lifetime. These were the photo-ops the Benetton ads had tried but failed to create. Designer duds look so *good* against rags. All the fashion mags agreed. Were they so willing to exploit her photos that they'd write any sort of twaddle just to sell magazines? The answer was resoundingly yes.

Why should I doubt that Diana *was* kind? I'm sure it never occurred to her to renounce her *whole* clothing allowance and donate it to land-mine victims so they could buy prostheses. I'm sure it never occurred to her that one pair of South Seas pearl-and-diamond earrings could fund a whole anti-land-mine charity for a year.

Then Diana made that bad career move with which many of us are familiar. She started to enjoy her freedom as a single woman, and she even went yachting with the Sheik of Araby. The golden-haired princess may indeed have been having sex with a dark-skinned Egyptian! She publicly broke the cardinal rule for golden princesses.

So even *before* Diana's death there were signs of media backlash beginning. Did we really want an A-rab stepfather for the heir and the spare? The tabloids had a field day with Dodi-Di. Pictures were "digitally enhanced" to show "the kiss." Diana was depicted as a mermaid of the Mediterranean, as Jackie O. had once been depicted as a mermaid of the Aegean. Ondines flashed their glittering tails, but black clouds were ominously hovering.

How could the Windsors ever be happy with the way Di had edged them all off the front pages? Di divorced was even better copy than Di married. Dodi-Di was lip-smackingly delicious. Think of the shopping sprees, the yachts, the far-flung houses. Think of the legions of designers, decorators, and jewelers who would benefit from this union! And then, suddenly, Di and Dodi died. My first thought was: Her Majesty's Secret Service did it. But I freely admit to having a conspiratorial frame of mind.*

The truth was, Di had gone as far as she could go alive. Virgins can't *stay* virgins and they mayn't be public whores, so they have to die. From Juliet to Sleeping Beauty, consider the fate of virgins. The kiss kills as often as it cures.

In death, the apotheosis of Diana was complete. She ascended to that realm inhabited by Marilyn Monroe, Evita Perón, Jean Harlow, Amelia Earhart, and Sylvia Plath—all dead while still young and photogenic. If there's anything the world disdains more than uppity *young* women, it's uppity *old* women. Dying young has *always* been a woman's best career move.

Let's face it: Diana's real tragedy would have been to outlive her looks and try to make it on good works alone. Suppose she had *looked* like Mother Teresa or even Princess Anne. Imagine what sentiments the press would have favored her with. Instead they adored

*Not as conspiratorial as the Egyptian press, however, which at the time of this writing is speculating about the Mossad's involvement in Di-Dodi's death. Their theory is that the Jews wanted Di dead so that she couldn't convert to Islam like her friend Jemima Goldsmith. Here is a conspiracy theory to demonstrate the irrepressibility of anti-Semitism even unto absurdity.

the icon who died at thirty-six and had the Marilyn Monroe song—"Candle in the Wind"—recycled for her.

The recycling of the song ought to remind us that the icon is stronger than the person. We needed a dead icon, we got a dead icon. After all, there is no princess like a dead princess to sell magazines.

Who knows what Diana was *really* like? She is an icon, and icons are judged largely on appearances. She *looked* kind. She was the queen of the photo op, the prime-time interview, the tabloid bestseller. Her goodness has been unquestioned.

The things Diana did for charity—attend black-tie benefits, pose for photographers—are indeed onerous (personally I *hate* both activities), but they are hardly as onerous as scrabbling for a living nine to five, sans nannies, sans chauffeurs, sans therapists. She probably was a dear girl (why should I doubt it?), and she was more empathetic than the usual Sloane Ranger, but she was, after all, still a Sloane Ranger. More curious than her own self-glorification, I find, is her glorification by everyone else.

Suppose that behind the mask there was another woman—a woman lost and confused about her role, like so many of us. She was a woman who wanted to leave the world a better place, wanted to be a good mother, a loyal wife, a private person. Diana the icon superseded this real woman. She was obliterated by the public Diana. And this is the deeper tragedy. We live in a world that so worships fame that we refuse to acknowledge how much fame distorts a person's life. When she was too young to know what she was doing, Diana made a Faustian bargain: She gave away her privacy forever.

Absorbed into that great pantheon of heroines, the sweet innocent girl she probably was hardened into iconography. Diana's tragedy happened long before her death. It happened as soon as her face hit the tea towels. She gave up real life for being the heroine of a public soap opera. And she could never go back to being real again.

*The longer I live the more I become convinced that the only
thing that matters in literature is the writer is first of all an
enchanter.*

—VLADIMIR NABOKOV,

THE NABOKOV-WILSON LETTERS

"Lolita is famous, not I,"* Nabokov said to one of the many
interviewers who came to interrogate him after the *succès de scandale*
of his most celebrated novel, *Lolita.* And like so many Nabokovian
utterances, it was both true and the mirror image of true. Lolita's
fame made her creator both a "brand-name" author—to use that
distressing contemporary locution—and an adjective. Very few

---

*Actually, Nabokov's passion for verbal accuracy was such that he responded to his interviews in
writing, on index cards, from the fastnesses of his retreat in the Montreux-Palace Hotel in Mon-
treux, Switzerland. The entire quote, which comes from the *Paris Review* (1967), is worth repeat-
ing: "Lolita is famous, not I. I am an obscure, doubly obscure, novelist with an unpronounceable
last name."

writers become adjectives. Joyce begat Joycean. Dickens begat Dickensian. Henry James begat Jamesian. Yet writers as unique as Jane Austen, Emily Dickinson, and Edgar Allan Poe did not become adjectives—perhaps because they are inimitable. All through my twenties I tried to write Nabokovian novels, but even I would be hard put to define the term. Novels full of doppelgängers, mirror images, and obscure words were what I yearned to create. When I found my voice, it proved the opposite of Nabokovian. I was doomed to be forthright and direct where Nabokov was labyrinthine, but I never lost my affection for Nabokov.

Vladimir Vladimirovich Nabokov, alias V. Sirin (Volodya to his friends), born on Shakespeare's birthday in 1899, became famous in 1958–59, at the fairly ripe age of sixty, through the notoriety of his fictive daughter Lolita, Dolly, Lo, Dolores Haze, of the soft brown puppy-body and equivalently gamy aroma.

Like most famous literary books, *Lolita* seduced the world for the wrong reasons. It was thought to be dirty. It has this in common with Joyce's *Ulysses,* Henry Miller's *Tropic of Cancer,* D. H. Lawrence's *Lady Chatterley's Lover:* It won its first passionate proponents by being banned. When it came to wide public consciousness, it was reputed to be a scandalous book about a scandalous subject: the passion of an aging roué for a twelve-year-old girl.

Since my literary debut was also steeped in scandal, I know intimately the ambivalent feelings of an author who gains wide fame and commercial acceptance through a misunderstanding of motives. Much as any writer craves the acceptance conferred by bestsellerdom, it is bittersweet to win this by being thought a pervert. Such ambivalence alone explains Nabokov's mocking reference to *Lolita*'s fame. Nabokov knew that he had been toiling in the vineyards of the muse since adolescence. The public did not know. Nabokov knew that he had translated *Alice in Wonderland* into Russian. The public did not know. With eleven extraordinary novels, a study of Gogol, an autobiography, numerous short stories, poems, and translations behind him, the author of *Lolita* was hardly a literary novice. His identity as a novelist, poet, and literary scholar had been honed and polished in three languages since he had had his poems privately printed in Saint Petersburg at the age of fifteen. He had certainly endured more terrible traumas than sudden fame. Fleeing the Bolshevik Revolution and escaping Europe with a Jewish wife in 1940 tend to make the publication of a scandalous book seem trivial. The generous, amused, self-mocking way Nabokov reacted to *Lolita*'s stardom contains within it all the paradoxes of a career rich in paradoxes, a career that seems to have the very symmetry and irony of the novels themselves.

It is almost superfluous to introduce *Lolita*—even on her thirtieth* birthday—because Nabokov, who thought an author should control the world of his book with godlike authority, anticipated all the possible front (and rear) matter any reader could wish for. We have the mock introduction by "John Ray, Jr., Ph.D.," a spoof on scholarly psychobabble and tendentious moralizing—two

---

*This essay was first published in the year *Lolita* turned thirty. She is now fifty-two.

things Nabokov detested as much as he detested Freudian symbol-mongering in literary criticism. As he often said to his students and interviewers: "Rely on the sudden erection of your small dorsal hairs. . . . Beware the modish message. Ask yourself if the symbol you have detected is not your own footprint." Since he wrote to achieve what he called "aesthetic bliss," since he believed that a literary work inhered in "the divine details," he would want his readers to "caress the details" in his own work as he, as a teacher of literature, taught his students to caress the details in Tolstoy, Pushkin, Gogol, Chekhov, Kafka, Flaubert, and Proust. His impersonation of "John Ray" in the foreword to *Lolita* is one of the most delicious of literary parodies, and his own afterword "On a Book Entitled Lolita" is, I believe, the last word on the subject of the sensual versus the pornographic. I always wonder why it is not quoted more often in those endless, predictable, and anesthetizing debates that go on about the nature of pornography and eroticism (to which I am inevitably invited).

Here is Nabokov on that dreary subject:

While it is true that in ancient Europe, and well into the eighteenth century . . . deliberate lewdness was not inconsistent with flashes of comedy, or vigorous satire, or even the verve of a fine poet in a wanton mood, it is also true that in modern times the term "pornography" connotes mediocrity, commercialism, and certain strict rules of narration. Obscenity must be mated with banality because every kind of aesthetic enjoyment has to be entirely replaced by simple sexual stimulation which demands the traditional word for direct action upon the patient. Old rigid rules must be followed by the pornographer in order to have his patient feel the same security of satisfaction as, for example, fans of detective stories feel— stories where, if you do not watch out, the real murderer may turn out to be . . . artistic originality. . . . Thus, in pornographic novels, action has to be limited to the copulation of clichés. Style, structure, imagery should never distract the reader from his tepid lust.

Tepid lust, indeed. Those who can't tell the difference between masturbatory stimulation and imaginative literature deserve, I believe, the garbage they get. The erection of small dorsal hairs is the issue here and not, as is commonly assumed, other sorts of tumescence.

Nabokov thought of *Lolita* as his best novel in English, and he had been trying to write it at least since his German expatriate days. Perhaps the literary artist is born, like a woman with all her eggs present in their follicles; they have only to ripen and burst forth— and ripeness is all. But sometimes it takes half a lifetime for them to ripen. Nabokov began what was to become *Lolita* as a novella in Russian called *The Enchanter* (*Volshebnik*), which he composed in the fall of 1939 in Berlin. It was his last work in Russian and his last work written in Europe before he, his wife, Vera, and his son, Dmitri, emigrated to America in 1940.

In *The Enchanter,* all the elements of *Lolita* are present: the lustful Central European lover with a whiff of madness, the nymphet who is aware yet unaware of her charms, and the marrying-her-mother theme. In *The Enchanter,* however, it is the nymphet's un-named lover (who in *Lolita* becomes Humbert) who is killed by a truck, not the nymphet's mother. Nabokov claims he destroyed *The Enchanter* soon after moving to America; but his memory apparently misled him, for the novella turned up in his files and was published in 1986. It seems a pale foreshadowing of *Lolita,* interesting as a cartoon for a future masterpiece. What is most fascinating is how the theme obsessed Nabokov until he finally got it right—the mark of a real artist. Sometimes one cannot write a certain book because all the elements for it are not yet in place: Life has to catch up with art, providing the flora and fauna of the fictive world.

One of the many glories of *Lolita* is the evocation of the American landscape, American slang, American teenagers of the fifties—all seen with the freshness only a twice-exiled European would bring. The difference between *The Enchanter* and *Lolita* is the difference between a postcard of Venice and a Turner painting of the same scene—and it inheres in the divine details. Even before *The Enchanter* was written, the idea for *Lolita* was present in Nabokov's imagination. In *The Gift (Dar),* Nabokov's autobiographical Russian novel (published serially in Berlin in 1937–38, and in its entirety in 1952 in New York) there exists this premonition of *Lolita:*

Ah, if only I had a tick or two, what a novel I'd whip off! From real life. Imagine this kind of thing: an old dog—but still in his prime, fiery, thirsting for happiness—gets to know a widow, and she has a daughter, still quite a little girl—you know what I mean—when nothing is formed yet, but already she has a way of walking that drives you out of your mind—a slip of a girl, very fair, pale, with blue under the eyes—and of course she doesn't even look at the old goat. What to do? Well, not long thinking, he ups and marries the widow. Okay. They settle down the three of them. Here you can go on indefinitely—the temptation, the eternal torment, the itch, the mad hopes. And the upshot—a miscalculation. Time flies, he gets older, she blossoms out—and not a sausage. Just walks by and scorches you with a look of contempt. Eh? D'you feel here a kind of Dostoevskian tragedy? That story, you see, happened to a great friend of mine, once upon a time in fairyland when old King Cole was a merry old soul.

The language of *Lolita* is as amazing in its way as the language of *Ulysses* or *A Clockwork Orange*. Nabokov has the same lexicographical itch as Joyce or Burgess, but because he learned Russian and English almost simultaneously in his privileged childhood, he likes to play the two languages off against each other. Like so many of the most original modern novelists, he started literary life as a poet. The poet, W. H. Auden says, has first to woo not his own muse but Dame Philology. Vladimir Nabokov wooed that mistress for years before surrendering to *Lolita*. The novel teems with loving lexicography, crystalline coinages, lavish listmaking—all the unmistakable symptoms of rapture of the word.

"Nymphet" was a Nabokovian coinage for this novel, as were the more obscure items "libidream," "pederosis," "nymphage," and "puppy-bodies." As with *Ulysses,* not a page fails to amaze; not a page fails to reward the most diligent rereading. (French critics pointed out that Ronsard had used the word "nymphette" to mean little nymph—a fact Nabokov knew—but he created an English term, which has stuck because we have no substitute to describe that feral girl-woman who drives the middle-age man mad.)

Lolita is a novel about obsession. It has this in common with *Death in Venice, Anna Karenina, Madame Bovary,* Shakespeare's sonnets, and even *Portnoy's Complaint.* Impossible obsession fuels literature. Many writers are obsessed with obsession.

The subject was hardly a new one for Nabokov—though the form the obsession takes is new in this novel: nymphage. Luzhin in *The Defense* is obsessed with chess; Sebastian Knight in *The Real Life of Sebastian Knight* with literary immortality; Kinbote in *Pale Fire* with regaining his Zemblan kingdom; Herman in *Despair* with killing his double, Fyodor in *The Gift* with transcending time through literary creation. (One could continue the list through all Nabokov's novels.)

In *Speak, Memory,* Nabokov's autobiography, he terms himself a "chronophobiac" (another delicious invention), and to a great extent *Lolita* is a book about chronophobia every bit as much as Shakespeare's sonnets are.

Humbert Humbert is in love with something that by definition cannot last. That prepubescent state he calls nymphage lasts from nine to thirteen, a fleeting four years, often less. The honey-hued shoulders, the budbreasts, the brownish fragrance of the bobby-soxed nymphet, are all destined to be abolished by the advent of womanhood—which Humbert despises every bit as much as he worships nymphage. Humbert's dilemma puts the dilemma of all obsessional lovers in relief. He loves what he can never possess. Time rips it away from him even as he dreams of possessing it. No Elizabethan poet writing sonnets about gathering rosebuds while ye may could convey this better than Nabokov does with his nymphet.

So the villain here is time. And the dilemma is the dilemma of the human being who foresees his own death. It is not coincidental that so many of Nabokov's heroes are doomed and so many of his novels are cast in the form of posthumous autobiographies. His subjects are nothing less than mutability and time, Eros and Death, the twin subjects of all real muse poetry.

Like so many Nabokovian narrators, Humbert Humbert is a man obsessed with an irretrievable past. When he refinds his nymphet in Ramsdale (even the place names in *Lolita* are full of sexual innuendo), he recognizes at once that he has discovered the reincarnated essence of his Riviera puppy love, who perished of typhus decades earlier:

It was the same child—the same frail, honey-hued shoulders, the same silky supple bare back, the same chestnut head of hair. A polka-dotted black kerchief tied around her chest hid from my aging ape eyes, but not from the gaze of young memory, the juvenile breasts I had fondled one immortal day. And, as if I were the fairy-tale nurse of some little princess (lost, kidnapped, discovered in gypsy rags through which her nakedness smiled at the king and his hounds), I recognized the tiny dark-brown mole on her side. With awe and delight (the king crying for joy, the trumpets blaring, the nurse drunk) I saw again her lovely in-drawn abdomen where my southbound mouth had briefly paused; and those puerile hips on which I had kissed the crenulated imprint left by the band of her shorts—that last mad immortal day behind the "Roches Roses." The twenty-five years I had lived since then tapered to a palpitating point, and vanished.

Time is what Humbert seeks to abolish. Time is the enemy of all lovers. Nabokov has caught the essence of obsession no less than Thomas Mann in *Death in Venice*. Obsession has a life of its own: The object, however irreplaceable and particular it seems, can change, though it is in the nature of obsession not to recognize that.

The obsession of Humbert with Lolita has been compared to many things: the obsession of the artist with the creative process, the obsession of the butterfly collector with his specimen, the obsession of the exile with retrieving a lost homeland (a characteristic Nabokovian theme). It is all these things, and more. And yet the book works, finally, because it is the story of a man maddened by an impossible love, the impossible love for an impossible object: a banal little girl who calls him "kiddo." Aren't all impossible, obsessional loves inexplicable to other people? Do our friends *ever* understand? Isn't that inexplicability the wonder and the terror of obsessional loves?

In looking for the "sources" of *Lolita,* we have to look no further than Nabokov's genius, but it *is* useful to remember that he translated *Alice in Wonderland* into Russian, and that Pushkin's *Eugene Onegin* is one of the seminal books in his life, as it is in the life of so many other Russian writers. As D. M. Thomas said of Pushkin, "The sexual and creative instincts in him ran as parallel as the twin blades of a skater." The same surely can be said of Nabokov, and nowhere is this clearer than in *Lolita.*

The publishing history of *Lolita* is almost as Nabokovian as any of Vladimir Nabokov's creations; it seems almost a case of life imitating art. Nabokov finished *Lolita* in the spring of 1954 and "at once began casting around for a publisher." Since *Lolita* is thirty this year—or at least her first American trade edition is—we should try to remember the state of American publishing in 1954, when I myself was in nymphage.

In those benighted days, it was impossible to obtain a copy of John Cleland's *Memoirs of a Woman of Pleasure* outside the rare-book room of a university library or a private erotica dealer. Believe me, I tried. Henry Miller's *Tropic of Cancer* and D. H. Lawrence's *Lady Chatterley's Lover* could not be purchased at your local bookstore. The raciest sex manual available to the panting adolescent was *Love Without Fear* by Eustace Chesser, M.D. And

A Stone for Danny Fisher by Harold Robbins was as close as most adolescents of the fifties got to "literary" sex education. Even Normal Mailer, in *The Naked and the Dead,* had replaced "fuck" with "fug." And though he was far more explicit in *The Deer Park* (1955), he was punished for it by the reviewers.

It is hardly surprising, then, that the typescript of *Lolita* was rejected by four major New York publishers. Although the novel contained not one "mural word" (as Nabokov put it), *Lolita* was a genuinely new creation, and genuinely new creations do not usually fare well until they have been safely certified. It was not only that *Lolita* dealt with forbidden obsessions: *Lolita* had the additional demerit of being literary. American puritanism is more comfortable with sex when it stays in the gutter than when it rises to the level of art.

Even more amazing than the responses of the publishers were the early responses of Edmund and Elena Wilson and Mary McCarthy to this masterpiece, which Nabokov thought "by far my best English work." I am amazed to read in the Nabokov-Wilson letters what the usually randy Edmund Wilson wrote to Nabokov of *Lolita:* "I like it less than anything of yours I have read." Mary McCarthy, who did not finish the manuscript, called the "writing terribly sloppy throughout." (See *The Nabokov-Wilson Letters* for 30 July 1954, 9 August 1954, 30 November 1954.)

Now, the responses of even the greatest writers to their contemporaries' books are not always accurate—for a variety of reasons not all of which have to do with envy. Virginia Woolf called *Ulysses* "an illiterate underbred book ... the book of a self-taught working man ... egotistic, insistent, raw, striking, and ultimately nauseating." Woolf happened to be a great literary critic as well as novelist—and here she was utterly misguided. Authors rarely recognize their contemporaries; often they are blind to them. For every Ezra Pound, Anthony Burgess, John Updike, or Henry Miller who is open enough to praise the new, there are a thousand Edmund Wilsons who say: "I wish I could like the book better." Even that regretful tone is rare; more usually authors attack the new with contemptuous relish, pronouncing it boring, sloppy, or underbred simply *because* it brings fresh vitality to the language. Something new in literature is often gloriously oblivious to old rules of decorum, old limits of literary expression; its vulgarity and vitality are frequently so intertwined that they cannot be separated.

That Nabokov was depressed by Wilson's response, we have on record from the Wilson-Nabokov letters. He had brewed this novel for twenty-five years in two languages: How could he not be depressed at presenting a rare vintage and having it pronounced vinegar?

Had Edmund Wilson not dubbed the book "repulsive," "unreal," and "too unpleasant to be funny," had he not conveyed these sentiments to his own publisher, the publishing history of *Lolita* might have been different. As it was, fate—which is such an important character in *Lolita*—arranged that *Lolita* have her first publication in English in France, in 1955, under the auspices of Maurice Girodias's Olympia Press (heir to his father's Obelisk Press, Henry

Miller's publisher).* Girodias, *père* and *fils,* had been publishing literary erotica and not-so-literary erotica for the expatriate market in Paris since the thirties. Though he was condemned by some as a porn king, praised by others as "the Lenin of the sexual revolution," the fact remains that Maurice Girodias was courageous enough to publish William Burroughs, Samuel Beckett, Jean Genet, J. P. Donleavy, Nikos Kazantzakis, and Nabokov's *Lolita* when others were too afraid of censorship to try.

I am privileged to count among my Nabokovian treasures a somewhat battered two-volume set of the first edition of *Lolita,* The Olympia Press, 8 Rue de Nesle, Paris 6^e, printed in August 1955 by S.I.P., Montreuil, France, 900 francs per volume. The printing was small, perhaps only five thousand copies, but big enough so that Graham Greene found a copy and pronounced *Lolita* one of the three best novels of '55 in the *Times* of London.

It was Greene who conferred the sort of literary blessing upon the book that John Updike and Henry Miller were later to confer upon *Fear of Flying.* Greene saw literature and language where others had seen only perversion and pornography. *Lolita*'s eventual triumph can be traced ultimately to his intervention. Following Greene's discovery of *Lolita,* Jason Epstein printed portions of the novel in the *Anchor Review.* Following that, Walter Minton of Putnam's and George Weidenfeld and Nigel Nicolson (of the U.K. firm that bore their names) entered into an arrangement with Giro-

---

*Jack Kahane. His son took Girodias, his mother's name, to outwit the Nazis.

dias to publish *Lolita* in the United States, the United Kingdom, and Canada. One third of the royalties were to go to The Olympia Press, but *Lolita* was at last to have mainstream United States and United Kingdom publication. The hero of this chapter in what came to be called *L'Affaire Lolita* is Nigel Nicolson (son of Harold Nicolson and Vita Sackville-West), who sacrificed his parliamentary victory in the Bournemouth elections in part because of his constituents' disapproval of his publication of *Lolita*.

It was widely assumed that *Lolita* would provoke legal action in England and the United States. The Olympia Press edition had been banned at one point in Paris at the request of British authorities. The novel was even debated in the British cabinet, but the publication proceeded without legal impediment. A New Zealand ban came later.

United States publication took place on 21 July 1958 (Putnam's). United Kingdom publication on 6 November 1959 (Weidenfeld and Nicolson). The U.S. edition hit number one on the *New York Times* bestseller list in January 1959; it was eventually nudged out of that place by another child of Russia, *Doctor Zhivago* by Boris Pasternak. Those were the days when literary books actually appeared on bestseller lists with some regularity.

Most of *Lolita*'s reviews paid more attention to *L'Affaire Lolita* than to the book. As if Nabokov's afterword did not exist, many journalists boringly debated the old literature-versus-pornography question. Not surprisingly, a number of the reviewers sound like the author impersonating "John Ray, Jr., Ph.D." Vladimir Nabokov

had an uncanny ability to anticipate everything in his novels, even
their critical reception. One exception to the generally banal level
of the commentary was Elizabeth Janeway's review in the *New York
Times Book Review*. Janeway, with her usual good sense and lack of
prudery, spotted the quality of the book right away and understood
that its tragicomedy was Shakespearean in nature:

> Humbert's fame seems to me classically tragic, a most perfectly
> realized expression of the moral truth that Shakespeare summed
> up in the sonnet that begins, "The expense of spirit in a waste of
> shame / Is lust in action": right down to the detailed working out
> of Shakespeare's adjectives, "perjur'd, murderous, bloody, full of
> blame." Humbert is the hero with the tragic flaw. Humbert is every
> man who is driven by desire, wanting his Lolita so badly that it
> never occurs to him to consider her as a human being, or as any-
> thing but a dream-figment made flesh—which is the eternal and
> universal nature of passion.

The great thing about masterpieces is that they seem always to
have existed, unopposed. Now that all the false starts, cavils, bans,
and bad reviews have been reduced to the blurry footnotes they
are, we have the book in all its glory, as if it had never not been.

Outrageous, inevitable, infinitely rereadable, *Lolita* at thirty is
as young as she was as a glimmer in her author's eye.

She has, in fact, defeated time—her enemy, her inspiration.

To her progenitor she gave worldwide fame and the chance to air all his earlier Russian novels in English translations. Engendered by a young, exiled author in Berlin, she bestowed upon the old American author he became ease, comparative wealth, and two more decades to complete his oeuvre.

The story ends in Switzerland overlooking a mirrory lake, "once upon a time in fairyland when old King Cole was a merry old soul."

POSTSCRIPT

"*Lolita* Turns Thirty" was originally commissioned by the Book-of-the-Month Club to serve as the introduction to a thirtieth-birthday facsimile edition of Vladimir Nabokov's *Lolita* (the Putnam's edition of 1958). It was later revised for publication in the *New York Times Book Review* (June 5, 1988), and it has been changed somewhat for publication here.

After writing about the curious publishing history of *Lolita*, I was fascinated to discover that Adrian Lyne's 1997 film of *Lolita* encountered similar problems. In May 1998, I interviewed Adrian Lyne for the *New York Observer* after screening the movie. My resulting article proved to be an update of censorship practices in the United States as they have evolved between 1954, when the manuscript of *Lolita* was turned down by every American publisher (it eventually went to Maurice Girodias's Olympia Press in Paris in

1955), and 1998, when Adrian Lyne's movie could not find theatrical distribution in the United States and was bought instead by Showtime, the cable channel.

Even the most literate audiences believe censorship to be a thing of the past—a problem faced by James Joyce and Bennett Cerf, Henry Miller and Barney Rosset, but absent from the cultural equation today. This is simply not true. Censorship is creeping back in a more insidious way today. Fear, self-censorship, and state-by-state prosecutions succeed where federal laws never completely could. If there were an American James Joyce ready to write a contemporary *Ulysses* today, it might not get published, let alone defended in court.

As attorney Martin Garbus (who was called in as a consultant on the distribution problems of Lyne's film of *Lolita*) told me, "Censorship today comes from both the right and the left—the private pressure groups—some feminists, regional censors like the Christian right, and conservative communities that bring pressure to bear on state and federal prosecutors. The struggle is very different from the sixties. It's more complex and more dangerous."

Few people are aware, Mr. Garbus said, that

federal prosecutors left over from "Operation Porn," a legal unit put together by Edwin Meese, give legal support and encouragement to state and local prosecutors. Groups like the American Family Association stage demonstrations to close down such films as *The Last Temptation of Christ* and threaten manufacturers with boycotts if they use people like Madonna as spokesmen [*sic*]. Utah, Alabama, and Georgia will prosecute materials that are perfectly safe in urban areas. The country is being broken down into pockets of safe and unsafe [areas].

In the case of Lyne's film of *Lolita,* threats from Dworkinite feminists—for whom women are always a tabula rasa defiled by the ever corrupting male—became a decisive factor in scaring off distributors. JonBenet Ramsey's murder was very much in the news in the fall of 1997 (when theatrical distribution was under discussion) and Milos Forman's film about Larry Flynt (*The People vs. Larry Flynt*) had encountered protests from Andrea Dworkin, Patricia Ireland, and NOW. The same group was also threatening to boycott *Lolita* for supposedly making the victim of incest appear as the aggressor. (They could not have seen the movie if they honestly thought that.) According to the Dworkinite fringe of feminism, all female adolescents are utterly pure of mind and only evil stepfathers can possibly corrupt them. Any book or movie that attempts to treat a young woman as a creature of ambivalence, of sexual longing, or of oedipal confusion, is bound to be on their see-no-evil list. We can only depict happy feminists on tractors selling Girl Scout cookies and/or recovering lost memories of sexual abuse by horrid male relatives. It was Adrian Lyne's ill luck to have made a fifty-eight-million-dollar art movie in such an atmosphere. If the Mormons didn't boycott the movie, the Dworkinites might.

Even though Mr. Garbus declared "the film was safe" from a legal point of view, the combined Dworkinite-Mormon threat was chilling enough to scare distributors away. Of course, distributors wouldn't honestly cop to their fear, but despite Mr. Garbus's legal assurances, the film never found theatrical distribution. Sometimes a threatened boycott is more effective than a real one.

For the assorted sins of being faithful to the classic novel, daring to present "every little girl's fantasy of replacing her mother" (said my nineteen-year-old daughter, Molly, who watched the movie with me), Mr. Lyne and his fifty-eight-million-dollar feature film were given the booby prize of going straight to cable in the all important American market. As of this writing, the Showtime channel was scheduled in August 1998 to broadcast for the first time in America a film that begs to be shown on the big screen.* *Lolita* has, of course, already been seen in theaters in England, France, Italy, Spain, and Russia and plenty of other places that are historically no strangers to censorship, but Americans are currently being "protected" from it by a combination of studio paranoia and troglodyte misunderstanding of the fact that art is not advocacy and advocacy is not art.

If you present the story of a wretch who seduces his stepdaughter, that does not necessarily make you a pervert or an advocate for perverts. Adrian Lyne the director has come smack up against all the problems Vladimir Nabokov the author faced in the fifties.

---

*Thanks to this protest, among others, the movie had a theatrical release in New York City, Los Angeles, and nationally in September 1998.

As Lyne ironically explained to me: "You can make a movie about cannibalism. You can make *Silence of the Lambs*. You can make a movie about necrophilia—*The Kiss*. But pedophilia is the last taboo. I think probably because it's too close to home. People want to believe that sexuality flies in conveniently at the legal age of eighteen, and it's just not true. I think back to myself as a kid. You're kind of an ungainly mess of sexuality at fourteen."

Strictly speaking, a girl between the ages of thirteen and seventeen is not a child, though legally she is a minor. If we are going to claim that girls between thirteen and seventeen have no interest in seduction, we will be hard put to explain the existence of all the industries that feed on their fascination with it: from music videos and CDs to makeup, magazines, and movies. Teenage girls are constantly exploited commercially in far worse ways than any *Lolita* may threaten. These forms of exploitation raise no eyebrows.

"What is awful is this atmosphere of fear which they rationalize by saying the movie is an art movie," Lyne told me. And the sad fact is that a genuine work of art is being pushed to cable when it clearly belongs on the big screen.

"[François] Truffaut said years ago that American directors like to make movies about heroes, while European directors like to make movies about people with weakness and vulnerability, and that's what fascinates me really," said Lyne. He has made such a movie, and he has succeeded beyond his wildest dreams. Lyne's *Lolita* is a tragicomedy as Nabokov intended.

Neither lover is completely innocent nor completely corrupted, and the audience is finally overwhelmed by the way both lovers doom each other to disappointment and death. Lolita is hardly an advertisement for the joys of sex with minors.

What is it about the movie that has occasioned this sad display of institutional cravenness? It is a beautifully made portrait of an impossible love whose principal tone is elegiac. It is a movie that paints the American landscape Nabokov chronicled with a surreal visual style that often evokes Diane Arbus's photographs, yet is perfectly faithful to Nabokov's outsider's vision of a forties America of sad trailer parks, dusty diners, and lonely desert gas pumps.

It is a movie whose eye can linger now on a fly caught on flypaper, now on a girl sucking a banana as if it were a cock, now on a chocolate soda with a large white turd of vanilla ice cream falling into it, now on a holocaust of moths in an electric zapper—while never letting us forget that the real enemy of Humbert Humbert and his Lolita is time itself. The lovers are doomed because Lolita must grow out of the very nymphage that attracts her lover. Besides Humbert doesn't really love anyone living, he is obsessed with a long-dead girl, his baby love from the South of France when he himself was a child of fourteen.

It is a movie that often evokes dreams—particularly nightmares—a movie whose dominant tone is sadness and loss, a movie that accomplishes the almost impossible feat of making a pervert sympathetic enough for us to want to spend a whole evening with him, yet wretched enough to make us understand what a dead end obsession is. Obsession, *Lolita* makes clear, can lead to nothing good. So this is a moral movie in the deepest sense of the term. It shows the stark contrast between obsession and love. It does not—like so many other movies—confuse them.

Lyne has also succeeded in capturing Nabokov's verbal humor. Stephen Schiff's screenplay deftly uses verbatim monologues from the book, which Jeremy Irons makes come alive in voice-overs. Visual and aural jokes abound—from Quilty's voice on the radio, half-heard by Humbert at the start of the movie, to the brief glimpse of a sign outside a motel where Humbert and Lolita stay which reads: CHILDREN UNDER 14 FREE.

Lolita's maddening combination of childish bubblegum-popping and siren gestures (learned from the *Photoplay* magazines she constantly reads) is also true to Nabokov's vision.

The movie has none of the overstatement of Lyne's $156-million-grossing *Fatal Attraction*. It is a restrained, understated piece of work on a subject we are no more allowed to address in 1998 than we were in 1955.

Here is the astounding thing about *Lolita:* It still has the power to shock. The oedipal myth it portrays is as much a subject for denial today as it was in the fifties—or for that matter in Sigmund Freud's day.

We continue to deny the reality of underage sexuality. With unconstitutional forays like the Child Pornography Act of 1996, we combat the very idea that such a thing exists. But we are still finding excuses to censor works of art while we let all sorts of trash fly free. *Lolita* is an elegy to lost love, not an exploitation movie. If it showed an adolescent girl carved up by cannibals it would have been released in thousands of theaters two years ago with remarkably little fuss. But because it deals with incest—that universal, yet universally denied phenomenon—it has been subjected to the dunderheaded ministrations of the political correctness police.

So censorship is still with us. Only it is even more dangerous today because it is decentralized, thus harder to attack. The idea of the artist as enchanter has succumbed to the idea of the artist as political threat. In many ways we were better off in the fifties, when censorship was called by its proper name.

*The form of government most suitable to the artist is no
government at all.*

—OSCAR WILDE

Pornographic material has been present in the art and literature of every society in every historical period. What has changed
from epoch to epoch—or even from one decade to another—is the
ability of such material to flourish publicly and to be distributed
legally. In elitist societies there are, paradoxically, fewer calls for
censorship than in democratic ones, since elitist societies function
as de facto censors, keeping certain materials out of the purview of
hoi polloi. As democracy increases, so does the demand for legal
control over the erotic, the pornographic, the scatological. Our
own century is a perfect example of the oscillations of taste regarding such material. We have gone from the banning and burning of
D. H. Lawrence, James Joyce, Radclyffe Hall, Henry Miller, and

other avant-garde artists early in the century, to a passionate struggle to free literature from censorship in midcentury, to a new wave
of reaction at century's end.

After nearly a hundred years of agitating for freedom to publish, we find that the enemies of freedom have multiplied rather
than diminished. They are Christians, Muslims, oppressive totali-
tarian regimes, even well-meaning social libertarians who happen
to be feminists, teachers, school boards, some librarians. This
should not surprise us since, as Margaret Mead pointed out forty
years ago, the demand for state censorship is usually "a response to
the presence within the society of heterogeneous groups of people
with differing standards and aspirations."* As our culture becomes
more diverse, we can expect more calls for censorship. So it is essential for us to understand what role pornography plays in our
lives and what value it has.

Our job is made tougher and more confusing by the fact that the
spate of freedoms we briefly enjoyed in the late sixties, the seventies, and the early eighties led to the proliferation of sexual materials so ugly, exploitative, and misogynistic that it is impossible to
defend them. Artistically, however, we may believe that the First
Amendment protects them. The door was opened to *Lolita, Lady
Chatterley's Lover, Tropic of Cancer, Couples, Portnoy's Complaint,
Fear of Flying,* but it was also opened to *Debbie Does Dallas, Deep
Throat,* and *Snuff.* There has been a deluge of pornography so of-

*Margaret Mead, "Sex and Censorship in Contemporary Society," in *New World Writing* (New
York: New American Library of World Literature, 1953).

fensive to women that it has understandably provoked the ire of many feminists. Pornography also became hugely profitable once legal restraints were lifted, and this in turn gave rise to another wave of reaction.

We stand at a crossroads now when many former libertarians and liberals suddenly want to ban sexual materials. The old dream of the avant-garde that freeing sexual oppression would free human beings from their inhibitions and limitations has withered. We think we are sadder and wiser about what sexual freedom leads to, but in truth we never really *tried* sexual freedom. We only bally-hooed its simulacrum.

I want to bypass a reappraisal of the so-called sexual revolution for the moment and look instead at the impulse to create pornography and the role it plays in works of art. We owe it to ourselves to *understand* the impulses toward pornography, eroticism, scatology, before resuming our contentious public debate about their uses and whether or not they should be restricted.

I use the terms "eroticism" and "pornography" interchangeably, because I have come to the conclusion that only snobbery divides them. At one time I thought of pornography as purely an aid to masturbation, eroticism as something more high-toned and spiritual, like Molly Bloom's soliloquy in *Ulysses*. Now I doubt that distinction. Every visual artist—from the anonymous sculptor of the bare-breasted Minoan snake goddess to Pompeii's brothel muralists to William Turner and Pablo Picasso—has been drawn to the erotic and the pornographic. So have literary artists throughout history.

Sometimes the urge has been to stimulate the genitals; sometimes the urge has been to stimulate the mind. Since the mind and the genitals are part of one organism, why distinguish between masturbatory dreams and aesthetic ones? Surely there is also an aesthetics of masturbation, which our society is too sex-negative to explore. At any rate, it is time to go back to the origin of the pornographic impulse and explore the reasons why it is so tenacious.

Mark Twain's *1601* is a perfect place to start. Although Mark Twain lived in the Victorian age and knew he could never publish his pornographic fancies officially, they nevertheless preoccupied his energies, and he was so proud of them that he sought to disseminate them among his friends.

In Mark Twain's case, pornography was an *essential* part of his oeuvre because it primed the pump for other sorts of freedom of expression. It allowed him the freedom to create a new sort of American vernacular, first-person narratives that drew on American speech patterns and revealed the soul of America as never before. Experiments with pornography, scatology, eroticism, allowed him to delve into the communal unconscious and create some of the most profound myths on which American culture is based.

Mark Twain's notorious *1601 . . . Conversation as It Was by the Social Fireside, in the Time of the Tudors,* fascinates me because it demonstrates Mark Twain's passion for linguistic experiment and how allied it is with his compulsion toward "deliberate lewdness."

The phrase "deliberate lewdness" is, of course, Vladimir Nabokov's. He always linked the urge to create pornography with "the verve of a fine poet in a wanton mood" and regretted the dullness of contemporary porn, where "action has to be limited to the copulation of clichés." Motivated by such lackluster lust, the connoisseur of pornography is impatient with all attempts at verbal dexterity and linguistic wit. One is reminded that Henry Miller failed miserably as a paid pornographer because he could not leave the poetry out, as his anonymous patron wished. Anaïs Nin fared better with *Delta of Venus* and *Little Birds*. For Henry Miller pornography mattered precisely *because* it aroused him to poetry!

Henry Miller's attitude toward the pornographic is an ancient one. Poetry and pornography went hand in hand in Roman, Renaissance, and eighteenth-century literature. The pornographic flights of Catullus, Ovid, Petronius, and Juvenal never sacrificed style. Boccaccio, Villon, Rabelais, Cervantes, Shakespeare, John Donne, and Andrew Marvell all delighted in making porn poetic. Jonathan Swift, Alexander Pope, and Laurence Sterne were equally drunk with lewdness and with language.

No creator should have to bother about "the exact demarcation between the sensuous and the sensual," says Nabokov. Let the censors worry about such hypocritical distinctions. The literary artist has another agenda: to unfetter the imagination and let the wildness of the mind go free. The pornographic verve of ancient literature was his inspiration: In this he would have recognized Mark Twain as a brother.

Choosing to write from the point of view of "the Pepys of that day, the same being cup-bearer to Queen Elizabeth," in *1601* Mark

Twain was transporting himself to a world that existed before the invention of sexual hypocrisy. The Elizabethans were openly bawdy.
They found bodily functions funny and sex arousing to the muse.
Restoration wits and Augustan satirists had the same openness to
bodily functions and the same respect for eros. Only in the nineteenth
century did prudery (and the threat of legal censure) begin to para-
lyze the author's hand. Shakespeare, Rochester, and Pope were far
more fettered *politically* than we are, but the fact was that they were
not required to put condoms on their pens when the matter of sex
arose. They were happy to remind their readers of the messiness of
the body. They followed a classical tradition that often expressed
moral indignation through scatology. "Oh Celia, Celia, Celia shits,"
writes Swift (in one of his so-called unprintable poems), and he
writes it as if she were the first woman in history to do so. Swift is de-
bunking the conventions of courtly love (as well as expressing his
own deep misogyny), but he is doing so in a spirit that Catullus and
Juvenal would have recognized. Satire lashes the world to bring the
world to its senses. It does the dance of the satyrs around our follies.

Twain's scatology serves this purpose as well, but it is also a
warm-up for his creative process, a sort of pump-priming. Stuck in
the prudish nineteenth century, Mark Twain craved the freedom of
the ancients. In championing "deliberate lewdness" in *1601,* he
bestowed the gift of freedom on himself.

Even more interesting is the fact that Mark Twain was writing
1601 during the very same summer (1876) that he was "tearing
along on a new book"—the first sixteen chapters of a novel he then

referred to as "Huck Finn's autobiography." This conjunction is hardly coincidental. *Huckleberry Finn* and *1601* have a great deal in common besides linguistic experimentation. According to Justin Kaplan in *Mr. Clemens and Mark Twain,* "both were implicit rejections of the taboos and codes of polite society and both were experiments in using the vernacular as a literary medium."

What is the connection between *Huck Finn* and *1601*? As a professional writer whose process of composition often resembles Twain's (intermittent work on ambitious novels, writing blocks during which I put one work aside and devote myself to other projects, and periods of lecturing and travel), I think I understand Twain's creative strategy. He was sneaking up on the muse so that she would not be forewarned and escape.

Every author knows that a book begins to live only when the voice of its narrator comes alive. You may have plot ideas, characters may haunt you in the night, but the book does not fly until the sound of its voice is heard in the author's ear. And the sound of one book's voice is as individual as the sound of a child's voice. It may be related to that of other offspring, but it always has its own particular timbre, its own particular quirks.

In order to find the true voice of the book, the author must be free to play without fear of reprisals. All writing blocks come from excessive self-judgment, the internalized voice of the critical parent telling the author's imagination that it is a dirty little boy or girl. "Hah!" says the author. "I will flout the voice of parental propriety and break free!" This is why pornographic spirit is *always* related to unhampered creativity. Artists are fascinated with filth because we know that in filth, everything human is born. Human beings emerge between piss and shit, and so do novels and poems. Only by letting go of the inhibition that makes us bow to social propriety can we delve into the depths of the unconscious. We assert our freedom with pornographic play. If we are lucky, we *keep* that freedom long enough to create a masterpiece like *Huckleberry Finn*.

But the two compulsions are more than just related: They are *causally* intertwined.

When *Huckleberry Finn* was published in 1885, Louisa May Alcott put her finger on exactly what mattered about the novel even as she condemned it: "If Mr. Clemens cannot think of something better to tell our pure-minded lads and lasses, he had best stop writing for them." What Alcott didn't know was that "our pure-minded lads and lasses" aren't. But Mark Twain knew. It is not at all surprising that during that summer of high scatological spirits Twain should also give birth to the irreverent voice of Huck. If *Little Women* fails to go as deep as Twain's masterpiece, it is precisely because of Alcott's concern with pure-mindedness. Niceness is always the enemy of art. If you worry about what the neighbors, critics, parents, and supposedly pure-minded censors think, you will never create a work that defies the restrictions of the conscious mind and delves into the world of dreams.

1601 is deliberately lewd. It delights in stinking up the air of propriety. It delights in describing great thundergusts of farts, which make great stenches, and pricks that are stiff until cunts "take

ye stiffness out of them." In the midst of all this ribaldry, the assembled company speaks of many things—poetry, theater, art,
politics. Twain knew that the muse flies on the wings of flatus, and
he was having such a good time writing this Elizabethan pastiche
that the humor shines through a hundred years and twenty later.
I dare you to read *1601* without giggling and guffawing.

In the last few years a great deal of pious, politically correct
garbage has been written about pornography. Pornography, the
high-minded self-anointed feminist Catharine MacKinnon tells us,
is tantamount to an assault on women and actually causes rape.*
Pornography, MacKinnon's comrade in arms Andrea Dworkin
asserts, is a *form* of rape.†

A chorus of younger feminists has at last come along to counter
these unexamined contentions. Pornography, says Susie Bright, is
necessary to liberation. Pornography, says Sallie Tisdale, is desired
by women as well as men. Pornography, says Nadine Strossen, is
guaranteed by the Bill of Rights.

But what about the Bill of Rights for artists? Could Robert
Mapplethorpe's photographs of lilies have existed without his photographs of pricks? Could Henry Miller have grasped human tran-
scendence in *The Colossus of Maroussi* without having wallowed in
the sewers of Paris in *Tropic of Cancer?*

I say no. Without farts, there are no flowers. Without pricks,
there are no poems.

---

*See *Only Words* (Harvard University Press, 1993).
†See *Letters from a War Zone,* 1993, or any of Dworkin's other books.

This is not the first time in history we have seen an essentially libertarian movement like feminism devolve into a debate about purity. The suffragists of the last century also turned into prudish prohibitionists who spent their force proscribing drink and policing pure-mindedness. One might argue that a concern with pure-mindedness is fatal not only to art but also to political movements.

Why does this urge toward repression crop up in supposedly libertarian movements? And why does this puritanical urge to censor the artist keep recurring? The artist needs to be free to play in the id in order to bring back insights for the ego. But the id is scary. It yawns like a bottomless *vagina dentata*. It threatens to bite off heads, hands, cocks, and to swallow us up in our darkest impulses. Society fears the id even as it yearns for the release to be found there. We retreat from dream and fantasy even as we long to submerge in them. Make no mistake about it: The primal ooze of creation *is* terrifying. It reminds us of how little control we have over our lives, over our deaths. It reminds us of our origins and inspires us to contemplate our inevitable annihilation.

Pornographic art is perceived as dangerous to political movements because, like the unconscious, it is not programmable. It is dangerous play whose outcome never can be predicted. Since dream is the speech of the unconscious, the artist who would create works of value must be fluent in speaking the language of dream. The pornographic has a direct connection to the unconscious.

I suspect this was why Twain was having such fun with *1601* the very summer *Huck Finn*'s adventures were burgeoning in his brain.

The filth of *1601* fertilized the garden of Huck's adventures. Like any literary artist who is in touch with his id, Twain instinctively knew that sex and creativity were interrelated. He could not fill *Huckleberry Finn* with farts, pricks, and cunts, but he could play in *1601* and prepare his imagination for the antisocial adventures he would give his antihero in the other book.

In his classic essay "Obscenity and the Law of Reflection,"* Henry Miller suggests that "when obscenity crops out in art, in literature more particularly, it usually functions as a technical device. . . . Its purpose is to awaken, to usher in a sense of reality. In a sense, its use by the artist may be compared to the use of the miraculous by the Masters." Here Miller means the *spiritual* masters. He believed that Christ and the Zen masters resorted to miracles only when such were absolutely necessary to awaken their disciples. The artist uses obscenity the same way. "The real nature of the obscene lies in its lust to convert," Miller says. Obscenity is used in literature as a sort of wake-up call to the unconscious. Obscenity transports us to "another dimension of reality."

So *1601* served an important creative function for its author. It awakened his freedom to experiment, play, and dream outrageous dreams.

Havelock Ellis once said that "adults need obscene literature, as much as children need fairy tales, as a relief from the obsessive force of convention." The urge toward obscenity is nothing more

---

*See *Henry Miller on Writing* (New Directions, 1964).

or less than the urge toward freedom. Those who condemn it are clearly afraid of the debauchery that freedom might unleash in themselves. They inevitably condemn what they are most attracted to. The censor is the one who slavers in private over books, films, and visual artifacts that he or she then proscribes for the rest of society.

Throughout history, the urge to censor has always been stronger in those most attracted to the freedom of the obscene. In quashing freedom in others, the censor hopes to quash it within.

"Liberation," says Henry Miller, "implies the sloughing off of chains, the bursting of the cocoon. What is obscene are the preliminary or anticipatory movements of birth, the preconscious writhing in the face of a life to be."

Miller goes on to say that the obscene "is an attempt to spy on the secret processes of the universe." The guilt of the creator when he or she knows that something extraordinary is being born comes from the knowledge of tampering with godlike powers, a Promethean guilt for impersonating the immortals. "The obscene has all the qualities of the hidden interval," Miller says. It is

vast as the Unconscious itself and as amorphous and fluid as the very stuff of the Unconscious. It is what comes to the surface as strange, intoxicating and forbidden, and which therefore arrests and paralyzes when in the form of Narcissus we bend over our own image in the mirror of our own iniquity. Acknowledged by all, it is nevertheless despised and rejected, wherefore it is constantly

emerging in Protean guise at the most unexpected moments. When
it is recognized and accepted . . . it inspires no more dread than . . .
the flowering lotus which sends its roots down into the mud of the
stream of which it is born.

Sexuality and creativity were not always divorced as they are
today and as they were in Mark Twain's day. All so-called primitive
and pagan art exhibits the marriage of sexuality and creativity—
whether in the form of giant phalluses, multitudinous breasts, or
pregnant bellies. But the divorce between body and mind that char-
acterizes the Christian era has led the artist to curious strategies of
creation and constant guilt for the possession of the creative gift.

We see this guilt as clearly in Mark Twain as in any artist who
ever lived. His creative strategies of intermittent composition, his
fear of working on a book once it became clear that the process of
composition would inevitably lift the veil and take him into the sacred and forbidden precincts, betrays his hypersensitivity to something we might call post–Christian creator guilt—if it weren't such
a daunting mouthful.

In primitive societies, the artist and the shaman are one. There
is no discontinuity between artistic creation and the sacred. The
shaman-artist creates in order to worship and worships in order to
create.

Not so the artist in our culture. Always racked by guilt for the
power of creativity *itself,* beset by censors within and without, our
artists are shackled by a sense of transgression so deep it often

destroys them. No wonder we use obscenity to break open the door, to lift the veil. No wonder we insist on our right to do so as if our lives depended on it. They do.

So the artist needs pornography as a way into the unconscious, and history proves that if this license is not granted, it will be stolen. Mark Twain had *1601* printed privately. Picasso kept pornographic notebooks that were exhibited only after his death.

But what about *access* to these works? Should access be restricted? And if so, how shall we decide to *whom* it shall be restricted, and how shall we decide who makes the decision? As I said earlier, this is a problem that arises only in heterogeneous societies. In homogeneous societies, tradition and taboo govern what shall be seen and what unseen, and the whole tribe agrees about it. There *is* no problem. But our society is multiethnic, multiracial, multisexual. What is offensive to a Muslim may not be offensive to a Unitarian. What is offensive to an Orthodox Jew may not be offensive to an assimilated Jew. What is offensive to a feminist may seem like free speech to a lusty adolescent. We do not even agree on the *definition* of obscenity.

Who shall make rules for the whole of society when society is so diverse and none of us agree on what obscenity is?

This is the problem we confront today. Add to it the relentlessly commercial thrust of our communications media and the fact that they are concentrated in fewer and fewer hands, and you see the danger we are in. Commercial television networks in America have "solved" the problem by editing out *anything* that may be offensive to *any* group who may petition their sponsors. Ban what is quirky, eccentric, imaginative, sexual, satirical, or strange, and the result will be the predigested baby formula American television offers. The whole country is in danger of becoming a Disney theme park whose main aim is to sell hamburgers, hot dogs, and copyrighted trinkets in the shapes of cartoon characters. Interactive media—whose main interaction is between credit card and digital order-taker—seems to be going the same way. Puritans have already attempted to ban sex in cyberspace, but apparently not selling. Selling is, of course, *not* considered obscene in America.

Margaret Mead says that all societies have two problems in relation to sex:

> how to keep sex activity out of forbidden channels that will endanger the bodies and souls of others or the co-operative process of social life, *and* how to keep it flowing reliably in those channels where it is a necessity if children are to be conceived and reared in homes where father and mother are tied together by the requisite amount of sexual interest.

We must keep people together to rear families, and we must raise children who can "focus their capacities for sexual feelings on particular persons." These two social tasks seem simple to effect, but they are not. Random sexual activity must be controlled, contained, ritualized—but not to the detriment of desire itself. Desire is necessary—not only for art but for binding parents together. Sex can be a destructive force or a cohesive one—depending on how it is used. Many primitive societies have allowed group sexual activities under particular circumstances—to propitiate the crops or to celebrate a wedding or feast. "An orgy for all which serves group goals ceases to be an orgy, and so is dignified," says Margaret Mead.

One of the reasons we are so negative toward pornography is that we do not see pornography as serving group goals. In this we may be mistaken. The former U.S. surgeon general, Joycelyn Elders, was forced to step down a few years ago after publicly averring that masturbation might be a good thing for adolescents—a far better thing than early sexual activity and parenthood. Such was the prevalent sexual hypocrisy of the United States that this eminently sensible statement caused an outcry. Given his own predilections, President Clinton should have awarded the Congressional Medal of Honor to Elders rather than forcing her to resign.

I cheered her. Any idiot can see that masturbation is less harmful than parenthood at twelve, thirteen, fourteen, fifteen. . . . But one may not say so publicly. We are supposed to pretend that sexual desire does not exist. Sexual desire *does* exist, and every society in history has expressed it in art, literature, jokes, dances, music, sacred rituals. Now we are faced with the possibility that the heterogeneity of our society may lead to our banning those universal expressions of human feeling.

I believe that censorship is always an evil to be deplored in a free society. A far better method of keeping inappropriate materials out of the purview of those we deem too young or too emotionally vulnerable for them is a system of rating or labeling visual or literary materials so that minors and those who seek to protect them can be forewarned. To restrict access to materials *by age* is *not* the same as to proscribe them. Parents who believe it is their responsibility to protect their children from the corruptions of television, movies, books, and the Internet have but to pull the plug on the machine (or lock up the books and magazines) when danger beckons. It is unfair for such parents to demand that the state control what they themselves cannot control. So, too, with puritanical sects. If they cannot dissuade their youths from wallowing in what is morally corrupting, what kind of moral leadership are they providing? Surely they cannot demand that the *state* provide for them the moral authority their priests cannot provide?

In place of censorship I would limit access, increase parental responsibility, and urge those who do not like our mass media to create their own competing media. If we ban whatever offends *any* group in our diverse society, we will soon have no art, no culture, no humor, no satire. Satire is by its *nature* offensive. So is much art and political discourse. The value of these expressions far outweighs their risk.

Oscar Wilde—who appears to have said everything—said of censorship: "In France . . . they limit the journalist and allow the artist almost perfect freedom. Here we allow absolute freedom to the journalist and limit the artist."

Like so many things he said, it is still true. This long after the centenary of Wilde's sentencing for "gross indecency," we ought to be wiser about restricting sexual expression than our predecessors were. In the name of protecting children, we cannot starve adults. In the name of social harmony, we cannot ban ecstasy. We *can* limit access based on age. I believe that is the *most* we *should* do. The enforcement may be spotty—but so, too, is the enforcement on banning nicotine for children or firearms to criminals. As long as we allow tobacco companies to addict our children to a cancer-causing substance, it is sheer hypocrisy to demand censorship of sexual materials on the grounds that they pervert and corrupt.

The well-meaning feminists who assert without evidence that pornography is rape, the evangelical Christians whose influence over their own children is so weak they want the state to bolster them, the authoritarian Muslims who read works of the imagination literally and thus proclaim fatwas against creative writers, cannot be our masters. Our concern must be with keeping intellectual and artistic excellence alive *even* in a pluralistic democracy. It is a tough challenge, and it tends to bring out the zealotry in the most academic ideologues. "Every idea is an incitement," said Oliver Wendell Holmes. Surely that does not mean we should banish ideas.

English law on the subject of pornography attempts to ban certain materials on the basis of their tendency "to deprave and corrupt." The Hicklin rule, on which nearly all British and American pornography decisions were based for over a century (and which has recently been revived by Catharine MacKinnon under another name), made the test for obscenity its tendency to "deprave and corrupt those whose minds are open to such immoral influences." The Obscene Publications Act of 1959 and 1964 modified Hicklin but still relied on the test of depraving and corrupting to define pornography and to distinguish it from those productions of human ingenuity which advance medical science or art or literature. We must admit that this is an inexact test, very prone to influence by political trends. The current United States law on pornography is equally bad. It asserts "community standards" as a test and begs the question of federal standards entirely.

So we are no closer to a good definition of obscenity than we *ever* were, and as our society grows more diverse, we are in for more chaos and confusion. If you factor in the problem that defenders of public morality are not always entirely sincere and are often motivated by low political ambitions, you see how thorny the dilemma is. In his memoir, *Murderers and Other Friends*, John Mortimer has a witty passage about this very subject:

> As defenders, we naturally found ourselves on the side of books and films which the prosecution was trying to ban. That didn't mean that we found these works particularly attractive; it's not necessary, when defending an alleged murderer, to believe that the best way to end an unhappy marriage is with a kitchen knife in the stomach. Prosecutors who seek to keep the purity of our national life unsullied can be similarly detached. Geoff and I did a long case about some questioned publication or other against a particularly jovial prosecutor who would push his way past my middle-aged

knees every morning and chirrup, "Give us a kiss, darling," as I sat gloomily preparing my work for the day. I used to write in a number of notebooks which had dark circles printed on their covers. In his final speech to the jury this prosecutor was saying, "And if this sort of publication is allowed, youth will be corrupted, authority will be undermined, family life will be in peril and civilization, as we know it, will grind to a halt." Then, glancing down at my notebook, he muttered, "Arseholes all over your notebook, darling!" and went on with his peroration. The truth is that the defenders of public morality are not always all that they seem to be.

Indeed not. We have to admit that history of censorship from Anthony Comstock to the present has not been a distinguished one. Moreover, people being people and motivated by power first, lust second, there is an imperishable human tendency to use censorship for political ends: to crush one's opponents, to keep dissenters silent, to prevent changes in the status quo, to keep women properly in our places. Whenever and wherever legal grounds for censorship exist, it is never long before they are used to crush the underdog, the nonconformist, the woman, the witch. Because censorship is such an obvious club put in the hands of the state, I am *mystified* by feminists who seek to renew its force. Perhaps they believe they are (or are soon to be) the state—in which case they are seriously deluded. A concern with "public morality" is—if not the last refuge of a scoundrel—the first foray of the fascist. First they burn books, as Heine said, then they burn people. For "books," read films, Internet, television, whatever.

And who profits from censorship? I maintain that those who own and control the fewer and fewer media conglomerates do. Through censorship laws, their hegemony over the airwaves, over the Internet, is protected. The Christian Coalition will at first seek to control the Internet with antiobscenity laws, but you can be sure that their definition of obscenity will *not* include rallying militia movements via optical fiber or proselytizing against gun control laws, environmental regulation, freedom of contraceptive choice, and abortion. One's enemy's agenda is *always* obscene. One's own is *always* moral.

For this reason alone, I am against censorship. I prefer the chaos of uncontrollable communication of all sorts to selective banning of certain materials. I do not think human beings can be trusted to be above politics and to promote the common good. One group's common good is another group's evil.

We are better off punishing rapists, making our streets safe for women and children, than banning pornography. We are better off spending time *raising* our children and teaching them values than attempting to police television, magazines, the Internet.

I suspect that calls for censorship are always the lazy person's way of influencing the minds of the young. The truth is, we teach our children by our own example and not by what we let them watch on television or plug into on the net. If we are hypocrites, they will be hypocrites, too. If we are honest about our beliefs, they will be drawn to honesty as well. Mass communications do not raise our children; *we* do. In attempting to control the airwaves, we are mimicking the dictator's agenda. We are making our media safe for selling, delivering the next generation of customers, and abdicating our own personal responsibility. Better to turn the television off than to turn off our own discrimination, parenting, and judgment.

The calls for censorship we have lately heard are an attempt to blame mass communications for all the seemingly insoluble problems of a violent and overpopulated world where wealth has increasingly become the only measure of worth. The truth is that mass communications are only a mirror of our values. They show us who we are and what we have become. If we dislike what we see there, we should cure the diseased body politic, not merely attempt to retouch its image. That is a way of doing nothing while reassuring ourselves of our zeal for reform.

I have an emotional tapeworm. Never enough to eat.

—ANAÏS NIN

Anaïs Nin: the very name conjures exoticism and eroticism. There should be a specific word for this heady combination. In fact, there is: her own name, Anaïs, which has become a perfume, a vast library of books, an almost museum-size collection of photographs, and of course the archetype of the contemporary writer as a woman.

Like any archetype, she is loved and hated—with the *same* evidence being used for each canonization, each attack.

Kate Millett saw Anaïs Nin as the first self-portraitist "of the artist as a woman." Millett suggests that "our form is autobiography," and she dubs Nin "Mother to us all."

Why are there so few positions in between adoration and detestation? Because Nin is seen as a representative of woman's psychological and sexual freedom. The response to her depends on the reader's degree of liberation. For women who seek freedom—artistically and sexually—she is the pioneer, validating our quest. For women who fear freedom, she becomes the target, evoking a furious response that may be only anger at one's self for being unfree.

To men she is an enigma—seductive to some for her sexual and literary sorcery (which have the same roots and in fact become one), but repellent to others for her manipulativeness, her old-fashioned nineteenth-century sexual romanticism, and the queasy-making, highfalutin tone her writing sometimes takes. Since few men have a visceral understanding of the problems women writers face, they may consider Anaïs Nin's strategies duplicitous, deceptive, seven-veiled.

What *are* the problems a woman writer faces? Let's get this straight once and for all. Virginia Woolf described them brilliantly in *A Room of One's Own* (1928), but half the world, apparently, hasn't heard.

First, there is the need for privacy and silence—which a woman's life often lacks. If she is a wife or a mother, even the care-taker of a brother, father, mother, aunt, or lover, she is assumed to *need* no private time or space. But writing cannot happen in a crowd.

Next, she lacks money to support her fulfilling herself—those few guineas a year Woolf's hypothetical woman writer needed. The guineas needed are inflated now, but they are usually earned by giving up the necessary time to write. Woolf's hypothetical woman writer had a private income—albeit small. As for husbands, they *used* to support wives, but they supported them on condition of certain services being performed—social, sexual, maternal, culinary. It is the rare husband, even today, who can free his wife from social appointments, family duties, child care, and let her mind find the spaciousness it requires. The wife who says, "I'm writing. I won't be home for dinner," is often the wife who is about to lose her job. Since men still have a preponderance of the world's money and women (except for a tiny elite) are dependent on men's attitudes, they must either change their men, tiptoe around them, lie to them, or get divorced and live alone.

These options are more than ever possible today. But a sense of family is hard to lose. Family warmth grounds the dreamer. Men who dream surely need this warmth, and their getting it is not always antithetical to their family affections. Women dreamers are still often asked to give up love.

These are only the domestic problems. What if a woman solves them somehow and goes out into the world to present her creative work? She finds that her sex is a built-in bias, that men rule the definitions of prestige, that her gender goes in and out of style every decade or so.

She also faces the whore/madonna dichotomy. Women who write about sex are presumed to be whores. (*Good* women write domestic novels, sweeping historical potboilers, romances that make no literary claims, or biographies of historical figures. Good women do not disturb the status quo.)

There is, of course, a little bit of room for rebels and renegades—especially if they are dead. Virginia Woolf is safely dead, safely modernist, safely categorizable as "Bloomsbury." Gertrude Stein is safely dead, safely modernist, safely categorizable as "lesbian." She doesn't worry male critics much because she's clearly *out* of their domestic and sexual spheres. She need not be judged by the prejudices of heterosexual love. Woolf and Stein are both sui generis at last.

But for women who live *in* the world, sleep with men, love their children, and dare to enter into the sexual debate through their books, the reception is much chillier and much contentious.

Anaïs Nin knew all these things long before my generation discovered them. She knew she had to survive, find time to write, have money to live, and somehow fulfill her sexual and literary potential. Even though she'd married very young to a man who did not particularly stir her sexually, she loved and needed him. While idealizing him recklessly, she knew that unless she was to live only half a life, she would have to perfect deceit. The same holds true for many women today.

Nin had been seduced and abandoned by her father in childhood, then brought up strictly by her all-suffering Catholic mother. She was at first so afraid of sexual love that she may have deliberately married a man who shared her fear, and her marriage to Hugh Guiler remained unconsummated for at least two years. He patiently waited for her to blossom, worshiping her as an angel-artist. She also began to write in a mélange of languages, none of which was wholly hers at first. (Spanish, French, and English warred for hegemony on her tongue.) So Nin developed various strategies essential to her as a writer/wife. To learn about sexuality without sacrificing her stabilizing marriage, she learned to deceive. It came easily to her because she was an expert at deceiving herself. She had blocked all her terrifying sexual memories from childhood.

To write her journals, she fictionalized them, even to herself. To publish her journals, she expurgated them. To be honest to history, she left manuscripts of these secret journals to literary executors who shared her vision; they saw to it that the journals were published after her death.

I am concerned here only with the first two of them: *Henry & June* and *Incest*. Nin managed to have them appear exactly as she wrote them, even though she had to wait for posthumous publication.

No married woman writer has ever succeeded as well in preserving all her work. Sylvia Plath's journals and literary remains were partly destroyed by Ted Hughes. Laura Riding repudiated her early art and hid herself by changing her name. Virginia Woolf committed suicide in her literary prime. Jean Rhys stopped writing for decades, sunk in alcoholism. Marina Tsvetayeva, Anna Wickham, Sara Teasdale, ended their own lives. Only Anaïs Nin and Colette went on writing as they ripened and left us all that they wished to leave.

But French women don't count. Even in the eighteenth century, they were allowed to be intellectuals while the rest of us were still hiding manuscripts under the embroidery hoop. Colette had a whole

French female literary tradition to draw upon. Few American and English writers could count on this. Nin presented her expurgated journals to the public in the seventies, but she left the most stirring stories for after her death. The first, *Henry & June,* appeared in 1986. It stunned with its sharpness and frankness. Decades after *Tropic of Cancer,* in an age when sex was all but discredited, *Henry & June* still seemed electrifying. It told the story of Anaïs Nin's love affair with Henry Miller from October 1931 to October 1932—a love affair which was also a ménage à trois.

This extraordinary love triangle between the seductive gutter-snipe Miller, his seductive wife, June, and the seductive Nin really becomes a quadrangle if you count Nin's husband Hugo's quiet, half-knowing part in it.

The bare bones of the story would be seductive, even if the principal characters were unknown.

A beautiful young writer, not yet thirty, is ensconced in the lush suburbs of Paris a few years after the crash of '29. Her banker husband, who was much richer when she married him, travels a lot, leaving her in the fantasy world of her villa, where she keeps her journal and dreams of being a member of the bohemian artistic set in Paris. Her father was a celebrated musician, who left the family when she was a girl. Her mother was an artist turned drudge. Her husband is her loving protector, but sexually they are incompatible. He longs to be an artist himself but works at the bank to support her and her whole family, including her disapproving Catholic mother. He is a WASP who went to Yale and was disinherited for marrying her. He loves her madly, but he is confused about what he wants to be when he grows up. He is sexually repressed and sexually hungry.

One day, at lunch with a lawyer she knows through her husband, our heroine meets a bohemian guttersnipe from Brooklyn, who is writing the book to end all books, the book to tell everything that is left out of books. This self-described "Brooklyn boy" is already nearly forty, and he talks as wildly and brilliantly as he writes. He's as much in love with literature, philosophy, and D. H. Lawrence as she is. He's fierce, feral, and drunk with life. His sexuality is powerful, but unlike his writing, he is courtly in pursuit.

She finds herself drawn to him and becomes entangled. Then, suddenly, his wife appears from America.

She is equally fascinating—a vamp, a flapper, a magic talker, a blond bisexual from Greenwich Village. She also dreams of becoming an artist of some sort.

She and the young writer/wife fall in love, or lust, or sisterhood—or all three at once. The three weave their webs around one another and around the writer's husband, who comes back to pay the bills and take everyone out to dinner.

The young writer and the Brooklyn wildman analyze both the vamp and the husband, and become passionate lovers in the process. They make love to the vamp (and challenge the husband)

through each other. The husband is aroused by all the frenzy in the
air, but he doesn't really want to discover why. Even when he
comes home to find the Brooklyn wildman in his bed, he is jollied
out of believing what he saw was betrayal by his magical muse of a
wife. As the quadrangle grows even hotter, the young writer discovers how to write more vividly, how to make love with her whole
self, how to surrender to a man and also to the muse. The Brooklyn
guttersnipe is equally inspired. He finishes his fearless book and
shows it to his inamorata. It is indeed "the last book" by "the last
man alive." With her encouragement, he goes in search of a publisher. Then the vamp comes back from a trip to America for the
final confrontation.

In this story, who is the muse and who is the creator? The two
women vie for the role of muse and the two men vie for the role of
lover. The young writer is sure she has created everyone. The
Brooklyn guttersnipe believes that he is the life force. The vamp
believes that both writers are stealing her soul. The husband believes he is getting a soul out of all this pain.

It's a hell of a story, and Nin tells it fiercely. Her good-girl
pudeur stripped away, she writes with a burning pen. Her sexuality
open, she seduces her husband, her analyst, her lover, her muse,
her lover's wife. The story is told with sure, searing strokes, with
no flowery prologues or codas.

But *this* story, in *this* form, will go unpublished until after the
author's death, at seventy-four. She refuses to publicly humiliate

her husband (and perhaps she also fears to expose herself),* so the version of it that first appears has pillow talk occurring instead in cafés. No wonder something seems to be missing! No wonder the prose often seems maddenly vague and wispy.

The year after the triumph of having written *Henry & June* into her secret journal, Nin began to tell another story, the story of her discovery of love from October 1932 to November 1934. This tome was only released sixty years later, as *Incest, from "A Journal of Love."*

The love in this case is still for Henry Miller (with whom her life and loins are still entwined), her husband, Hugo, who has become more sexual, her first analyst, René Allendy (whom she once loved but now abandons), her second analyst, Otto Rank (with whom she is currently entranced), Antonin Artaud, the actor-poet, and Joaquin Nin, her father, the musician, whom she seduces in revenge for his having seduced and abandoned her in childhood. She triumphs over his Don Juanism with her far stronger impersonation of Doña Juana.

It's a "Journal of Love" unlike any ever published before. It dares to describe the ultimate act: incest. What does she feel? What does he feel? No other writer before her dared this much. If Henry Miller wanted to write what was left out of men's books, Anaïs Nin succeeded in writing all that has been left out of women's books for

---

*I once asked Anaïs Nin why she had expurgated the sexual scenes in her diaries, and she replied: "Because I was aware that any woman who wrote frankly about her sex life was never again taken seriously by literary critics." "But, Miss Nin," I protested, "that is exactly why we must do it." This exchange took place at the 92nd Street Y in 1971 or 1972. Nin remains correct. Women who write about sex are still denigrated.

centuries. (Only in the last few years has the incest taboo been breached in women's writing.)

The central incident in *Incest* (at least in the present retelling of the story) is Anaïs Nin's seduction of her father (or her father's seduction of her).

I notice that our language contains no word for mutual seduction—but it really *was* that. After much letter-writing fore-play, many regrets about not having truly known each other as child and parent, the two come together at Valescure-Saint Raphaël, at the now defunct Coirier's Grand Hotel, each of them temporar-ily fleeing another life.

They discover how alike they are in their sexual selves. Joaquin Nin y Castellanos discovers his daughter, his double. Anaïs discovers her father the myth as a mere man—a rather rigid, fussy, controlling man of almost fifty-four who suffers from lumbago and regrets.

Like any father figure, he seduces her by telling how his wife failed to understand him—but in this case his wife is her mother!

Like any daughter figure, she confesses her past, her hurts in child-hood, her love affairs. She is seeking absolution—but in this case he is the *author* of her primal hurts. All the love affairs have sought in vain to assuage them, but now she has the real thing in her snare.

She confesses that all her journal-writing was for him, that her craft has always been an attempt to bring him back.

He in turn confesses that his whole life has been tainted by his abandonment of her, that he has been seeking her everywhere, in other women, but now he has "found [his] match."

They discover that they both love to go to the same hotel room with other lovers, delighting in their own duplicity, aroused by the secret knowledge of betrayal. They discover also that they are mirrors of each other; they discover, in short, the perfect narcissistic love. They are both picaresque heroes, both afraid of intimacy, both flirts and illusionists, who flee. But they cannot flee each other.

Nin's father teaches her own faults, exposes her own defects of character. She is both attracted and repelled by him.

He confesses: "I don't feel toward you as if you were my daughter."

She confesses: "I don't feel as if you were my father."

And with that (and a little more psychologizing), he kisses her mouth. And then comes "a wave of desire." And then, though she is both "terrified and desirous," she "melts," and he "emptied all of himself in me . . . and my yielding was immense, with my whole being, with only that core of fear which arrested the supreme spasm in me."

She holds back her own orgasm and retreats at once to her room to be alone, feeling "poisoned by this union." She is guilty but suddenly in possession of some primal mystery. The mistral blows so hard it cracks the windows. She feels both humbled and defiled.

"The sperm was a poison," she writes in her journal, feeling she has succumbed to "a love that was a poison."

She longs to run away but must know the end of the mystery. So she stays on, succumbing again and again to her father's passion, never having an orgasm yet being filled with his sperm, so "overabundant" that she walks down the hall to her room "with a handkerchief between [her] legs."

He claims he wants to replace her other lovers, but despite his orgies of repeated penetration, he fears the loss of his *riquette,* his virility. He fears that she is young and will abandon him for younger men. He admits jealousy of Hugo, of Henry, of all the letters she receives from them daily. But for all his supposed twinship with Anaïs, he fails to have an inkling of *her* feelings—her utter confusion and bewilderment, her embodiment of the incest taboo in her failure to find orgasm, her sadness, her remorse. She is *tormented* about lying to everyone to achieve this gloomy union; he fails to understand that, too.

What is remarkable about Anaïs Nin's telling of the tale is not only the description of physical incest but the willingness to record all her feelings about it, even before she fully understands them. The taboo is so strong that most women writers have mythicized and disguised these feelings, in fiction and poetry as well as in autobiography. I felt that I was reading a story never told before. Not only is the father dissected, but the daughter's feelings are anatomized.

Only once have I confronted such material in my own writing and it took me wholly by surprise. In my third novel, *Fanny, Being the True History of the Adventures of Fanny Hackabout-Jones,* I was unwittingly drawn into an incest myth. My heroine was raped by her stepfather and later learned he was her biological father. The incest was wholly unintentional, and it astounded both heroine and author. Several adapters of the book for stage and screen have been adamant about changing this one part of the book. The incest taboo is that strong.

Nin broke this primal taboo in her life and she also had the audacity to write about it. It's true that the prose in this episode becomes filled with "unreality"—a word Nin uses often when she is confused by emotional contradictions.

Henry is real; Hugo is real; Rank is real; even the elusive Antonin Artaud is (almost) real. But her father dissolves in a poisonous mist, and when he cries and says he cannot let her go, she is all the more determined to leave. She rationalizes away his bad character, embellishes his sensitivity, tries in every way to idealize him. But he comes across as a weak and selfish man who knows neither his own heart nor his daughter's, a man incapable of either filial or genital love.

The *"padre-amour"* section (note that Anaïs uses Spanish and French in describing it) is the shortest of the book, though it provokes the title. All Nin's actual diaries had fevered titles, like *La Folle Lucide; Equilibre; Uranus: Schizoidie & Paranoia; The Triumph of Magic; Flagellation . . . Audace; The Definite Appearance of the Demon, or Flow—Childhood—Rebirth. Incest* is faintly commercial by comparison, and the brashness of the title may actually be a liability. Nevertheless, it is psychologically true to the book. Anaïs Nin's multitudinous seductions were all incestuous at heart. She was forever wooing and winning her mythic father by mimicking his behavior. He was the Zeus who ruled her mental universe.

The first part of *Incest* tells of Nin's waning ability to idealize Henry Miller (though their affair continues), of her starting to see Henry as "a perverse, irresponsible child" whose fierce honesty can be "another way of hurting."

But *Henry & June,* for which she is seeking publication while writing *Incest* (through William Aspenwall Bradley, the agent she found for Henry), is seen by her as too soft on Miller, too idealizing. This response thwarts publication but makes Nin more determined than ever to continue writing her unsparing daily journal.

In fact, it is just the *dailiness* of the journal that makes it revolutionary. *Incest* goes on to explore Hugo's discovery of his wife's affair (through reading her journal) and Anaïs's Scheherazade-like ability to talk him out of what he has read (and seen), claiming her journal to be erotic fiction based on fantasy. She swears to Hugo that there is another, still *more secret* journal, which reveals her innocence. Wanting to believe, Hugo believes and forgives. Anaïs is left with her husband's quiet kindness and her own ravening guilt. She is both elated and depressed by her ability to be so many women at once—playing each part with utter conviction.

In *Incest,* she complains that Henry stops reading her writing, that he has thousands of faults. Yet she still sometimes dreams of "finding Hugo a woman who can make him happy" and departing for another life with Henry.

Six months after the first meeting, her father comes to her house in Louviciennes and makes love to her again. He pleads for utter fidelity between them, knowing fidelity is impossible for them both. This time she feels nothing but compassion for him (which disguises her need for revenge).

She becomes involved with Otto Rank, her second psychoanalyst, who demands that she give up her diary, her "opium," and leave it in his hands. This ultimate surrender propels their love affair. Father commands are always aphrodisiac to Nin. Through Rank, Nin is able to dismiss her father as a lover. She finally tells him what a narcissist he is and hardens her heart to all the men in her life. She feels herself becoming a "primitive woman" who loves at least four men at once. With her new power, she persuades Jack Kahane to publish *Tropic of Cancer* after a vacillating two-year wait. She underwrites the publication with money borrowed from Rank. But still her own journals remain unpublished.

In London, she meets Rebecca West and finds herself more admired than Henry. This is a special kind of validation.

In May of 1934, she discovers herself pregnant with Miller's child. A heroic struggle begins in her mind between Henry the child-man and little Henry, the fetus. She knows that Henry wants no rival in a child; and she knows that she cannot present Henry's child to Hugo. She imagines a war between the child and her artist self. Over Hugo's objections, she goes to a *sage-femme* to abort the child.

It is a life-changing sacrifice she is making, and she is well aware of the cost. She describes the labor and the stillbirth with a vividness that still makes me cringe and weep on the tenth rereading. The expelled fetus becomes an abandoned child like herself: "So full of energy my half-created child that I will thrust back into the *néant* again. Back into obscurity and unconsciousness, and the paradise of non-being. I have known you; I have lived with you. You are only the future. You are the abdication."

Then comes the battle of birth, the futility of pushing out a dead baby. Anaïs stops pushing and the doctor rages at her and causes her deliberate pain. "The pain makes [her] howl."

Finally the little sacrifice is pushed into the light. It is a girl baby, perfectly formed, perfectly dead.

With this act, Anaïs feels she has delivered herself as an artist. She has killed the woman in herself, committed female infanticide both on her child and on herself.

With one act, she has repudiated her mother, her father, Henry, Hugo, Rank, and all the men who want to possess her. She will never face abandonment again.

Tropic of Cancer, that other baby, bursts into the world. Henry is launched, and accordingly she loses interest in him (though he does not in her). She sails for America with Rank, to become a psychoanalyst.

What Nin has created here is nothing less than a mirror of life. The fluctuations of moods, the flip-flops from hate to love that mark our frail humanity, are seen in *process,* as never before.

Nin was doing what Proust, Joyce, and Miller were doing, but she was proceeding from within a *woman's* consciousness. Where Miller is often impossible to follow because of his plotlessless and stubbornly nonlinear time, Nin is always lucid. She reflects the change of mind and mood by an accretion of precise descriptions, not by the loopy repetition we often find in Miller.

Nor does she veil her story in ancient mythology and clever coinages like Joyce. But she has the same modernist urge to explode time and abolish space. The space inside the mind is all that interests her.

If Nin was such a pivotal and important figure in the history of modern literature, why has she been so maligned?

The first reason is obvious: sexism. The second is also obvious: our unique cultural fear of sexuality. The third reason is equally obvious: What she has created is new (a kind of writing that hybridizes autobiography and fiction). Since we belong to a species that fears the new for no other reason than because it is not old, Nin's creation of a new form is troubling.

But Nin has also been deeply misunderstood because of the *sequence* in which her work appeared.

For years she was the great unpublished author, whispered and gossiped about, known for her literary love affairs and vast artistic and psychoanalytic acquaintanceship. The few novels that appeared under her name were written in an obfuscating experimental style and issued from precious avant-garde publishers. Even her book on D. H. Lawrence was known only to a coterie.

In the early seventies, with the rebirth of feminism, the so-called second wave, Nin was published to a large hungering audience, but published in ways that obscured the immensity of her achievement. The books were expurgated to spare the feelings of husband Hugo and countless others who were still alive.

Nin's reputation rose with feminism and fell with its repudiation. It rose with the movement for sexual liberation and fell when that movement retreated in the Reagan-Thatcher-Bush years.

Now, in the age of AIDS panic, uncut Nin journals are gradually reappearing. But Nin is out of fashion as a contemporary feminist, because the political winds have shifted. She is a seductress in a time when all seduction is presumed to be rape, a sensitive chronicler of inner emotion and psychoanalytic transformation when all that is wanted from women writers is angry agitprop which repudiates Freud and all "dead white males."

But the largeness of her contribution will remain for other times, other politics. Like Colette, she told the inner story of a woman's life from girlhood to old age. She committed neither suicide nor creative suicide. She was indefatigable (as every artist must be), and she left a body of work that other women writers can build upon. We can love her or hate her. Either emotion will be useful for our future writing. But she is there like a mountain. She must be climbed.

There are signs that as this century ends, her innovations have become part of our literature. The incest taboo has been broken. Autobiography and fiction have been merged into one form. Women writers have a degree of freedom undreamed of by her generation. And the unexpurgated journals will keep on coming. They will continue to be attacked by women who are afraid of freedom and by men who like women that way. But for our daughters and grand-daughters, they will be there. When tomorrow's women are ready, they will read Anaïs Nin and be transformed.

Future generations will discover her with the excitement we felt when we discovered Virginia Woolf, Colette, Simone de Beauvoir, Edna St. Vincent Millay, Jean Rhys, Zora Neale Hurston, Angela Carter, Sylvia Plath, and Anne Sexton.

She will give confidence to women writers who need to validate their own subject matter.

Perhaps that's the greatest influence a writer can have on the future: to inspire new practitioners of the craft. They will adore her, detest her, debate her, rewrite her, reinterpret her. And why not? She is mother. And mother is the earth from which we spring.

Weep and you weep alone!—What a lie that is! Weep and
you will find a million crocodiles to weep with you. The world
is forever weeping. The world is drenched in tears. . . . But
joy, joy is a kind of ecstatic bleeding, a disgraceful sort of
contentment which overflows from every pore of your being.
You can't make people joyous just by being joyous yourself.
Joy has to be generated by oneself: it is or it isn't. Joy is
founded on something too profound to be understood or
communicated. To be joyous is to be a madman in a world
of sad ghosts.

—HENRY MILLER, SEXUS

All of us, if we are honest, know that art is a fart in the face of
God. Only the establishment artist, whose work exists principally
to justify the injustices of the status quo, flatters himself that he is
godlike. The renegade, the maverick, the rebel, the Henry Miller,

the Petronius, the Rabelais, the Blake, the Neruda, the Whitman, knows that in part what makes his life's work valuable is its criminality. If somewhere along the line he is *not* banned, burned, deprived of his livelihood, cursed by the academics, denigrated by the self-appointed guardians of art, then he knows he is doing something wrong.

Henry Miller was such a criminal.

On the bottom of his letter paper was printed: *When shit becomes valuable, the poor will be born without assholes.* Other sheets gave the following quote from one of his friends: *Henry, sometimes I'm obliged to sleep in my car—but when I have to take a shit, I go to the Beverly Hills Hotel.*

If Henry used the word "shit" a lot, it was because no other word so well conveyed what he thought of the world. But the word became clean in his mouth. He purified the excrement of life and made it roses. "I want a classic purity," he once said, "where dung is dung and angels are angels." He knew that angels could not be angels without dung, that a world of angels would be devoid of literature.

Those who criticized him—those who, to the end, denied him his place in the pantheon of poets—were in part, unknowingly, reacting to the fears his honesty roused in them. Like Swift, he lashed the world to bring it to its senses. Like Swift, he was a heartbroken lover of mankind, a naïf pretending to be a cynic. "Just a Brooklyn boy . . ." he often said of himself.

Sometimes I used to think that the critics who hated Henry were really suffering from nooky envy. He seemed to spend so much time fucking, and fucking so *guiltlessly*! How could the perpetually guilty be anything but envious? But even in his fucking he was literary. My former husband Jonathan Fast once asked him if he had ever *really* screwed a woman with a carrot, and he laughed uproariously and denied it—though he always maintained his books were autobiographies, not novels.

I disagree with him here. The Henry Miller of the novels is surely a comic persona, a picaro, a quester, a hero in search of the Holy Grail.

"What is a hero?" Henry once wrote: "Primarily one who has conquered his fears." And in the *persona* of Henry Miller, the *real* Henry Miller created a fearless alter ego, one who never quailed at a cunt, never wilted, fainted, or failed. As the ancient hero was fearless in battle, the modern hero must be fearless in bed. Thus has our sphere of heroic action shrunk from a meadow to a mattress!

The fearless hero Henry Miller impersonated was often his opposite. Anaïs Nin described his fear of travel, his sensitivity to dislocation, and his extreme dependence on her—and on the other women in his life. I have always thought his impersonation of Braveheart (or Braveprick) stemmed from his massive insecurity. He deluded the world so well that he almost deluded himself.

Henry Miller admired the gurus and the sages even more than he admired the poets and the painters. Moreover, he knew that the essential characteristic of a sage is his gaiety. He would have agreed with Yeats's line "Their ancient glittering eyes are gay." And so were Henry's eyes—even the blinded one—till the end.

I imagine him singing hosannahs on his deathbed and muttering to the maker of the cosmos. His death was clearly a much-sought release, at which all his friends and family rejoiced. I hear that he rejoiced, too. Trapped in an ailing body, he had failed from year to year. He deserved better than such frail flesh, and even in his death he has not left us.

I met him when he was already an old man—met him through literature, not life. Though he never read his contemporaries (except I. B. Singer), though he was said by his detractors to be a sexist and an anti-Semite, though he was blind in one eye and tired quickly, he was coaxed by a friend into reading *Fear of Flying*, and he responded with a torrent of applause, enthusiasm, and unpaid agentry. Many of my foreign publishers were a gift of his enthusiasm.

He was the most generous writer I have ever known (and I have known one or two who, in their generosity, flouted the general rule that writers hate all other writers except the safely dead). He tirelessly wrote to German, French, Japanese, Dutch publishers on my behalf. Asked to do nothing, he did everything—from writing a preface to the French edition of my novel, to writing an essay on the op-ed page of the *New York Times* about it (an essay from which the word "horny" had to be deleted as unacceptable to a "family newspaper").

I was bowled over by his kindness. Day after day the letters arrived—written in black felt pen on yellow legal sheets or on his own stationery with its curious aphorisms printed at the bottom. My own replies were rather stiff at first. How to cope with the excitement of having a living legend actually writing to *me*! It was daunting. But Henry's letters were so loose and spontaneous that you had to respond in kind. Having freed himself, he freed everyone he touched; it was his great gift. There was no question that I would see him when I went to California.

I came at the most awful and wonderful time in my life. An early marriage breaking up, a film promised of my first novel but turning to heartbreak before my eyes, sudden notoriety that alarmed me as much as it delighted me. Henry's house in Pacific Palisades became a refuge of peace in this maelstrom. At his dining room table, listening to him talk of Cendrars, Picasso, Brassaï, John Cowper Powys, Marie Corelli, Gurdjieff, Knut Hamsun, Lawrence Durrell, and Anaïs Nin (and Isaac Singer, whom he—and I—admired above all living writers), I felt safe and protected even in the city of the Lost Angels!

Henry was frail when I met him in 1974. Only rarely would he let me take him (and his friends) out to dinner—usually at the Imperial Gardens, a rather seedy Japanese restaurant on the Sunset Strip, which was his favorite eatery in Los Angeles. More usually, Twinka Thiebaud, his cook and devoted caretaker, made us dinner at home and Henry held forth for the assembled throng. His house was full of young people, often including his kids, Valentine and Tony, and Henry would feed everyone—as, in his Paris days, everyone had fed him. In the last months (when I had already moved to Connecticut), it was rumored that one or two of these young people may have exploited him. But that first autumn I knew him, he was still well enough to write in bed, to emerge for garrulous meals before he grew tired and had to be wheeled back into his room, to grope his numerous nubile visitors, though not (he always maintained) to fuck them. He lived his last years (as he wrote in a letter to me) in the most delicious erotic fantasies. Now and then he copped a feel—though not of *my* breasts. I was not his physical type at all (he adored lithe Asian women), or maybe he thought of me as too bookish, for he always made a great point of how literary I was.

Henry indeed loved women, but he loved them more for the imaginary women he created through them than for the women they actually were. He was a true romantic even in his rebellion against romanticism. Like most romantics, he did not always see people with perfect clarity. He loved or he hated. When his love failed, he often repudiated the love object totally. When a friend died, he ceased to think about him. He claimed he never mourned. He lived in the present more completely than any person I have ever known. For this alone, he shone out from other men as an enlightened soul.

But he *hated* his reputation as a pornographer and longed, despite himself, for literary respectability. He accepted the Légion

d'honneur with predictable derision but with unpredictable grati-
tude, and each year he lusted deeply after the Nobel Prize. Each
year, at his urging, *all* his friends and disciples recommended him.
Each year, the dynamite factory passed him by.

When a publisher had the temerity to suggest that Henry and
I collaborate on a book to be titled, humorlessly enough, *A Rap
on Sex* (a sort of companion piece to Margaret Mead and James
Baldwin's *A Rap on Race*), Henry wrote back: "In the first place I
am not an expert as you dub me—and secondly, though it may well
be profitable, there's something in the idea that stinks."

I thought the idea stank, too, but I was not yet able to be so blunt
in a letter to a publisher. *A Rap on Sex*, indeed. This never-written
book's title, complete with unconscious pun, sounds more dated
today than a title of a book by Marie Corelli—who happened, by
the way, to be Queen Victoria's favorite author as well as Henry
Miller's.

His contradictions were many. Victorian and bohemian, schnor-
rer and benefactor, sexual guru and tireless romantic, he made
women up out of pen and ink (and often watercolor). Did he make
up his autobiographies, too? In a way, he did. In a way, we *all*
make up our autobiographies. He was more of a fabulist than he
would have admitted—though the very word would have made
him puke. He was "just a Brooklyn boy—don'tcha know?" and if
he was the great force that liberated literature (I nearly wrote *liber-
ature*) in our age, he knew it in his gut but did not know it at all in
his brain. He desperately sought public recognition of his genius,

and in the pursuit of that recognition, he gave far too many interviews and entertained far too many con men. Thus are even enlightened souls seduced by the lust for recognition! That we denied him such final pleasures is a measure not only of official literary meanness but of his own greatness: He still—even to the end—had the power to shock the hypocrite, the faint of heart, the literary pantywaist.

I hope you get your Nobel Prize in heaven, Henry, sent up on blasts of dynamite.

. . . sitting at the table, thinking of the book I have written,

the child that I have carried for years and years in the womb

of the imagination as you carried in your womb the children

you love . . .

—JAMES JOYCE TO NORA JOYCE

Only a man (or a woman who had never been pregnant) would compare creativity to maternity, pregnancy to the creation of a novel. The comparison of gestation to creativity is by now a conventional metaphor, as largely unexamined as the dead metaphors in our everyday speech (the arm of a chair, the leg of a table), but it is also inexact.

Although the *idea* for a poem or novel often comes as if unbidden, a gift from the muse, and although at rare moments one may write *as if* automatically, in the grip of an angel who seems to speed one's pen across the page, most often literary creativity is sheer hard work, quite different from the growing of a baby in the womb, which goes on despite one's conscious will and is, properly speaking, God's miracle. It seems hardly to belong to the individual woman who provides it with a place to happen. The growing of the fetus in the womb is DNA's triumph, the triumph of the genes, the triumph of the species. The woman whose body is the site of this miracle is only being used by the species temporarily, in its communal passion to survive.

The writing of a book may be seen as the muse working through the voice, hand, and will of an individual creator, but that individual creator must labor hard indeed to be worthy of serving as a vessel to the muse. She is a stern taskmistress and will withdraw her favors from the lazy, the slovenly, or the self-pitying artist. Nature, on the contrary, is all-forgiving. Any womb, any woman, may be the vessel for continuance. Assent is hardly even necessary: only a healthy womb and the will not to deliberately destroy the fetus.

How much more passive pregnancy is than creativity! Creativity demands conscious, active will; pregnancy demands only the absence of ill will. Maybe the desire to compare them arises from the artist's ancient wish that creativity be as effortless, easy, and unconscious as the creation of a fetus. Or perhaps the male artist's desire to compare the two arises out of his yearning for the female capacity to create life. Like most forms of envy, it is useless. One might as well envy the hummingbird for being able to stand still in midair, or the flounder for having two eyes on one side of its head. Whatever joys there are in pregnancy (and there are many), they are not the joys of consciousness. Pregnancy is perhaps most enjoyable to the intellectual woman precisely for that reason.

This was certainly true for me. All my life, until I became pregnant, I had mistrusted my body and overvalued my mind. I had sought a very high degree of control over my body. I never became pregnant, not even "accidentally," until well after my thirty-fifth birthday, having spent a year or more consciously wishing for pregnancy and trying to become pregnant. Before that I had dreaded pregnancy as a loss of control over my destiny. I had fantasies of death in childbirth, the death of my creativity during pregnancy, the alteration of my body into something monstrous, the loss of my intelligence through mysterious hormonal sabotage, of my energy, my creativity, my looks.

But I should have known that the ruler of the cosmos is nothing if not a joker—and all the opposite things happened. For the first time in my life, I controlled my weight effortlessly; my face grew thinner, my skin clearer, my eyes brighter. I never felt sick or lacked energy. I worked as hard at my writing as I ever had in my life. In fact, I worked with greater consistency. I wrote a whole book of poems, continued productively writing the novel I'd begun a year before becoming pregnant, even undertook a grueling book tour in my fifth and sixth months of pregnancy. Certainly I worked as hard as I did partly to undercut the myth that pregnant women are somehow incapacitated (or else "too fulfilled" by burgeoning life to need creative work as well), but mostly it was a case of genuinely feeling wonderful and very much myself (now liberated from the gnawing anxiety that I would never have a child). Whatever pregnancy "fulfilled" in me (and I do not underestimate that fulfillment at all), it was of a wholly different order than the one I seek through my creative work.

Pregnancy felt particularly good to me, I think, because it was an affirmation of life for a romantic who, like most romantics, had once worshiped death. At twenty-five I wished "to cease upon the midnight with no pain," with Keats and Sylvia Plath, but by thirty-five I had turned away from the idealization of poets who died of tuberculosis or had committed suicide, and I wanted to prove to myself that both poets and women could be survivors. It was a turn from infatuation with martyrs to respect for survivors, from worshiper of sickness to affirmer of health. And having a successful, easy pregnancy was a way of telling myself that the core of my being was healthy and could confer life not only upon myself but on others as well.

Since the nineteenth century, artists and intellectuals in our society have worshiped illness, as if it were illness that propitiated art rather than art that conferred a temporary reprieve from illness. This is one unfortunate legacy of nineteenth-century Romanticism. It also implies that the mind can be nourished only at the expense of the body: the opposite of the classicist's pursuit of healthy mind in healthy body. Critics sometimes fault artists for being too prolific, as if creativity were a material substance, a sort of natural resource that could be depleted by too wanton use. In fact, the contrary is true. Both creativity and health are self-replenishing; the more they are used, the more they regenerate and flourish.

Bodily health and artistic creativity were seen as complementary, not opposing, characteristics by the Greeks and Romans, and it was only when the scourging of the flesh came to be considered of spiritual benefit by the medieval Christian church that we began to move toward the modern attitude that mortification of the flesh somehow encourages the creative powers of the mind. The nineteenth-century worship of suicidal or consumptive poets, alcoholic and insane creators, is a twisted outgrowth of the medieval view that the mind can flourish only at the expense of the body.

Women inherit a double legacy of mistrust in regard to the body. First, they share the Western Christian heritage that dictates chastity and mortification of the flesh as prerequisites to the spiritual life. But they also inherit the medieval church's primitive attitude toward womankind, childbearing, and the female body. For a woman artist, the choice of physical robustness coupled with fertile creativity has been particularly fraught with all sorts of practical difficulties. We tend to forget that until the advent of dependable birth control (which is less than a century old), childbearing was not optional for women. Except for the deliberately abstinent or accidentally sterile, pregnancy was too compulsory to be experienced as a *choice*. But even after the advent of birth control, complex social and psychological forces conspired to make all but the most adamantly individualistic women marry, then bear children for most

of their adult lives. Pregnancy could hardly be seen as an affirmation of life and health when it was so compulsory, so full of dangers
for mother and child, and so *constant*. It often did herald the end of
other forms of creativity. The fact that many women artists avoided
pregnancy like the plague and then referred to their books or paintings as their "children" is hardly surprising.

I belong to one of the first generations of women artists for whom
pregnancy is *not* compulsory. Despite the psychological pressures
for motherhood that still exist, not to mention the ubiquitous
threats to reproductive freedom, I and my contemporaries are free
to look at creativity and maternity in wholly new ways.

Jane Austen and George Eliot did not have that option. Even
Edith Wharton and Virginia Woolf were not really able to regard
childbearing as a choice. The legacy of Victorian womanhood was
too close and too frightening. In Wharton's time and Woolf's, the
only way for a woman artist to combat the Victorian stereotype of
"the angel in the house" was either to play the devil or to claim that
they were mothers of books, not children.

For years I was determined not to have a child because the
women writers I admired most had avoided maternity. If childlessness was good enough for Jane Austen, Emily Dickinson, and Virginia Woolf, it must be good enough for me. Yet the desire for a
child gnawed at me. Images of childbirth kept bursting forth in my
poems. Precisely because I was so afraid of childbearing, I was
drawn to it. Only by doing the things I feared the most had I progressed in my life. Having a child seemed to me a rite of passage I

would be a coward to avoid. What point was there in having passed a whole incarnation in a female body without experiencing all the potentialities of that body? It would be like being incarnated as a bird and never flying. Still, I hesitated. Childbearing had always taken too much of a toll on women. It had always meant jeopardizing the things writers needed most—peace, quiet, the lack of interruption. It had meant diluting passions that one wanted undiluted for one's work. It was not only the drudgery of childbearing that seemed threatening, but the pleasures. Babies are most distracting when they are most delightful. Besides, it had taken me years to free myself of the guilt I felt toward the men in my life when I shut myself away to write. How could I ever deal with the guilt created by a creature who would actually need me for its physical survival?

Of course, there was no way to solve all these dilemmas in advance. I would have to take the plunge and find the answers later. I would have to give up my constant need for the illusion of control. Control of the future is a delusion anyway, since the future always defeats our most carefully made plans. I came to the conclusion that whatever was lost by introducing this element of uncertainty into my life would be more than repaid by the new experiences and insights it might bring. By thirty-five I knew that art cannot exist without life. Plenty of artists who were careful to limit their lives (in the hope of screening out all interruptions) wound up with nothing to write about at all.

I tried to hedge my bets as best I could. I did not become pregnant until I found a man who I thought really wanted to share all aspects of child rearing with me, and I waited for a time in my life when there was enough money for help. Whether this made me cowardly or prudent, who can say? All I know is that I did the only thing I could do at the time. For the first thirty-five years of my life, writing was so much more important to me than anything else that I would not risk *any* turn of fate that might jeopardize my own still shaky self-confidence as a writer. It had taken me years to form the *habit* of writing, and I wasn't about to give up that necessary daily meditation. Women who bear children *before* they establish serious habits of work may never establish them at all, however easy their economic circumstances may be. Having been defined first as mothers, they may never be able to see themselves in another light, and the demands of their children may always drown out the demands of their books.

I only know that I am grateful to have been born into a time when it was possible for a woman to delay childbearing until other life patterns were firmly established. We have to acknowledge that in many ways this is the best time for women the world has ever known. The discrimination against us is still rampant and virulent. Given how many practical obstacles stand in the way of most of us doing creative work at all, the malignity with which that work is often treated is nothing less than criminal. But the fact that we can choose when and whether to bear children has improved our lives to a degree unthinkable for the thousands upon thousands of mute, toiling, laboring generations of women. The very fact that no generation before ours has really been in a position to challenge the lie that creativity and maternity are one and the same makes us privileged beyond any earlier generations. And that privilege rests almost entirely upon motherhood remaining a choice. Choice is the key to all our freedoms—even the freedom to dwell seriously on the meaning of pregnancy and childbirth. As long as motherhood was constant and compulsory, women could not examine motherhood honestly, nor could men resist idealizing it.

I think we have never quite considered the implications of the fact that most of the literature about pregnancy and birth has been written either by men or by women who forswore childbearing in order to do their creative work. Even after women writers began to be mothers as well as writers, they often resisted writing directly about their experiences, for fear of male chauvinist criticism ("Don't wear your ovaries on your sleeve") or for fear of seeming trivial. Pregnancy and childbirth were often considered minor, foolish, "female" subjects. Women writers who aspired to the heights of Parnassus often disdained such subjects as their male mentors had taught them to. So the lie that creativity and maternity were somehow interchangeable continued unchallenged for generations. Even in our own day, it has been insufficiently examined.

Neither the women who denied the childbearing urge in order to create books, nor the men who had wives to bear children for them, were in a position to chart the terra incognita of pregnancy and childbirth. Both were prejudiced parties, partisans of the party of childlessness. Women who had children because it was inevitable also lacked the power to examine their fate. Trapped first by their own bodies, then by society, how could they not feel fury at their helplessness, however much they may have loved the infants they produced?

Now we stand at a literary crossroads made possible entirely by childbirth having become a choice. All efforts to withdraw that choice must be seen as efforts to put women back into the mute rage from which we have so recently emerged. What untold wonders would world literature contain if it told the story of pregnancy, childbirth, and childbearing as well as the story of childlessness! What untold stories might we hear if mothers as well as fathers were able to relate their tales? The history of world literature has often been the literature of the white man, the childless white woman. How different it looks now that mothers are writers, too! A book's creative demands on its author end at the moment of completion—while a baby begins to call forth true creativity only after it emerges from the unconscious Eden of the womb.

A man in the house is worth two in the street.

—MAE WEST

The perfect man—for any woman—is the man who loves her constantly and fucks her frequently, passionately, and well; who adores and admires her; is at once reliable and exciting; an earthly Adonis and a heavenly father figure; a beautiful son, a steady daddy; a wild-eyed Bacchic lover and a calm, sober, but still funny friend. Can you find all these attributes in one man? Not bloody likely! And if you find them, will they endure for all the various passages of your life? Not bloodly likely.

Given this problem, what's a woman to do? Having two or three men simultaneously would seem to solve the problem—if it didn't create so many logistical snafus. What happens, for example, when lover number one and lover number two decide to arrive on the same train for the same weekend? What do you do about birthdays and Christmas? Or Hanukkah, for that matter? A partial solution to this problem is to have one WASP and one Jewish lover—with perhaps a Zen Buddhist or an atheist thrown in for good measure so holidays can be staggered. But then you stagger, too. Because the fact of the matter is that nobody can spend 100 percent of her time getting laid, arranging to get laid, administering TLC to a variety of men with a variety of needs. And what woman worth her salt wants to be involved with a man whose needs she cares nothing about?

A divorced male friend of mine recently said to me, "When I was married, I spent perhaps twenty percent of my time getting laid. Now that I'm divorced, I spend eighty-five to ninety-percent of my time getting laid." There's the problem in its essence: Putting together one perfect man out of two, three, or four slightly imperfect candidates is just too time-consuming and tiring. We are finally driven to monogamy not by morality but by exhaustion. One candidate wins out over the others, and we succumb to the blandishments of one (hopefully) perfect man. This solution has on its side: convenience, honesty, simplicity, and stability. But *does* it have stability on its side? Our divorce statistics show that our monogamies tend to be serial; that sooner or later both spouses begin playing around; that most children born today can expect to grow up in single-parent households by and by (or to become somebody else's stepchildren). The old European system—if one can call it that— of stable marriage, accompanied by a series of fairly stable liaisons, starts to look better and better when we consider the wreckage of our lives, and our children's lives, under our present shambling system of serial monogamy.

A beguiling young man once said to me, "Marry as often as you like, but promise me I'll be your only lover." He was paraphrasing Oscar Wilde, but his wistful plea had true longing in it: the longing for some stability in an unstable world. If marriage no longer provides that, then perhaps our love affairs will. I treasure the fantasy of marrying and marrying and marrying, yet having only one lover through it all. But fantasy it is. I am neither young enough, nor foolish enough, nor unscathed by divorce enough, to want to endure the psychological wreckage of splitting up yet again. That leaves me, like everyone else, in search of the Holy Grail of the perfect man—wherever, and whoever, he may be.

Knowing full well that life is too surprising, rich, and strange for love ever to come in the form of a prearranged, predictable, prefabricated model, I nonetheless feel the temptation to put together a sort of police composite of the perfect man.

Okay. He's beautiful—but not without some craggy imperfection in his features: a nose that once was broken, or slightly crooked teeth. He's enormously intelligent but never pedantic; his intelligence is suffused with humor. Most important of all, in fact, is his sense of humor. He can laugh in bed. And though he's indefatigable in bed, he's not obsessive about sex. He doesn't think of it as a performance, and he doesn't berate himself if he doesn't have a constant erection, nor does he expect his woman to berate him.

He's relaxed about sex; has a sense of fun about it; is passionate without being priapic.

These qualities are rare enough in a world where sexual performance has become as obligatory as sexual abstinence—or the pretension to it—once was. The worst by-product of the so-called sexual revolution is the substitution of performance for passion. For many men, sex has become yet another area of dire competition. One young man of twenty-four—the son of a writer friend of mine—confessed to me that from ages sixteen to twenty-one he never "allowed" himself to have an orgasm with a woman, because he was so concerned with pleasing his partners. "Here were all these women like you and my mother writing all these books and articles about how men were so insensitive to women's needs. So I figured that the main thing was to give the girl as many orgasms as possible. I got so *controlled* I couldn't even come myself. Now I just say 'fuck it.' Let's bring back the John Wayne image of manhood, when men could prematurely ejaculate and not care!"

What this young man didn't consider in his supposed nostalgia for the John Wayne image is that *no* man of John Wayne's generation could have been sitting at a dinner party (at his mother's house) having such an intimate conversation with his mother's friend. Something *has* changed forever in men as a result of the sexual revolution and the women's movement, and that change can be summed up as greater openness. Not only are men able to talk to women about sex, but men of twenty or so and women of thirty-five or so often wind up talking themselves right into bed—an explosive combination long celebrated by French novelists and moviemakers but curiously neglected in the supposed land of opportunity. Even so, no one (of any age) seems quite immune to performance mania. Our society, having collectively decided that sex is acceptable, if not quite optimal, without love, seems to have replaced the desideratum of endless love with the desideratum of endless erection. When sex becomes as competitive as racquetball or the stock market, surely some essential quality has been lost.

My perfect man, then, is not a slave to performance. He doesn't ask, "How'm I doing?" in bed. He doesn't have a nervous breakdown if he can't get it up one night, and he is secure enough to know that he is liked for his brains and humor and not just his cock.

What other qualities does he have? Generosity, tenderness, a willingness to be wrong occasionally, a sense of playfulness, a recognition that the best sex happens when the partners are playmates and share each other's fantasies. He doesn't have to be rich; his generosity can take the form of making eggs Benedict on a Sunday morning or chopping firewood, or sending roses when I feel rotten. He is not judgmental; he doesn't throw fits about stupid stuff—like the wrong turns I take in the road or the way I have my canisters lined up on the kitchen shelf. He is mature enough to know that life is too short to spend in acrimony over trivia. He doesn't borrow my classic car and wreck it; he gives me a back rub if I've had a lousy day. He doesn't run off and fuck my best friend if I'm neglecting him because I have a deadline, and he can amuse himself happily, not spitefully, if I'm on a business trip. He adores children and dogs but doesn't necessarily try to woo me through my child (my dog is altogether another matter). He doesn't demand fidelity of me if he isn't prepared to give it himself, and he doesn't get involved in sex games he can't handle (like telling me it would turn him on if I fucked his best friend, then clobbering me—or leaving me—because I fucked his best friend). An honorable man, he has that old-fashioned quality: integrity.

He is reasonably unambivalent emotionally, so you know where you stand with him, and he doesn't blame others for his own fears and inadequacies. Does this paragon exist? "Actually, the perfect man is Mel Diamond—a dry cleaner in Flatbush," said a friend of mine, "but he doesn't want it generally known for fear he'll be ravished by swarms of hungry women." (If anyone named Mel Diamond is reading this, rest assured that my friend's choice of your name was pure coincidence. Lie back and enjoy the swarms.)

"The perfect man is someone you love who also loves you," said psychologist Mildred Newman.

"If I had to single out one quality," said singer-songwriter Carly Simon, "I'd say it was a sense of joy."

"There is no such thing as a perfect man, and no one even gets close," said Helen Gurley Brown. "The way to be a happy person is never to even try to attain perfection! It is totally absurd to think there is such a thing. Having said that, I'll say the perfect man overtips, undercriticizes, and would not run the air conditioner in January."

"The perfect man is in touch with his vulnerability and love; he has softness and tenderness and is not afraid of his feminine side," said Diane Von Furstenberg. "Also, you only find him when you're not actually looking."

I agree with all these definitions of perfection. "Perfection is terrible; it cannot have children," wrote Sylvia Plath in one of her *Ariel* poems. She was alluding, I think, to the fact that perfection is final, closed, and leaves no room for growth. And certainly when we search for the "perfect" man, we know full well that if we found perfection it would be quite inhuman. We love people, ultimately, for their humanity; not because of their perfection but in spite of their imperfection. A man who was a "perfect ten" in looks would terrify me. When I think of the men I have loved most, and the things I found most endearing about their appearance at the height of our passion, I always remember their small imperfections: a crooked front tooth, slanting or shaggy brows, eyes of slightly different hues. Even Quasimodo would be lovable if he had the right smell and touch.

Which brings us to another one of the great imponderables of life: Why does one person's scent turn you on, while another person's smell repels? Is it all a question of pheromones or of decisions made in the DNA before our conscious minds even have a chance to consider them? (Pheromones are substances long recognized in the insect world and now beginning to be isolated in humans, which account for otherwise unaccountable attractions between one individual and another.) For that matter, why does one person's touch excite while another's does not? These things baffle me more and more as I continue through my life. Surely I have chosen my mates capriciously or badly, since three of my marriages proved perishable. Or *have* I chosen badly? Was it just that I chose different traveling companions for different stages of my journey, and because my calling as a writer made that journey complicated, the traveling companions could not necessarily be permanent ones? This last, fairly optimistic explanation pleases me more than the notion that I am ever doomed to bad, or neurotic, choices.

My first husband was a fellow college and graduate student at a time in my life when my studies were of paramount importance to me. We read Shakespeare together in bed and immersed ourselves in medieval history, eighteenth-century literature, and old movies. We were soul mates at one period of our lives, but then our souls changed. My second husband represented stability, order, and sanity at a time when I was diving down into my unconscious to retrieve my first real poems. I needed him to haul me up when I felt I was succumbing to the rapture of the deep, and he fulfilled that function well. Once I learned how to do it for myself, his role became more and more artifact, and his deficiencies—humorlessness, in particular—more and more apparent.

My third husband shared with me the longing for a child, the passion to create a life around reading and writing novels while rearing our daughter. For a time, we also were powerful soul mates, but then, too, our needs and our souls changed. Is this failure, or a complex kind of destiny? I prefer to think of it as the latter. Each of these choices had its own peculiar logic at the time it was made. The fact that the union could not endure doesn't really invalidate the choice. Each of the three marriages had its joys. The third had six years of great happiness before the final terrible year of pain.

Perhaps my life has been more complex because of the blessing/ curse of becoming a celebrated writer, a public figure, a woman whom the media have sometimes chosen to see as scandalous. But in essence I believe my fate (and the stages of development through which I found it, or it found me) has not been so very different from that of other women of my generation.

Raised to believe we needed men as parental figures, we grew up into a world where we had to assume burdens our mothers would have thought of as masculine: earning a living, managing money and taxes, not to mention shoveling snow and changing tires. We found ourselves more capable of nurturing men than of finding men who could nurture us. Raised to believe ourselves weak (hence in need of male support), we increasingly found ourselves strong. The men in our lives, we discovered, depended on us more than we did on them. We started out looking for daddies and wound up finding sons. We were ready to enjoy the deliciousness of this kind of relationship, but saw, too, that it did not come without a price tag attached. What eluded us, most often, was finding true partners.

In this odyssey from the search for daddies to the finding of sons, I have been very much like many women of my time. In my twenties, unfledged in my career, I married a father figure; in my thirties, well established in my career, I felt free to choose a man merely for his "sense of joy." When even that proved to have its own problems, I hesitated and stayed single for eight years. I still regard this as the most critical period of my life. When I remarried, I was ready for a true partner and I married someone I had come to consider my best friend. It was a marriage unlike any other I had made. It continues to grow in unpredictable ways.

I think it is usual for women in their twenties, especially ambitious, committed career women, to marry men less for their sexiness and joie de vivre than for their sustaining, supportive, daddylike qualities. Once having achieved professionally, though, we chafe under the commitments we've made to Daddy, and we want playmates, soul mates, beautiful boys, luscious young men, without regard to whether or not they can pick up the lunch tab or remember to telephone when they say they will. Some cynics see this as a role reversal, women taking the prerogatives men had for years, but I see it as a logical development of women's growing emancipation. For centuries women had no choice but to sell their sexuality for social status. Now that we can earn our *own* social status, our sexuality has suddenly become very precious to us and not a thing to be bartered.

"Does this mean that women have their own version of the whore/madonna split?" Nancy Friday asked me when I discussed this theory with her. Must it always be either/or? I wonder. The perfect man would surely *combine* beautiful boy and steady daddy, but alas, that combination rarely turns up. "The sort of men who buy one life insurance are never much fun in bed," my novelist friend Fay Weldon said.

Ah, but one wishes they were! True, most successful women will opt for joie de vivre and sex appeal over life insurance—we can buy our own life insurance—but every long-term relationship still requires reliability as well as a sense of joy. There are problems with all relationships not based on true equality; sooner or later an unequal partnership has to become equal or break down. (If, for example, a woman gets involved with a much younger or much less successful man, either he has to grow to become an adequate mate for her or the relationship will founder.) Some of the loveliest love affairs seem doomed from the start, and maybe their savor comes from their essential brevity, but it is easier nonetheless to make things last with a true partner.

Where on earth does one find a true partner? For years I despaired of finding one myself. At this evolutionary stage in the relations between the sexes, women are often more enlightened by their lives than society permits men to be. Still an underclass, women have all the insights of an underclass: a self-deprecating sense of humor that punctures pomposity; a view of the overclass from the ass up, so to speak; a social perspective that only an outsider can have. All these things force us to grow. This is the shit out of which our roses flower.

Men, on the other hand, continue to constitute an overclass—as proved by the fact that they *consider* themselves not a class but merely representatives of humanity. They still tend to be coddled by women, from mothers onward, and they are deprived of the chance to have their pomposities punctured. Some exceptional men over-come this state of affairs, but many do not; they merely slip into the grooves society has prepared for them and go their way in blinders. Of course they're confused by female strength and female free-dom, and of course they're vulnerable—more vulnerable in certain ways than women. But they have not seen their entire world turned upside down in this generation. Female sexuality may astound them, but the society in which they function is largely ruled by members of their own sex.

I do not at all mean to imply that one gender or the other has gotten a rawer deal from the sexual and feminist revolutions—incomplete as these two revolutions are. Both sexes have been shaken to the core, and both sexes are reeling from the shocks. Whether men or women suffer more is not the issue. It is not even ascertainable, I think. But for a variety of reasons, women have been forced to have certain insights into society that are largely un-available to all but the most empathic, artistic, intelligent men. It is therefore terribly hard for most women of my generation to find true partners. Not bed partners, not fun partners, but men who will shoulder burdens equally with us and who also possess that quality of joy Carly Simon and I so treasure.

Ah—the dream of the true partner. He is, after all, "the perfect man." Do we find him? Or do we train him? Do we grow him in our gardens or import him from the moon? And if we find him, will he go mad at twenty-five or into a depression at thirty, or wind up fucking baby-sitters at forty? Can we love him without coddling him? Can we make demands on him without being left? Can we find a balance between giving and taking? Can we receive as graciously as we give?

Our analysts tell us the answer lies within ourselves, that when *we* are ready, the perfect man mysteriously comes along. It all sounds very Pollyannaish to me. I have known women who were ready for years: So ready and so self-reliant, in fact, that they judged men by standards of perfection impossible to meet—and eventually got used to being partnerless. They even discovered they liked it. The journey remained the same, but the traveling companions changed. The true partner had eluded them for so long that they stopped seeking him.

I thought I had given up on the perfect man, but I never really did. I simply readjusted my notions of perfection. As I came to understand that I had character defects, I was willing to have a partner who had them, too.

The perfect man is, after all, the one who sees the best in you and who holds you to your own beau ideal even when you waver. Because he loves both who you are and what you can become, his vision helps you become more truly yourself. As you grow sure of yourself in his love, you generously mirror his best self as well.

I used to be intrigued by the things that ended relationships. Now I am most fascinated by what allows them to continue. A marriage that lasts is always in a state of metamorphosis. The perfect man transforms the perfect woman. They know each other by their willingness to be transformed.

The ultimate sexist put-down: the prick which lies down on the job. The ultimate weapon in the war between the sexes: the limp prick. The ultimate banner of the enemy's encampment: the prick at half mast. The symbol of the apocalypse: the atomic warhead prick that self-destructs. That was the basic inequity that could never be righted: not that the male had a wonderful added attraction called a penis, but that the female had a wonderful all-weather cunt. Neither storm nor sleet nor dark of night could faze it. It was always there, always ready. Quite terrifying when you think about it. No wonder men hated women. No wonder they invented the myth of female inadequacy.

—FEAR OF FLYING, 1973

Viagra is the perfect American medicament. It raises the Dow-Jones and the penis, too. If you were ever wondering whether the stock market was a metaphor for male potency, here's your answer.

According to a venerable old Wall Streeter of my acquaintance, young Wall Streeters are predicting it will lower the divorce rate. That's a major concern in the age of equitable distribution. If you can still fuck your wife, maybe you don't have to give her (and her lawyer) half your ill-gotten gains.

To judge by the speed with which the new impotence drug is selling out, Bill Clinton may be the only man in this country who has the option of whipping out his dick. Walking through analyst-and-urologist-land on the Upper East Side, I spotted several "We have Viagra" or just "Viagra" signs on pharmacy windows.

Selling for a hardly accidental ten dollars a pill, this cure (nick-named the Pfizer Riser) for what urologists and euphemists call "erectile dysfunction" is being marketed directly to the consumer— in this case, the aging baby boomer whose significant other is threatening to get a younger man unless he shapes up. Pfizer Inc.'s stock prices surged 21 percent between February 1 and March 28, 1998, posting the highest price-earnings ratio of any pharmaceutical stock in recent memory. By April 24, the numbers had risen even higher, and a split was rumored.

What amazes me about Viagra is this: Impotence is apparently so widespread that there are thirty million sufferers out there, but until the advent of Viagra, the condition was not one much talked about at cocktail parties, in trading rooms, or in doctors' offices. Internists used to report that they could tell an impotence sufferer about five minutes into the interview, because he was so tongue-tied and reticent. But all of a sudden, Viagra has smoked erectile dysfunction out of the closet and onto the information superhighway.

"Took just one before dinner Friday night at 7:30 and after dinner played with my wife, by 8:15 I had a raging hard-on easier than I'd experienced in the last 10 years," reported a happy Internet correspondent. But there is a downside to Viagra for at least one virile e-mailer, with the nom de guerre "Billy B": "I got sick to my stomach after each orgasm." Undaunted, Billy B persevered: "Within the next half hour of more playing, I was hard again." Friday night was erection-packed, and Sunday morning was even better. After a weekend of trial and error, our guinea pig reported that the pill worked best on an empty stomach. "I did experience heartburn all Sunday night," he added, but it didn't seem to dampen his enthusiasm for the drug.

The pill has not been out a month, and already the Internet reports a rip-off called Viagro, which bills itself as the "herbal analog of the new impotence pill." This pill claims "no severe or moderate side effects." It goes on, however, to say that "the most commonly reported side effect was fatigue in the morning." Are they warning or boasting?

"Man, is it refreshing," raved a woman called Brenda, "to have an open discussion on such a vital yet sensitive issue!"

Things were not ever thus. Back in 1973, when my heroine Isadora Wing said in *Fear of Flying* that the ultimate feminist existential dilemma was "a liberated woman face-to-face with a limp prick," critics were not always kind.

It was bad enough to encroach on forbidden male territory in writing of female sexuality (which Norman Mailer had appropriated with his short story "The Time of Her Time"); to reveal the darkest male secret—that even tough guys were not always hard—was the ultimate literary faux pas. Men were in charge of literature then, and they also wanted to be seen as in charge of erections.

But erections were starting to get iffy as women were starting to demand sexual pleasure. The game had begun to change. Men were expected to please women as women had once been expected to please men. This made a lot of men very nervous, nervous enough to lose their erections. Frank O'Hara, Henry Miller, and Norman Mailer had never had such problems, at least to hear them tell it. Apparently all they ever had to do was fend off women raving over what indefatigable lovers they were.

The tricky thing about the penis, I am told by informed sources, is that it doesn't always listen to reason. A man may be madly in love and his penis may not know it. A man may be madly in lust but his penis may be on strike. A man may distrust a woman, and his penis may be otherwise informed (think of Samson and Delilah).

In the seventies, this was a big subject of discussion. I remember getting an urgent call from the actress Bibi Andersson in Stockholm when I was vacationing on Capri one summer.

"There's a new Swedish book called *Man Cannot Be Raped*," she said with great excitement, "and only you can write the screenplay. Only you understand." The idea was that men could boycott liberated women with the mutiny of their organs, and wasn't it just awful? I certainly thought so.

What was a liberated woman to do? Viagra promises to change all that. Or does it? After all, we've been promised pills to change the world before, and the world has had other ideas.

I certainly remember all the talk (back in the early days of Ovulen) that the birth control pill would utterly change sexual behavior. It was even posited by pundits that women would stop having babies. But pills do not really change the mating game, except temporarily. After everyone had fucked around for a while and contracted sexually transmitted diseases, free love stopped looking like a panacea.

Researchers insist that Viagra does not constitute a sexual revolution, but nobody seems to believe them. It will not create "sexual virtuosos," they warn. Or virtuosi. It "does not alter libido or desire." The same was said about powdered unicorn horn, but human optimism is hard to quash. Americans believe in pills more than we believe in God.

"Welcome to the post-pill paradise," said a fictional adulteress in John Updike's sexual-revolution novel of the sixties, *Couples*. There hasn't been a pill to cause such excitement since those palmy days when the whole sexual landscape seemed about to change, and then we got Richard Nixon, who mostly wanted to fuck the country.

I have often argued that the sexual revolution was mainly a media myth. Despite the fact that women's sexual standards have risen as male organs have wilted, it can still be demonstrated that young women like older men with money and that mating is as determined by economic imperatives as it ever was.

Twenty-five years ago, it didn't look as if that would still be true today, but certain eternal verities seem to have reasserted themselves. Money is money, and it remains sexy. Not all women have turned into Constance Chatterley as a result of the birth control pill, and I don't expect that all men will turn into Mellors the gamekeeper as a result of Viagra. Even if rich old men can now dose themselves with Viagra, the drug may be a stronger force for sexual conservatism than for sexual liberation.

Indeed, rich old men may be the only ones who can afford it. Many health maintenance organizations refuse to pay for Viagra. (They all claim to be studying the situation.) Apparently America's puritanism still dictates our definitions of health. Is the implication that sex has nothing to do with good health? Maybe things will change when hordes of angry impotent men storm their HMO's with placards reading "Help Keep America Hard."

You've probably heard by now that, like all great scientific discoveries, Viagra's discovery was serendipitous. The active ingredient, sildenafil citrate, was first developed as a drug to alleviate angina. Though cardiac patients participating in trials for the drug still got chest pains, they were happily distracted by their newfound erections. They demanded increased supplies of the experimental drug. It seemed sildenafil citrate boosted production of nitric oxide in the nerve endings of the penis, which in turn brought blood to boost the penis itself.

Researchers had stumbled on an impotence treatment that did not require nasty implants or injections into the penis. Those last-resort treatments have already been decimated by the arrival of Viagra. Now the little elves at Pfizer are trying to figure out a way to market it to clitorally challenged women as well.

But the name seems wrong. I suggest Pfizer conduct a contest for renaming the drug to sound less like Miracle-Gro. Viriltas, Virilissimo, Virilita—something like that. Or perhaps we should name it after our president, who appears to be one of the few men who don't need it.

So the problem that once had no name now seems ubiquitous. Urologist Dr. Ridwan Shabsigh told a *New York Times* reporter: "The prevalence is stunning." Impotence has become a subject of dinner-party conversation. Will bowls of Viagra pills become the status symbol that bowls of cocaine were in the seventies, or that bottles of Prozac were in the eighties? Have we gone from searching for serenity to searching for stiffness?

Perhaps the pill of the nineties will cause a revolution in fiction as well as one in the bedroom. Never, it seems, have young writers been so cynical about the delights of sex. But signs are everywhere that America is longing to cast off the sexual political correctness of the last decade. Surely that was responsible for endangering orgasms. The Viagra craze shows, if nothing else, that American men want their erections back. And so do American women.

To have "It," the fortunate possessor must have that
strange magnetism that attracts both sexes.

—ELINOR GLYN

Sex appeal is a quality of mystery and accessibility both at the same time. It is out there shimmering for you—slightly out of reach. It is related to beauty, but it has nothing to do with perfect features or a perfect body. It is related to physical passion, but it is in no way hydraulic. Human beings are most aroused by fantasy and dream, not by swollen red vulvas—like baboons—or by erect feathers like peacocks. One reason sex videos and X-rated cable channels do nothing but *anesthetize* some of us is that they make sex too literal, too available.

Surely I am not the first to say that our primary erogenous zone is the brain. But this is why some people are erotic for kindred spirits only, and not for everyone. Then there are others—Marilyn

Monroe and Paul Newman are examples—who seem to evoke that quality of mysterious sex in *many* people. At the heart of this universality is their appeal to daydream. But I'm not interested in talking about movie stars and media images; I'm interested in the sexuality each of us has and often does nothing to tap.

What makes a woman or a man sexual? Is it a question of scent, of pheromones? Or is it a question of evoking *yearning*?

When we read about the lives of the great courtesans and heroines, we always hear that they had physical flaws but they knew instinctively how to stimulate yearning. They made themselves selectively unavailable. Of all the women Henry Miller loved, the only one he never *stopped* loving was one who was married to another: Anaïs Nin. She came and went—off to her husband, Hugo, back to Henry, off to her analyst lover, Otto Rank, off to her social life, her voluminous journals, the drama of her daily life. Henry wanted to marry her, but she would not marry a vagabond/pauper/novelist. She made her house outside Paris (in Louviciennes) into a cave of dreams. There she entertained her admirers in a setting she controlled. Her journals became another snare. Often she would read her lovers selected sections of her journals to arouse them. Sometimes these journals would deal intimately with *other* admirers. She wove a web made of words, of costumes, of mysterious disappearances. Henry Miller mistreated many of the women in his life, but he never mistreated Anaïs. Her unavailability, above all, prevented it.

Many women know that it is better to be a mistress than a wife. Mistresses are never associated with the broken water pipe or with the baby vomit on the silk blouse. Mistresses receive their lovers at appointed hours. They insist on controlling the light show and the sound effects. (I am not speaking of unwilling mistresses, longing to become wives. I am speaking of wise women who know what they have.)

What is their principal lure? Fantasy and dream.

The people I have loved most deeply in my life are those who have shared the water main breaks with me. But the people I have fantasized about most obsessively were those who were never present for life's disasters. They have been ubiquitous in my dreams, oddly absent from the dailiness of my life.

Is this odd? Not quite. Always, daily life is anaphrodisiac. Daily life is the necessary evil. Fantasy is the *relief*.

We all want both: "The flesh and the vision together" (as Anaïs Nin said of Henry Miller's writing). But our lives defeat us. We are mired in the quotidian. Perhaps the appeal of elegant brothels to nineteenth-century gentlemen was just this lure of a secret world out of time, a world where erotic fantasy reigned.

I have often fantasized about creating a world like this for women. Liberated women have too *little* fantasy in their lives to refresh them. They run from the school meeting to the lawyer's office, to the teaching gig, to the writing table—and where is the space for renewal except in their dreams? The men of today have also lost those special islands of bliss. Instead they are offered the grossness of sex by video or online. It simply won't do.

A few years ago, computer wonks used to engage in an activity called (in America, at least) "hottalk." On their video screens, they would exchange fantasies with other computer wonks, whom they never met. They'd call themselves names like Lady Chatterley or Rambo. They'd sign their love notes "Tarzan" or "Jane." They were looking to reestablish fantasy in our all-too-literal world. They were looking for new fables and fairy tales of sex. They wanted to get away from the literal sex offered in the sex shop. They longed to return to the fantasy that makes the flesh rise. Françoise Gilot has said that "the best way to be attractive is to be playful about life, *playing* in the sense of being an actress." This is profoundly true. We respond to those people who bring out the playmate in us. We respond to those people with whom we can be characters in fairy tales, characters from history. A woman who has the ability to evoke the playful boy in a man will never lack for lovers. She can be bald under her wig, toothless under her bridgework, flabby under her girdle—but if she can make a man feel he is a boy again, she will be loved and made love to. Chaucer's Wife of Bath knew this secret—despite the gap between her teeth.

Or maybe *because* of it. Françoise Gilot knows it. Women who have it never lose it. Perhaps it can be learned, but perhaps not.

Most women let themselves be led astray by the glossy images in slick magazines. These images imply that we have to be anorexic models or bodybuilders to be lusted for—or even to be loved. Nothing could be further from the truth. The stress on being perfect actually *turns off* lust. Have you ever watched the studs and studdesses in health clubs? In front of the mirror, they are lusting *only* for themselves. The truly sexy woman evokes not an image of herself in the mirror but the image of the man she stimulates as a laughing little boy. He loves her for the way she makes him feel.

Gilot, that wonderful witch, also says that "love is perhaps a Utopia." She says that the essence of love is not wanting anything from the other but *pleasure*. In our daily lives, everyone *wants* something from us. Imagine meeting a person who wants only to laugh, to touch, to make you feel *good*! What a relief! Wouldn't you do anything for such a person?

The poet Neruda describes adulterous lovers as sailors on beds "high as ocean liners." The image evokes the solitary sea and the splendid isolation of lovers. Sometimes adultery is just the desire to have a place where no one wants anything of you but pleasure. You don't have to answer the phone. You don't have to be a big girl. You don't have to shop for groceries. You don't even have to swear undying commitment. All you have to do is play.

We all need mystery and danger in our lives. And sometimes we are attracted to someone, almost telepathically, because we understand that *this* is the gift that person brings. Wishing very hard, the other person catches our wish and sends it zinging back. This is deeply erotic. Sometimes the *zing* doesn't end in bed. Sometimes a touch on the hand or the neck or a phone call late at night proves enough. Sometimes your whole life changes, and you end up building new bookcases and hanging new curtains. But your fantasy has been awakened, and you are reborn. Without fantasy neither woman nor man can live. Why do we have to learn that again and again?

Surely a king who loves pleasure is less dangerous than one
who loves glory.

—NANCY MITFORD

It's hard to be a novelist in the age of soap opera. The slow accretion of five hundred well-wrought words a day seems pointless
beside the dizzying and breathless plotlines served up by the evening
news. The semen-stained dress! The tape-recorded confessions! The
thrilling revelations of dubious details that seem to vanish over-
night. All the national soaps tend to blend into one: the brothers
Menendez, O. J. Simpson, Monica Lewinsky. They burn brightly
for a while, then disappear into the archives of old news.

But they preempt the other stories we might tell, hound the subtler tales off the screen. And we are the losers. We tell each other
stories to get human truths. And there is no truth in the national

soap opera—only sound and fury. But the national soap opera has such power to absorb all our storytelling energy.

We turn to these tales to show us shadows of our own lives. And shadows are all they show. But they do track our changing mores. Just a few years ago, the mere hint of monkey business was enough to bring a presidential candidate down. (Remember Gary Hart in 1990?) Now the evening talk shows are full of jokes about White House knee pads, and nobody seems to care.

Are we bored with sex? Has the soap opera mentality so permeated politics that we are unsurprised by these revelations? We know that presidents are flawed and interns will be interns. Or is it that we are going back to a pagan view of the gods, in which they partake of all our most human failings and we laugh, seeing ourselves in them?

I think we are witnessing the delayed effect of all those revelations about FDR and JFK that have filled our cultural discourse for the last several years. We learned belatedly that our heroes had feet of clay. Now we learn about their feet of clay contemporaneously. That's the only difference.

Bill Clinton fits nicely into the Zeus archetype of king of the gods. Why should he be bound by bourgeois constraints? We expect a larger-than-life appetite from this larger-than-life leader.

JFK got us ready for this. So did LBJ and FDR. Though the press protected them while they were alive, the last two decades stripped them of their secrets.

Since we already know the worst about Bill Clinton, the verdict of history can only ennoble him. Already it seems he is being redeemed.

I happened to be in France at the height of the Lewinsky-Willey madness—right before the Paula Jones case against President Clinton was dismissed. "Of course the president cannot tell the truth about all these women," said a French friend. "A gentleman never tells the truth about ladies. It would be rude."

I had a vision of Bill Clinton addressing the nation at prime time:

"I am a gentleman," the president says, "and a gentleman must always be discreet. To set an example for the nation, let me say I never touched that woman or that woman or that woman or even that woman, for that matter. . . ."

The French believe that the president's penis is entitled to privacy. Apparently Americans are starting to agree. I came home to an article in the *New York Times* about people turning off their TVs when the president's sex life was mooted. Just as we don't want to think of our parents having sex, it turns out we don't want to contemplate the president's penis too closely. Or is it that we don't like his notion of foreplay? Whipping it out seems unromantic. Maybe we want a little candlelight and champagne. A little soft music?

Have we forgotten that the president is the alpha male of the tribe, and the alpha male gets the youngest and the most nubile females with or without foreplay? It's like that with chimps, gibbons, and even presidents of the United States. What the alpha male wants the alpha male gets. It was Evelyn Lincoln, JFK's secretary, who reported having to beat the women off with sticks. Does it count as sexual harassment if women are harassing the *president* for sex?

Let's be honest about this. Why do guys *want* to be president? It's not for the rubber-chicken dinners.

Anyone who has ever watched women falling all over one another to date fat middle-aged moguls should have no doubt about the desirability of the president's penis.

When we are confused by the current political scene, we ought to look to the animal kingdom for guidance. A recent political cartoon showed elephants, zebras, and antelopes looking at Bill and Hillary Clinton and saying: "They have strange mating habits."

But their mating habits are all too predictable. "Power is the ultimate aphrodisiac," said Henry Kissinger. And he wasn't even as cute as Bill Clinton.

Italy is a dream that keeps returning for the rest of your life.

—ANNA AKHMATOVA

Whenever I go anywhere *but* Italy for a vacation, I always feel vaguely disappointed, as if I have made a mistake. All too often I have changed my plans and left—a ski resort in the French Alps, a fairy-tale mountain town in Switzerland, a *mas* in Provence—to get to Italy as soon as possible. Once across the border I can breathe again. Why bother to go anywhere, I think—in those first ecstatic moments of reentry—but Italy?

What is the fatal charm of Italy? What do we find there that can be found nowhere else? I believe it is a certain permission to be human, which other places, other countries, lost long ago. Not only is Italy one of the few places left on the planet where fantasy runs unfettered and free (where, as Luigi Barzini said in *The Italians,* "even instruments of precision like speedometers and clocks are made to lie in Italy for your happiness"), it is also one of the few places that tolerate human nature with all its faults. Italy is the past, but it is also the future. It is pagan but it is also Christian and Jewish. It is grand and tawdry, imperishable and decayed. Italy has seen marauding armies, fascists and communists, fashions and fripperies, come and go. And it is still, for all its layers of history, a place that enhances existence, burnishes the present moment.

Consider the Italian art of making the small transactions of life more pleasant. One of my earliest memories of this comes from my very first trip to Italy. I remember a train conductor who, when I was nineteen and by mistake riding in a second-class carriage with a third-class ticket, refused to charge me the *supplemento* I readily proffered. He said (in Italian, in which it sounds even better than in English): "Signorina, you have given Italy the gift of your beauty; now let Italy give this small gift to you." The implication, of course, was that my beauty was so large that the gift of a piddling *supplemento* could not possibly compensate for it. Nor was the conductor coming on to me; he scarcely believed that I would be led to fall in love or lust with him by means of this mild flattery. Rather, it was Italian charm at work. And Italian charm often consists of a delicious combination of rule-bending and harmless flirtation. Now imagine how that exchange would have gone in Germany—the country of *ordnung* and charmlessness. No wonder the Germans themselves come to Italy when they want a holiday!

If the seven deadly sins seem somewhat less deadly in Italy, the Ten Commandments slightly less rigid and more malleable, it is because of this rule-bending humanity of the Italians. It is a country that not only tolerates contradictions—it positively encourages them. The Italian shrug embodies this philosophy. It says: *Things have been this way forever and always will be this way.* Why buck *la forza del destino*? And even the rigid northerner relaxes and has another glass of wine.

Your trip there will never quite go as planned. This is part of the *avventura*. There may be strikes, mixed-up reservations, maddening *imbrogli* of all sorts. But they will be charming *imbrogli*—you can count on that. They will be charming because the Italian people are charming. A lost reservation in Germany is a Walpurgisnacht; in Italy it is an opera buffa. Being in Italy is rather like being in love—with a whole country. So what if people have been in love before? So what if Italy has been a tourist trap for, at least, a thousand years? So what if everything you say in criticism—or praise—of Italy has already been said? Writers yet unborn will say it all again, blissfully unaware that anyone has said it before. They will fall in love with Italy all over again as if she were a virgin who had never been seduced. Italy is hardly a virgin, but then few seductresses remain virgins for long.

The first place I knew in Italy was Florence—or rather Bellosguardo, a lovely hilltop perch (*suburb* is too banal a word) looking down on the duomo from a yew-studded prominence. As a college junior, I lived in the Torre di Bellosguardo—a thirteenth-century tower adjoining a fifteenth-century villa, studied Italian and Italians, and fell madly in love with Italy.

The moon was brighter in Italy. The geraniums were pinker and more pungent. The wine was more intoxicating. The men were handsomer. *Cipressi* were more poetic than yew trees. Italian had more rhymes than English. It was the language of love, the language of poetry. I thought my impressions were original. I filled notebooks, aerograms, and sheets and sheets of something we then called "onionskin" with my banal musings. If I had known then what I know now—that a thousand years of similar musings by similar young musers preceded me—would I have felt diminished? Thank God I *didn't* know. I felt special, chosen. Italy has the power to confer this sense of chosenness.

I went back to Bellosguardo a few years ago and stayed in the same villa (now a lovely small hotel owned by the charming and erudite Amerigo Franchetti) with my daughter, Molly, who was at the *least* charming age of teenage daughters: thirteen going on fourteen. Because she knew I adored this part of Italy and had wonderful memories of it, she whined in the car from Arezzo to Florence, whined while passing through beautiful hill towns, whined at gas stations, at phantasmagoric autogrills, whined as we threaded our way past a traffic jam created by a procession in honor of Nostra Signora del Autostrada. She hated Florence, hated our room in Bellosguardo, hated the swimming pool, the restaurant, and of course her mother— until I had the inspiration of emptying a bottle of icy San Pellegrino on her head. Whereupon she threw her arms around me and said: "Mommy, I love you!" Is this part of the fatal charm of Italy?

Trips like that have taught me a lesson. For me the secret of being happy in Italy now is to live life *all'italiana*. That means I no longer even *attempt* to tour, but I stay in one place and live life by the eminently sensible Italian schedule: walk in the mornings and evenings, eat and rest in the middle of the day.

In the last few years I have concentrated on two particular sections of Italy: Tuscany and Lucca, the Veneto and Venice.

I discovered Lucca almost by accident. My friends Ken and Barbara Follett had rented a place called Villa San Michele right outside Lucca in a town called Vorno, and they invited us to come and stay. Since the Follett clan never stir on summer holidays without room for their five grown daughters and sons, various pals and partners, cousins, siblings, and Barbara's Labour Party colleagues, they have to rent enormous houses. Molly and I joined this happy throng; later my husband sprung himself from New York and met us.

Lucca is west of Florence on the autostrada, past Montecatini, the spa town, and just short of Pisa and Livorno. You first see Lucca from a ring road surrounding a walled, gated Tuscan city with bicyclers cruising the wide parapets and cars parked outside the impressive walls of the Centro Storico. There is a lovely restaurant on the walls (Antico Caffè delle Mura), a Roman coliseum turned into a honeycomb of dwellings during the Middle Ages, medieval streets, a glorious duomo. Lucca is surrounded by a variety of small country towns where you can stay, making the city a destination rather than a stopping place.

Villa San Michele at Vorno is entered through narrow stone gates opposite vineyards above which dramatic hills rise. It is a sprawling fifteenth-century villa, once a ruin, with gorgeous views and an ample swimming pool. Little hills covered with vineyards rise around it.

What did we do there? Mostly *far niente*. The joy of vacationing in Italy is *far niente*. The teenagers slept till at least noon every day. The grown-ups—if you can call us that—wrote, faxed, and telephoned in the morning, then after lunch lazed by the pool. If we went to Lucca to bike around the walls or shop or see works of art, it was never until three-thirty or four. I remember one lunch that ended at six in the afternoon, with Neil Kinnock playing sixties folk songs on his guitar while the whole group sang along. I remember passionate political discussions while we all sat topless around the pool. I finished a chapter of *Fear of Fifty* called "Becoming Venetian" while sitting near that pool with a yellow legal pad balanced on my knee. I remember a cruise we took along the coast to snorkel and swim in the Golfo dei Poeti. When we stopped for lunch at Portovenere, we overlooked the white marble quarries of Carrara (where Michelangelo had his marble quarried). The joy of Italy often consists of doing ordinary things in extraordinary settings.

Since Lucca was originally a Roman encampment (founded in 180 B.C.) that became a medieval and Renaissance city, it has the layers of history characteristic of Rome and Verona. The arches of its coliseum were long ago filled in with houses, and the central stage remains as a vast piazza.

Lucca reached its zenith as a trading town in the eleventh, twelfth, and thirteenth centuries. Between the fourteenth and eighteenth centuries, she remained an independent city-state like Venice—until Napoleon conquered them both.

No one leaves Lucca without admiring the white Carrara sepulchre in the duomo of the beautiful Ilaria del Carretto done by Jacopo della Quercia in 1406. Ilaria was the young wife of Paolo Guinigi, one of the fifteenth-century bosses of Lucca. I forget how she died. I'm sure I deliberately blank out her story because I loathe stories about young women who die at tender ages. I would rather see monuments to women who survived their first loves and went on to have several more.

Napoleon Bonaparte was so fond of Lucca that he wanted to keep it in the family. First, he made his sister Elisa Duchess of Lucca; later he promoted her to Grand Duchess of Tuscany.

Lucca still has a taste for luxury. The food remains excellent even in little *pizzerie*. The city is full of posh jewelry shops displaying antique and modern treasures. There are wonderful shoemakers— one of whom (Porselli) makes slippers for the dancers of La Scala. I never leave without ballerina flats in half a dozen colors. How can you ever go wrong in a town with good shoe shops?

We liked that summer sojourn in Lucca so much that the next summer we rented a house about twenty minutes from the Folletts', on the other side of the city walls, in a town called San Macario al Monte. Molly brought two friends. I invited my best friend, Gerri Karetsky, to share the house with us, and her son Bob joined us on his way home from the Maccabea games in Israel. Our place was a farmhouse rather than a palazzo but it was spacious and had lots of bedrooms, a great pool, and spectacular views.

I've found that houses with spectacular views often have spectacularly tricky roads leading to them, and this place was no exception. The road fell away in places like the corniche road along the Dalmatian coast—after the shelling.

Once ensconced upon our promontory, we discovered a comfortable rustic house with lovely views of other hilltops, a swimming pool with a vine-shaded pergola, silvery olive trees, dark *cipressi,* and both sunrise and sunset views. From our house, it was a ten-minute drive to Lucca, fifteen minutes to the Folletts in Vorno at Villa San Michele, and only half an hour to Pisa, with its duomo and fabled leaning tower, and the seashore towns nearby.

Between Lucca and Pisa there are sweet country inns, restaurants in gardens, restaurants on hilltop terraces, both splendid and modest. The jolliest meal we had was at a hilltop trattoria whose kitchen was closed when we arrived but where the most obliging *patrone* put out, with great panache, cheeses and salami and prosciutto for us. This nameless trattoria is nowhere as famous as Vipore, Il Giglio, La Mora, or the other starred places around Lucca. Again, it was the kindness of the people that made it so exceptional.

Since Molly is a Leo, born on August 19, she has celebrated almost every birthday in Italy since she was five. Her fifteenth summer was one of our best times—we celebrated with all the Folletts, their guests, and our guests at Villa La Principessa, a beautiful country villa-hotel with a garden restaurant full of huge chestnut trees.

We had a horseshoe-shaped table. The teenagers captured the middle and the grown-ups commanded the ends. We had invited Molly's nanny of ten years, Margaret Kiley, to come out of retirement and spend two weeks of this summer with us in Italy. Between our crowd of Jongs, Burrowses, Karetskys, and friends, and the Follett and friends clan, we rarely stirred without twenty people.

Fortunately, Italians find that normal—since *they* rarely stir without twenty people. Parties of family, friends, big kids, little kids, are not only tolerated in Italy, they are considered simpatico—which makes Italy perhaps the most sympathetic place in the world for a family vacation. There's no place where children are not encouraged and few places where they are not treated as full-fledged guests.

A villa on a hill about five minutes from ours sold excellent local wine, and the simple meals we made at home were as memorable as the ones in restaurants. Sitting out on our terrazzo under the rising moon, eating *prosciutto e melone* and grilled local fish, drinking inexpensive local wine, playing various games of charades with the kids, was better than any evening out.

What is this fatal charm of Italy? Why does it reflect us back to ourselves like a mirror that obliterates wrinkles, takes off pounds, and gives our eyes a devil-may-care sparkle? Why does Italy remain the country of the Saturnalia—the feast when everything was permitted? Is it because the pagan past is still alive in Italy and Christianity is just a thin veneer that scarcely covers? To wake up on a Sunday morning in Italy and hear the roosters crowing and the bells pealing is one of life's greatest pleasures. To take a walk or a run in that tintinnabulation is even better. The mornings are cool; the birds career from hill to hill; the bells seem to have been created not to draw worshipers to church but—like so many things here—for your particular pleasure.

If you stay long enough and transform yourself from tourist to habitué, the headwaiters will also call you *Maestro* or *Contessa* or *Dottore* or perhaps even *Commendatore*. To Italians this gentle flattery is almost meaningless; only Americans take it even semiseriously. Typically, we at first fall madly in love with this flattering overstatement, and somewhat later, when we discover it is only a form of social lubrication, we pronounce all Italians liars and fakes. Actually, both reactions are wrong. Naked truth, the Italians believe, can always do with some enhancement.

I had visited Venice many times as a tourist from my teens on but had never lived in the Veneto for extended periods until, when my daughter was small, I was researching and writing my Venetian time-travel novel (later published as *Shylock's Daughter*). To spin this tale of an actress who comes to Venice to make a movie of *The Merchant of Venice*, travels back in time, and falls in love with a young Will Shakespeare in the sixteenth-century ghetto of Venice, I not only submerged myself in literature about Venice and the Veneto but resided there as well. My unmethodical method is to live in a place, read everything about it, and let the ideas for the book germinate out of the interaction between the atmosphere and my unconscious.

Venetians have decamped to the foothills of the Dolomites and built summer villas there ever since the days of Palladio. Since I sensed that my dashing young Will Shakespeare and my older actress heroine, Jessica Pruitt, would eventually round out their *avventure* in the Palladian villas of the Veneto, I made it my pleasant obligation to see every Palladian villa, every hill town, every church—major or minor. Since my sixteenth-century Jessica was Jewish, like Shakespeare's, I also immersed myself in the Jewish history of Venice, the story of the Venetian ghetto, and the traces of Jewish life in Bassano, Ásolo, Montebelluna, Castelfranco.

I discovered that there were some towns, like Castelfranco, that had had thriving Jewish populations throughout the Middle Ages; that there had been pogroms caused by blood-libel accusations even among the tolerant Italians; that Jews were welcomed as bankers when there was need for their leavening financial efforts but often thrown out when they became too successful, as elsewhere. I came to understand why Jewish mothers all wanted their sons to become doctors in medieval and Renaissance Venice. The doctor did not have to wear the yellow hat identifying him as a Jew, and he could leave the ghetto after curfew. Many of the doges of Venice had Jewish doctors. To be a doctor meant unparalleled freedom for a Jewish man.

The winged Lion of Saint Mark that adorns most public buildings reminds us that most of the hill towns of the Veneto were dependencies of the thousand-year Venetian Republic, La Serenissima. Starting in the sixteenth century, noble Venetian families began to build country estates in the foothills of the Dolomites to escape the heat of the summer, do some serious gentleman farming, cultivate vineyards on these steep slopes, and escape from Venice when politics or economics required a graceful retreat. Venetian noble families used to cruise up the Brenta from Venice with barges full of servants, retainers, animals, and enough clothes for the elegant court life they transported to the country. The fine art of making the pilgrimage to the rural estate was refined and perfected in Italy—like so many civilized pleasures.

Our outpost in the hills of the Veneto on this occasion (and many subsequent ones) was an artist friend's farmhouse, perched on a precipitous hillside above Ásolo. It is reached by a breathtaking dirt road whose steep margins remind you not to drink after dinner (in one of the charming cafés in Ásolo's main square) if you want to make it home. The road can be washed out in mud season, but in summer it usually holds. The house is simple and full of paintings; the view is stupendous. It is almost impossible to find. In short, it is the perfect place to write. As in many Italian places, you live outside in the good weather and eat overlooking tiny twinkling hill towns balanced on neighboring hills.

My friend's farmhouse is within fifteen or twenty minutes of the Villa Barbaro at Maser, with its Veronese trompe l'oeil frescoes and extravagant fountains. It is also relatively near the Brenta River and the Brenta Canal, where the Villa Foscari (Malcontenta) stands. Vicenza, Bassano del Grappa, and the shoe factories of the Veneto (where nearly all the most beautiful designer shoes in the world are made) are also very close.

Ken and I spent a perfect day wandering through Marostica with its chessboard square and *castel superiore* (the fortress perched on a hill above the town). We discovered wonderful olive oils infused with truffles in the local trattorie and bags of dried mushrooms from the surrounding woods. Of the many good restaurants of the Asolean hills, Al Ringraziamento in Cavaso del Tomba is my new favorite. Even though it has a star in Michelin, it is extremely simple—white tablecloths, local wines, a fireplace. The great pleasure in the Asolean hills is just living *all'italiana*. There is even a verb for it in *la bella lingua—asolare—*the art of idling Ásolo style.

Ásolo and Venice are two halves of a perfect sojourn in the Veneto. If I want to conjure up Venice, I imagine myself lying on the bed in the room in Dorsoduro where I wrote *Serenissima,* looking up at the shimmering ceiling, seeing the light show of reflections of the rippling water. Laughter wafts across the canal. Fragments of conversation float under my open window. Dogs bark. Bells ring. Only the occasional plash of an oar or the furious roar of an outboard motor interrupts the silence. Venice remains a place where individual voices matter.

The first place where I stayed in Venice, when I was nineteen, was the youth hostel (*ostello di gioventù*) on the island of Giudecca, not far from Palladio's church of the Redentore. Since then I have stayed in hotels of every sort—from modest *pensioni* to the deluxe Gritti and Cipriani. But the most Venetian way to stay in Venice is to rent an old house in Dorsoduro or a crumbing fifteenth-century palazzo on Giudecca (with a courtyard full of old roses), far from the tourist centers. You have to be enough off the beaten track to let the watery rhythm of the city infuse your consciousness.

Then there is the quiet—the unearthly quiet of one of the last places on earth without cars.

I recommend that you fall in love in Venice and pursue (or escape) your forbidden love down the narrow *calli*, through the *campi*, under the *sottoportegi*. If you can't snare a lover for yourself, Venice will surely provide one—even if that lover is only the city herself.

Venetian love affairs, like Aschenbach's with Tadzio, inhabit some ideal realm, but they rarely prove durable when reality dawns. Perhaps that's the whole point. Venice accretes into the form of a yearned-for lover to teach us something about time, about beauty, about mutability. If a thousand-year republic can fall, Venice tells us, then even the greatest loves are transitory. Venice is our earthly correlative for mutability. Her most moving shrines—the ancient Jewish cemetery on the Lido, the mortuary island of San Michele, the ghetto in Cannaregio, the Redentore and Santa Maria della Salute (both built after plagues ended)—are shrines to Thanatos as much as much as they are shrines to Eros.

Venice is the place where those two great powers marry.

Sometimes I think I go back to Venice especially to dream. My Venetian dreams are always rich and strange. The water breeds them as I fall asleep, floating on Venice as if she were a boat. There are always many-chambered palazzi where princesses dance until their shoes are full of holes. All the players in my past mingle as they glide through the same dream ballroom. I wake up to the air shuddering with bells and aromatic with the scent of coffee.

I think it was Hazlitt who said that the only thing that could
beat this city of water would be a city built in the air.

—JOSEPH BRODSKY

It is like no other place on earth. You arrive from Tokyo, New
York, Paris, Delhi, Rio, Rome, and the first thing you notice, de-
scending from whatever earthbound vehicle has brought you—
train, plane, automobile—is that your equilibrium rocks a little
with your first step onto the shimmering liquid surface. For this is
the lagoon city (or rather it is two cities: one above and seemingly
solid; one below and reflected in the waters), and that slight wobble
tells you everything about its essence. It is the city of mirrors, the
city of mirages, at once solid and liquid, at once air and stone. The
stones themselves are thick with history, and those cats that dash
through the alleyways must surely be the ghosts of the famous
dead in feline disguise. Many noted artists, after all, died here:

Wagner, Browning, Diaghilev—though some, like Dante, merely died of maladies contracted on their last visit. These illustrious deaths have given the city a certain spooky patina and a faintly macabre reputation—like New Orleans, only more so. Or maybe it is the time-stopped nature of the place, the fact that so many vistas still look exactly as they do in Carpaccio or Bellini paintings (except for the television antennas, of course), which gives you the sense that you can turn a corner and stroll into the past.

The first time I came to Venice I was a student of *la bella lingua* in Florence. I came alone, by second-class railway carriage, a small spiral notebook in one hand and a ballpoint pen in the other, for I already knew that Venice existed in part for English-speaking writers to write about. Shakespeare, Byron, Browning, Ruskin, James, all had succumbed to its spell.

I came down the steps of the railroad station and was at once elated by the gleaming band of water I saw before me. (I had yet to spot the dead cats floating, or the raw sewage, or the masses of detergent bubbles, or the plastic bottles.) I was besotted with the idea and the reality of Venice, and that besottedness has never quite left me—despite the fact that I now know La Serenissima far too well to be a rhapsodist merely of her beauties. Still, on my many return visits, I have never failed to reexperience that first burst of elation, that Aha! of recognition, part physical, part literary.

On my first trip to Venice, I remember sitting in the Piazzetta reading Byron, amazed to be just a stone's throw from the place that inspired these words:

I stood in Venice on the Bridge of Sighs,

A palace and a prison on each hand;

I saw from out the wave her structures rise

As from the stroke of the enchanter's wand:

A thousand years their cloudy wings expand

Around me, and a dying Glory smiles

O'er the far times, when many a subject land

Looked to the winged Lion's marble piles,

Where Venice sate in state, throned on her hundred isles!

And then a very Venetian thing happened. A young man attracted by my dreamy expression, the poetry I was reading, the notebook, or something sensual in the ancient stones themselves, came up to me bearing a bunch of violets.

He was a tourist, too, a Chinese doctor from Australia, and he was shy—not the sort of person who accosts American college girls with violets. As we spent the day touring the palaces, the works of art, I realized that only Venice could have released him from his shyness. Venice does that to people. Just as it releases their longings, it also allows unpredictable things to happen.

One summer night a few years ago, I was dining with friends at a little outdoor restaurant on a canal in Dorsoduro. Another acquaintance came by in his boat, a brightly colored Torcello fishing boat, stopped to join us for coffee, and then invited us for a ride along the canals at midnight. One of our party was a violinist from the Fenice Theater, and he took out his fiddle, sat cross-legged on the prow of the boat, and played Mozart for us. As we rowed through the maze of little canals, the oars dipping and splashing in the inky water, the music filling the air, Venetians opened their windows and came out on their balconies to shout "Bravo!"

The mythical Venice may be hard to grasp on a steamy day in midsummer when this city of 338,000 seems to swell to twice that number, with the tourists milling about the Piazza San Marco, dutifully feeding scruffy pigeons, having their pockets picked, and listening to wheezy bands playing "New York, New York" (for reasons that will never be explained). But come back in November or December, in February or March, when *la nebbia* settles upon the city like a marginless monster, and you will have little trouble believing that things can appear and disappear in this labyrinthine city, or that time here could easily slip in its sprockets and take you, willingly or unwillingly, back.

Most of the summer tourists make a predictable forty-eight-hour pilgrimage from the railroad station to Piazza San Marco, swarm there briefly between the two columns (not realizing it was here that criminals were strung up and that Venetians believe it brings bad luck to walk between them), see Saint Mark's Basilica and the Doge's Palace over the heads of thousands of others of their kind, take a gondola ride, for which they pay about one dollar a minute and during which they have the curious pleasure of seeing the ubiquitous Japanese tourists rowing six abreast down the Grand Canal to the strains of Neapolitan music ("Come Back to Sorrento" is played for the same reason as "New York, New York," I guess).

I have a friend in Venice whose family has been historically prominent for the last thousand years, whose palazzo looks down upon one of the main serenade routes of the gondolas. Last summer, a merry family of Americans with four boys rented the *piano nobile* of this palazzo, and it was the younger boys' great joy (and my daughter's as well) to watch for gondolas and as they went by to throw things down to them: not bucketfuls of water (as sometimes happens in Venice) but trinkets, sweets, paper gliders. Such largesse suggests another of Venice's sly realities: the age-old pecking order of tourists.

There are the yachts that dock for a week or two, discharging mysterious international billionaires and setting all the gossips in Venice abuzz about who has been invited to cocktails, who to dinner, and who to set sail for Yugoslavia and Greece. There are the movie stars, who go to the Hotel Cipriani to toast and tryst, or to rest up after toasting and trysting. There are the affluent Americans, who schlepp from the Cipriani pool to Harry's Bar and back again, buying gold jewelry en route at inflated prices.

Those who rent a palazzo on the Grand Canal look down upon those who merely stay at the Cipriani or Gritti for a week, who in turn look down on those who come to the railroad station, stay for two days in a fleabag near the Piazza San Marco, and go away, sure that they've seen Venice and that it is ruinously expensive, dangerous, full of tourists and pickpockets.

All these things it surely can be, in any season, but it is also true that there are parts of Venice—the Giudecca, Dorsoduro—where you can live in midsummer and rarely see another American, and that many of Venice's most faithful recidivists never go near the Piazza San Marco in season and wouldn't, if caught there by mistake, dream of buying a gelato there. Not only is a San Marco gelato four times the price of a gelato in a true Venetian neighborhood, but there is no place to stroll and eat it in peace.

Venice has always attracted artists from abroad. Some, like Turner, found in her their true subject; others, like Corot, admitted that Venice defeated them. Venice still attracts artists. Arbit Blatas, the Lithuanian artist who first visited Venice in 1934, when Blackshirts were marching on the Riva degli Schiavoni, now lives and works on the Giudecca (one of the largest islands of Venice) with his wife, Regina Resnik, the retired opera singer.

Arbit Blatas explains that Venice attracts him as a painter because its surface "is constantly metamorphosing. Painting Venice is almost like being a restorer, peeling off the layers to find the picture after picture underneath. Venice is inexhaustible because the shifting light and the drifting fog keep changing her face. In the winter, Venice is like an abandoned theater. The play is finished, but the echoes remain. When you walk in the winter fog, there seems to be no division between water and embankment. You feel that you can walk through walls, through sky, through time."

Regina Resnik reminded me that "the Giudecchini say that the Venetians see only the Giudecca, while the people on the Giudecca look always at Venice." This is true. From her kitchen window, La Resnik sees the Dogana, the Doge's Palace, the campanile in the

Piazza San Marco. "There are times when the fog is so thick, you can't see out," she said. "But when the fog lifts, the Serenissima is always there. She's the anchor of my life."

When the Austrians built the railroad bridge connecting the mainland to Venice in 1846, they ended the city's island status. But it is still almost as hard to get to as if it were an island. (Venice, built on one hundred eighteen small islands, is crisscrossed by about one hundred fifty canals and spanned by about four hundred bridges.) Even the most aristocratic Venetian, with the grandest family palazzo, must carry his own bags out of the railroad station to the *vaporetto* or through the maze of little streets that surround the large parking area at Piazzale Roma and wend his way through the labyrinth of Venice on foot in order to get home again. Of course, there are *motoscafi*, water taxis, but they are wildly expensive and their drivers often are querulous about taking passengers to the smaller canals when the tide is low. As one friend says, "Venice seems to take delight in humbling us all, reducing us to footsore pilgrims dependent on our strong legs and comfortable shoes." If you are lucky enough to have a friend who meets you with a boat, then you sail into Venice in glory, feeling for all the world like Marco Polo come home. Otherwise everyone walks.

What was I searching for on all my trips to Venice? At first I thought it was Venetian art—painting, sculpture, architecture, music—all of which Venice has in glorious abundance. Of course, I loved Palladio, Longhi, Vivaldi, Albinoni, Bellini, Carpaccio, Veronese, Tintoretto, but as a writer I was also drawn to the gentle style of life that creation requires, a style far easier to achieve in Venice than in a city like New York.

I began spending summers in Venice with my family, renting apartments or houses there, and I grew to love the easy pace of the days, the way one activity flows into the next, the quiet, the light that glimmers inside as well as outside the houses. Venice may be the only city on earth where you can see the shimmer of canal water on a ceiling. So uniquely Venetian is this phenomenon that there is even a phrase for it in the Venetian dialect: *fa la vecia,* which translated literally, means "to do as the old woman does," or "squint." If your bedroom faces a canal, you wake up to this delicious shimmer on the ceiling, provided you do that very American thing—sleep with your shutters open. You also awaken to the joyous sounds of water lapping on stone and to bells pealing from the city's many campaniles. Even the sounds of Venice are kind to the ears—compared, say with the sounds of New York.

But Florence also has bells, if not lapping water, and Rome has grander fountains. And not every Venetian bedroom is situated on a canal. What, then, makes Venice so special? I think it finally has to do with its being a moated city, cut off from time. Not only do many places in Venice look exactly as they did four or five hundred years ago, but the ghosts of decades and centuries past seem trapped within the ancient stones, trapped by the water that moats the city. For certain susceptible souls, Venice seems to cast a spell, making them return again and again until, somehow, they unwork the spell or succumb to it. "I want to die in Venice," said a beautiful Brazilian lady I met once at a garden party. "And so I know I want to live in Venice."

To die in Venice may seem romantic, but alas, the final resting place may be shockingly impermanent. The Jews lie peacefully in the Antico Cimitero Israelitico out on the Lido, in sacred ground given them by the Venetian Republic in 1386, but the Christians who are buried on the island of San Michele have only a twelve-year lease, after which their bones are dug up and flung upon something the Venetians ominously refer to as "the bone island." Only the famous dead of San Michele are exempt from this fate. Ezra Pound, Diaghilev, Stravinsky, will not be displaced so long as their fame lasts. This is another Venetian irony. Fame is important not only before but after death. Venice is in some ways like Hollywood. Even dead, one is only as good as one's last reviews.

After many trips to Venice, a novel began to be born for me out of the stones. It started, like my historical novel, *Fanny,* with a sense of place. As *Fanny* was a sort of homage to eighteenth-century literature and the landscape of England, so my Venetian novel was born out of my love for Venice and my sense that the stones held a story for me.

The story took shape, little by little, like a mosaic. The overall picture was not clear to me at first. But as I came back, year after year, writing purely for my own pleasure in Venetian notebooks with marbleized covers, I discovered a heroine who was a Shakespearean actress, who had come to Venice to make a film of *The Merchant of Venice,* and who, through a series of strange incidences and coincidences, finds herself back in the past (with a sixteenth-century adventure to pursue before she can return to her own time). As I wrote my novel in Venice and its surroundings, and as I read every book about the city I could lay my hands on, I had the sense that Venice was using me as an amanuensis, as she had used many writers before me—and will use many more after me.

Since Venetians love to share the love of their city, my Venetian friends were wonderfully helpful with research. Marino Zorzi, the director of the Marciana Library, shared with me the volumes and volumes of handwritten diaries of Marin Sanudo, Venice's great Renaissance voyager. Count Girolamo Marcello introduced me to the state archives of the Serenissima, housed in a library in his palazzo since the fall of the Venetian Republic, in 1797, and gathering dust there awaiting her resurrection (at which time the Marcellos must restore them to the state). Finally I was taken on a tour of the Arsenale by Maurizio Crovato, an expert on Venetian boats. Before I could be admitted, I had to endure a security check more suitable for the NASA space center than for an arsenal that has been virtually a museum for centuries. Venice may no longer be the terror of the tides, but she relinquishes her image as a great imperialist power slowly, if at all.

On a freezing afternoon a year ago, I wandered through the Arsenale trying to imagine it in its heyday, when a galley could be assembled and equipped in one day. Such traveling back and forth in time is somehow easier in Venice than in other places. In fact, that is one of the reasons writers love to work in Venice, whether they are writing about the city or not.

Some writers come to Venice to submerge themselves in their own pasts. "We have been coming to Venice for some twenty years," the late Leo Lerman told me once, "and in these last years, I've been working on a long book of memoirs." Then, as if quoting from the work-in-progress, he said: "Venice, seeming so remote from the Manhattan of my long, long ago childhood, is closer to that childhood than the Manhattan in which I live today. I hear the island sounds, I smell the sea and the salt air, and I am plunged into my remote past. Above me I see the skies of my early boyhood. I am transported. Then, too, in Venice there is also the stable, intricate Proustian social structure that I imagined as I rode high on the upper deck of the Fifth Avenue bus past the mansions of the powerful and great. . . . These mansions frequently derived from the Venetian palazzi I look out on every day from my windows on the Grand Canal."

When I began my novel about Venice, I knew I was following in a venerable tradition, but at first I didn't realize how venerable. The Italian scholar Marilla Battilana suggests that for English writers, "Venice itself has become almost an archetype." It represents the distant Oriental city, a Xanadu reached by means of a perilous sea journey, a labyrinthine place to which one voyages in search of love but in which instead one encounters subterfuge, disguise, and betrayal. According to Battilana, writers through the ages created what might be considered a "composite myth of Venice"; they have also immortalized Venice as the city of justice, a city where a wise sovereign dispensed a higher justice than can be found elsewhere in the sublunary world.

Venice was apparently first mentioned in English literature in the fourteenth century, in a book called *Mandeville's Travels*. At that time it was already seen as an exotic place, a sort of European Cathay to which one traveled en route to the Holy Land. But the city's literary reputation for sin and depravity began with the Elizabethan Roger Ascham, who in his book *The Schoolmaster* (1570) so inveighed against the lechery and depravity of Venice that he made all Englishmen eager to visit the city. "I learned, when I was at Venice," wrote Ascham, "that there it is counted good policy, when there be four or five brethren of one family, one only to marry, and all the rest to welter with as little shame in open lechery, as swine do here in the common mire." If that wasn't designed to lure lusty young Englishmen down from London, what was?

And down they came. Thomas Nashe, a contemporary of Shakespeare, not only was lured to Venice but left and wrote a book called *The Unfortunate Traveller* (1594), in which he took the Venetian myth even further along. Fornication and deception thrive in Nashe's Venice, and another major element in the composite myth of Venice is introduced: master and servant exchange identities in order to savor the Venetian mysteries. Inevitably they encounter Venetian justice and find it both severe and Solomon-like.

It was Shakespeare, however, who established forever the Venetian connection between love and justice (*The Merchant of Venice*) and the Venetian connection between love and death (*Othello*). The inamorata and the judge are, in fact, fused in *The Merchant of Venice*—and disguise and hidden identities are important to the action. With Shakespeare, the myth of the lagoon city is complete and its two poles are established. In the comedies, love mates with justice ("The quality of mercy is not strain'd"); in the tragedies, love mates with death ("I kiss'd thee ere I kill'd thee").

After Shakespeare, Ben Jonson, Thomas Coryat, Sir Henry Wotton, Thomas Otway, Daniel Defoe, Joseph Addison, Lady Mary Wortley Montagu, Oliver Goldsmith, Lord Chesterfield, all added to the myth of Venice. But it was with the Gothic novelists, the so-called pre-Romantics, that Venice truly came into her own for Anglo-Saxon writers. Ann Radcliffe set *The Mysteries of Udolpho* (1794) in a Venice she had never seen. It was clear that if Venice had not existed, it would surely have been invented for the Gothic tales of virgins in jeopardy that have proved to be a durable literary genre even in our own time.

To the Romantic poets Byron, Shelley, and Wordsworth (Keats never got to Venice), Venice meant something more: a place to reflect on the lapsed glories of ancient civilizations, to muse gloomily on the passing of all mortal things, and to ponder the eternity of the poetic spirit. The decadence of Venice was the focus, and Venice herself became a moral lesson for the English—showing how their country, too, could decay if they didn't watch out.

To modern writers from Henry James to Thomas Mann, Venice has been the city of love and death, and this association has been echoed by contemporary filmmakers. Venice is the place where artists go to be reborn (but often die), the place where love yields to death, and the waters close, mercifully or indifferently, over all. Of the two poles of the mythical Venice shaped for us by Shakespeare, we have chosen the tragic pole. It is hard to imagine a contemporary novel or film set in Venice that is not Gothic, macabre, replete with ghosts and mirages.

It is also hard to tell how much of the city's spell is life and how much is literature. The two are by now so intertwined that it is impossible to untangle them. Walking the streets of Venice in a writer's fog, one can imagine Shakespeare coming to the ghetto to research *The Merchant of Venice;* Byron swimming home along the Grand Canal after a fete, with his servant rowing behind him, carrying his clothes; Browning staying on alone in the Ca' Rezzonico after Elizabeth Barrett's death; Henry James writing in the Palazzo Barbaro, then taking a stroll in the Campo Santo Stefano below. That Venice has so often sat for her literary portrait is, in fact, a part of her essence. She is like some grand decrepit prima donna surrounded by aging portraits of herself, or an old movie star showing you her yellowing clippings; she is the world's dowager city.

Contemporary writers also find Venice enormously compelling. Joseph Brodsky, Gore Vidal, Mary McCarthy, and Jan Morris have written wonderfully evocative travel books about her.

What troubles the writer in Venice is the same thing that delights her: Everything that can be said about Venice has already been said by somebody. Henry James even exulted in this fact. "It would be a sad day indeed when there should be something new to say," he wrote. Gore Vidal quotes this with evident satisfaction in *Vidal in Venice.*

In our disposable twentieth-century society, Venice matters more than ever. Compared with a New York that compulsively rebuilds whole neighborhoods every three or four decades, Venice seems to be permanence itself. But she, too, is in peril—that has always been part of her allure. The water is rising (or the city sinking, depending on which expert you ask). Hydrocarbon pollution from Mestre, Venice's industrial neighbor, has weakened the stones beyond redemption. The canals, no longer cleaned the way they used to be, are filled with muck to a height of several feet.

Whenever the perilous high tides hit, they reactivate the eternal discussion about saving the city from the ravages of twentieth-century industry. Many Venetians believe that the canal dug in the lagoon to accommodate large oil tankers has opened Venice to the fury of the tides in a way never before possible. The mythical Venice is imperishable, but the physical Venice is another story. Its survival may depend upon a decision to banish the large oil tankers, thus allowing the lagoon to resume its previous level. No such decision has yet been made, and the chronic dilatoriness of the Venetian authorities may well doom the city to the fate of Atlantis.

My Venice is the Venice of winter, the Venice of Dorsoduro, the Venice of fog. Walking down the Zattere in *la nebbia,* wearing rubber boots against the high water, one finds it hard to tell where terra firma leaves off and sky and water begin. The city seems to hang in the air like a mirage. Sounds bounce off the waters and deceive you with their closeness or farness. Figures appear and disappear around corners. The past beckons. It is quite possible to believe that it can take you and never give you back.

There is no use whatever in trying to write a book unless you
know that you must write that book or go mad, or perhaps die.

—ROBERTSON DAVIES

Despite all the cynical things writers have said about writing
for money, the truth is we write for love. That is why it is so easy to
exploit us. That is also why we pretend to be hard-boiled, saying
things like no one but a blockhead ever wrote except for money
(Samuel Johnson). Not true. No one but a blockhead ever wrote
except for love.

There are plenty of easier ways to make money. Almost *anything* is less labor-intensive and better paid than writing. Almost
anything is safer. Reveal yourself on the page all your life, and you
are likely to be rewarded with exile, neglect, or imprisonment. Ask
Dante, or Emily Dickinson, or Oscar Wilde. Scheme and betray
your friends, and you are likely to be rewarded with wealth, public

monuments, and relentless homage. Tell the truth, and you are likely to be a pariah with your family, a semicriminal to the tax authorities, and damned with faint praise by your peers. So why do we do it? Because saying what you think is the only freedom. "Liberty," said Camus, "is the right not to lie."

In a society in which everything is for sale, in which deals and auctions make the biggest news, being an amateur (one who does it for love) is the only remaining liberty. Do it for love, and you cannot be censored. Do it for love, and you cannot be stopped. Do it for love, and the world of money and business envies no one more than you. In a world of tuxedos, the naked man is king. In a world of bookkeepers with spreadsheets, the one who gives it away without counting the cost is God.

I seem to have known this from my earliest years. I cannot remember a time when I *didn't* write. Notebooks, stories, journals, poems—the act of writing always made me feel centered and whole. It still does. It is my meditation, my medicine, my prayer, my solace. I was lucky enough to learn early (with my first two books of poetry and my first novel) that if you are relentlessly honest about what you feel and fear, you often become the mouthpiece for others' feelings as well as your own. People are remarkably similar at the heart level—where it counts. Writers are born to voice what we all feel. That is the gift. And we keep it by giving it away.

It is a sacred calling. The writers I am most drawn to see it as such: Thomas Merton, Pablo Neruda, Emily Dickinson. When I am most perplexed, I return to my roots: poetry. I consider myself a poet who supports her poetry habit with novels and nonfiction. I know I am lucky to have supported myself as a poet for twenty-five years without ever writing a book I did not believe in. The novel is more elastic than the poem. It allows for social satire, cooking, toothbrushes, the way we live now. Poetry, on the contrary, boils things down to essences. I feel privileged to do both. I am grateful to have found my vocation early and never faltered. I was also blessed to encounter controversy and criticism early. They forced me to listen to my inner voice, not the roar of the crowd. This is the most useful lesson a writer can learn.

Lately, memoir is all the rage. Once again, we keep hearing dire warnings about the death of the novel. As one who has written frankly autobiographical fiction (*Fear of Flying*), historical fiction (*Fanny; Serenissima* or *Shylock's Daughter*), and memoir (*Fear of Fifty* and *The Devil at Large*), I think I've begun to understand how the process of making fiction differs from that of making memoir. A memoir is tethered to one's own experience in a particularly limiting way: The observing consciousness of the book is rooted in a historical person. That historical person may be rich and subtle, but he or she can never be as subtle as the interplay among various characters who all grow out of aspects of the author. In the memoir, the "I" dominates. In the novel, the "I" is made up of many characters' "I"s. More richness is possible, more points of view, deeper imitation of life.

When I finished *Fear of Fifty*, I felt I had quite exhausted my own life and might never write another book. What I eventually discovered was that I was liberated rather than exhausted. Having shed my own autobiography, I now felt ready to invent in a new way. I wanted to write a novel about the twentieth century and how it impacted the lives of women. I wanted to write a novel about a Jewish family in the century that nearly saw the destruction of the Jewish people.

I began with a year of reading history and literature. And when I started to write again, it was in the voice of a woman who might have been my great-grandmother. Liberated from my own place and time, I found myself inventing a woman's voice quite different from my own. What I took from my own family history were certain historical markers. The family began in Russia and came to America. They were artists, writers, malcontents. But as I started to invent this alternate family history, I found myself at play in the fields of my imagination. Characters sprang up like mushrooms after rain. I couldn't wait to get to work in the morning, to see what I thought and who was going to embody it.

Eventually I found that I had four heroines, born in different decades, and they were all mothers and daughters. Each had a distinctive voice, each a different way of looking at the world. Each was me and not me.

Graham Greene once said: "The main characters in a novel must necessarily have some kinship to the author, they come out of his body as a child comes out of the womb, then the umbilical cord is cut and they grow into independence. The more the author knows of his own character the more he can distance himself from his invented characters and the more room they have to grow in."

That seems to be precisely right. A novelist can come to this wisdom after shedding the skin of her own autobiography. That doesn't mean that characters are totally unrelated to the author. They share an affinity. But affinity is distinct from identity. The real person remains fixed. The character can fly.

A character who is not oneself may even access some deep memory in the brain that seemed lost forever. Fictional characters excavate real memories. Flaubert, after all, claimed to be Emma Bovary, gave her his restlessness and discontent. In some ways an author may be freer to expose himself in a character unlike himself. There is liberty in wearing a mask. The mask may become the condition for speaking the truth.

The line between novel and autobiography has never been as blurry as it is in our century. And this is probably a good thing. The novel endures because it is a supremely elastic form. It mimics truth. So if we are most convinced by autobiography in our age, even fiction will mimic that genre. Genres themselves matter less and less. The most enduring books of the modern era are, like *Ulysses*, full of exposition, narrative, dramatic writing, and even poetry.

What I require of a book is that it kidnap me into its world. Its world must make the so-called real world seem flimsy. Its world must trigger the nostalgia to return. When I close the book, I should feel bereft.

How rare this is, and how grateful I am to find it. The utter trust that exists between reader and author is like the trust between lovers. If I feel betrayed by the author, I will never surrender again. I must believe in the author's honesty in order to be swept away.

Movie companies may sell "product placement"—the Coke can in the shot, the Nike sneaker on the star's foot—but an author who did this would lose all credibility. We expect ethics from authors if not from politicians. We want them to be authorities—the place where the buck stops.

This is why it is so hard to start a new book. You must find the right voice (or voices) for it—the timbre that convinces even the writer of her own authority. Sometimes it takes years to find the tone of voice that unlocks the story.

The books we love best kidnap us with the first line. "Whether I shall turn out to be the hero of my own life, or whether that station will be held by anybody else, these pages must show" (*David Copperfield*). "You don't know about me, without you have read a book by the name of 'The Adventures of Tom Sawyer,' but that ain't no matter" (*Huckleberry Finn*). "There were 117 analysts on the Pan Am flight to Vienna and I'd been treated by at least six of them" (my own modest contribution). It's a question not only of an arresting opening—the writer's best trick—but of letting the main character's quirks show at the same time. And it's easier to do in first person than in third. But third person also relies on voice. All writing does.

You must do it for love—as I began by saying. If you do it for money, no money will ever be enough and eventually you will start imitating your first successes, straining hot water through the same used tea bag. It doesn't work with tea, and it doesn't work with writing. You must give all you have and never count the cost. ("Sit down at the typewriter and open a vein," as Red Smith said.) Every book I have written has subsumed all the struggles of the years in which I wrote it. I don't know how to hold back. Editing is what I do later—cutting perhaps hundreds of pages. But in the writing process, I let it all hang out. Later I and my editor chop. When the book is finished, I feel empty and bereft. I have to wait for the words to fill me up again.

Generosity is the soul of writing. You write to give a gift. To yourself. To your reader. To God. You give thanks for having been given the words. You pray to be given words another day.

Laurence Sterne knew this: "I begin with the first sentence and trust to Almighty God for the second." Amen.

Flesh is merely a lesson.
We learn it
& pass on.

People always ask where poems come from— and the truth is that not even the poet knows. Especially not the poet.

A line comes into your head. Or an image. If you are waiting in attentiveness for a poem to knock on your skull, you catch the line and write it down. Or maybe you catch only a fragment of the line and then allow it to suggest another and another and another. Sometimes the line or fragment waits for years in a notebook for you to pick it up again. Sometimes it is lost. But as with a dream fragment, it is important to catch whatever you can. By its toes if necessary. The rest of the body may follow.

"The Buddha in the Womb" started like that. "Bobbing in the waters of the womb" came into my head. And then the poem followed.

Or I followed the poem. It is hard to tell whether the poet follows the poem or the poem descends like Mary Poppins on a kite string.

What was the occasion for the poem? A headstand. I was practicing yoga. Inverted in the headstand, I thought: What if I were pregnant and the fetus was right side up because I was upside down? Paradoxes breed poems.

So I am balanced on my head. I love seeing the world upside down and experiencing the rush of blood to the brain—a cheap, natural high. And then an imaginary baby appears, glowing behind my solar plexus. His little skull glows with the light, the energy, the *prana*, that I have transmitted by imagining him. Any form of creation is an energy exchange. Creation breeds light and heat.

I was definitely not pregnant. I did not even admit I *wanted* to be pregnant. But I was at that dangerous age in a woman's life—early thirties—when twenty years of clockwork menstruation have made their point: "You were born to breed and die and the heart breaks either way" (as I said in another poem written then).

So I was toying with the *idea* of fecundity if not with fecundation itself. And I imagined a pregnant me in the headstand posture, wondering about the creature within.

THE BUDDHA IN THE WOMB

Bobbing in the waters of the womb,
little godhead, ten toes, ten fingers
& infinite hope,
sails upside down through the world.

My bones, I know, are only a cage
for death.
Meditating, I can see my skull,
a death's head,
lit from within
by candles
which are possibly the suns
of other galaxies.

I know that death
is a movement toward light,
a happy dream
from which you are loath to awaken,
a lover left
in a country
to which you have no visa,
& I know that the horses of the spirit
are galloping, galloping, galloping
out of time
& into the moment called NOW.

Why then do I care
for this upside-down Buddha
bobbling through the world,
his toes, his fingers
alive with blood
that will only sing & die?

There is a light in my skull

& a light in his.

We meditate on our bones only

to let them blow away

with fewer regrets.

Flesh is merely a lesson.

We learn it

& pass on.

The poem I pulled out with the first line is really a poem about
our spirit's passage *through* flesh to get *beyond* flesh. It asks: Why
make a baby if we are only spirit? Why make a baby if we are
doomed to die? And it answers: Because the soul expands through
creation even if the created thing is impermanent. Permanence is
not our business, but creation is.

And *who* is the creature we create, really? The creature is "infinite hope," a "little godhead," the promise of future life. The creation may be a poem, one's own Buddha nature, the hope of
outlasting the fate of ordinary mortals, who sing and die. The
point is we create because we *must*, because we are creatures whose
self-definition implies creation.

We are makers, mothers, fabricators, poets. Even if our creation
does not endure, our need to create is eternal. This passion to create defines our humanity. It explains why we resonate with a
creator-godhead. We share the urgency to replicate ourselves, to
make creatures and name them, to set them in the midst of predica-

ments and tell their stories. "Since flesh can't stay, we pass the words along," I said in a poem called "Dear Keats." And I still believe it. Words are our antidote to mortality.

"The Buddha in the Womb" has often been anthologized with poems about motherhood and pregnancy. In fact, I was not pregnant when I wrote it—but my imagination was. It is one of many poems I've written that meditate on generativity and creativity: a woman's ability to create with her body and also create with her mind.

Women tend to be obsessed with this duality—at least during our childbearing years. We find it confusing that two forms of creativity are available to us, and we tend to think we have to choose between them. Most women poets grew up in a world where womanhood was not honored, nor was motherhood. The poetry we read did not even *include* motherhood. The women poets we studied and honored were the divine exceptions—the divine Dickinson, Millay the mad flapper, Marianne Moore, who lived virginally in Brooklyn with her mother. There *were* women poets who had been mothers—Muriel Rukeyser and Adrienne Rich among others—but the difficulty of their choices was not honored. Poetry, we were made to feel, was the preserve of the childless. And women were born to be either nurses or mothers.

My generation was destined to change all this. Of course, we could not know that in our school days. We were destined to breed poets like Eavan Boland, who would later comment on the fact of growing up in a world "where the word *woman* and the word *poet* were almost magnetically opposed." Nor did you have to be Irish to feel the force of those powerful magnets. They were felt in America, too, felt strongly enough for a poet like Sylvia Plath to feel she had to kill her mythic "Daddy" to become a poet at all. Felt strongly enough for a poet like Anne Sexton to live in conflict between the poet and the mother and to make that conflict the essence of her work.

The women poets who grappled with these paradoxes sometimes gave their lives for them. Poetry was a dangerous art for a woman. Virginia Woolf asked: "Who shall measure the heat and violence of the poet's heart when caught tangled in a woman's body?" You felt that a woman poet had to renounce her life as a woman or else renounce her art. The woman poet had to cut a deal with the devil. She had to put her heart on the chopping block in the kitchen and watch it drain itself of blood.

The baby or the book? This fearful symmetry has haunted every woman writer I have known who chose to be a mother. It is not surprising to find that it informs our work. "The Buddha in the Womb" is for me an early exploration of this dilemma. At the time, there was no actual baby to consider. Later there was. I returned to the theme with more self-knowledge in *Ordinary Miracles,* and I wrote many poems for my daughter, Molly, which are about poetry and motherhood and the similarities and dissimilarities between them. But whether I resolved the conflicts posed in "The Buddha in the Womb" remains to be seen. In "The Birth of the Water Baby," the deep identification between mother and daughter makes moot the paradox of wanting/not wanting to become that dualistic being—a mother.

Little egg,
little nub,
full complement of
fingers, toes,
little rose blooming
in a red universe,
which one wanted you less
than emptiness,
but now holds you
fast,
containing your rapid heart
beat under its
slower one
as the earth
contains the sea . . .

The mother *is* the child and the child the mother, so how can there be any question of choice between them? How can you choose between two creatures that are one?

In "Anti-Conception," the strangeness of one creature's bringing forth another is contemplated.

Could I unthink you,
little heart,
what would I do?
Throw you out
with last night's garbage,

undo my own decisions,

my own flesh

& commit you to the void

again?

The mother-poet decides that she must get out of the way and let creation happen. She thinks of herself as publisher, producer, midwife to the baby's grand spectacle:

you are the star,

& like your humblest fan,

I wonder

(gazing at your image

on the screen)

who you really are.

Though the poems in *Ordinary Miracles* are among my favorites, they are not as edgy as "The Buddha in the Womb"—written before there was an actual child to distract me from the paradox.

The child and the poem are forever diverse. One grows and changes. The other remains fixed in words. The two forms of creation forever mock each other. But flesh is the lesson for both. Flesh, however, is perishable. If anything does, words remain. We learn them and pass on. Knowing this, we write as if our lives depended upon it. They do.

> *Poetry does not necessarily have to be beautiful to stick in*
> *the depths of our memory.*
>
> —COLETTE

People think they can do without poetry. And they can. At least until they fall in love, lose a friend, lose a child or a parent, or lose their way in the dark woods of life. People think they can live without poetry. And they can. At least until they become fatally ill, have a baby, or fall desperately, madly in love.

> I care not for heaven and I fear not hell
> If I have but the kisses of his proud, young mouth . . .

wrote Moireen Fox in a poem called "The Faery Lover." And it is hard to imagine a better conjuring of that cliché "madly in love." Instead of a dead metaphor, we have a living image—an image with color, speed, defiance. We have the love, the mad yearning for the lover, and we also have the feelings the love evokes—all in two lines. We know that it is a love not only to die for but to go to hell for. And we know that the speaker—whoever she may be—is a furious, passionate person, someone who throws caution to the winds. We know more about her from two lines than we know about many people we have conversed with for hours because we know her thoughts *and* her feelings. We know the tone of her voice: incautious, passionate, proud. We know that she is free and ready to pay the price for freedom. We know this woman's character in just two lines.

Only poetry can do that. Only poetry gives us language packed with feeling and personality. Which is why there are times in life when only poetry will do. Interestingly enough, they are the times when we feel most vulnerable, most human.

"The blood jet is poetry," said Sylvia Plath, "there is no stopping it." And that is another example of why only poetry will do at certain times. "Blood" tells us: essential, necessary for life, spillable. "Jet" tells us: moves fast, moves under pressure, once turned on not so easy to turn off. The language of poetry is heightened, emotional, imagistic, condensed. It concentrates meaning as a perfume concentrates flowers.

I said we need poetry most at those moments when life astounds us with losses, gains, or celebrations. We need it most when we are most hurt, most happy, most downcast, most jubilant. Poetry is the language we speak in times of greatest need. And the fact that it is an endangered species in our culture tells us that we are in deep trouble. We treat our poets as outcasts, lunatics, starvelings. We give least respect to those who give us most.

Our public attitude toward poetry and poets shows that spiritual needs count for little in America. We may take care of the outer being, but we allow the inner being to languish. The skin, not the soul, has all our care—despite lip service to the contrary. And many of us are dying for want of care for the soul. The poet is the caretaker of the soul; in many civilizations, the poet's contribution is central.

Poetry need not consist only of images. It can be declarative utterance packed with meaning. When Yeats directs that certain words be inscribed on his tower ("Inscription at Thoor Ballylee"):

And may these characters remain
When all is ruin once again

he is giving us an image of time's carelessness. He is pointing to mutability. Shakespeare is also obsessed with time. Its passage spurs his most passionate utterances.

"Devouring time, blunt thou the lion's paws" is an image embedded in a command. It is as if, for the moment, the poet assumes God's perspective, rather than the human vantage point.

And why shouldn't the poet have God's perspective—if only temporarily? As Anne Sexton once said to me: "We are all writing God's poem." The identity of the poet hardly matters. What matters is that the blood jet of poetry continues to spurt.

The blood jet is endangered in our culture not only because we do not respect our poets (poets can survive neglect if they are true poets: think of Emily Dickinson) but because we are destroying both solitude and the ability to *enjoy* solitude. Try to find a place without mixed media, traffic sounds, deafening music, distracting advertisements. You have to be a billionaire to escape the noisy overstimulation of selling that is ubiquitous in our cities, suburbs, airplanes, airports, and trains. Solitude has started to feel strange to us. We walk into the house and immediately turn on the TV for company. The sounds of silence seem peculiar. But poetry, like all creative work, is triggered by solitude. When Yeats described the "bee-loud glade," in "The Lake Isle of Innisfree," you knew he had listened to bees, not traffic. How loud the bees are in the bee-loud glade is known only by those of us who refrain from walking through the meadow with a boom box or a Walkman. Constant audio and video "input" drown our own "output." The "wild mind" (as poet Natalie Goldberg calls the poetry-producing place in our brains) needs space to dream and retrieve images. We have nearly lost that space. Perhaps we have willfully abolished it. But frenzied consumption of material things cannot do for us what poetry can.

Where does the poet go to find necessary solitude? And where does the reader of poetry find the space to *read or to hear*? The truth is, both writing and reading are endangered. But the need for poetry is such a basic human need that it adapts itself to new circumstances. When so-called mainstream publishers stop publishing poetry and ignore the needs of young people for poets of their own generation, the young turn to poetry slams and coffeehouse readings. Or to rap music. When the book world turns its back, poetry springs up in the world of music. An oral medium, it returns to its root: the tongue.

Which brings us to poets reading and poetry as a medium for both ear and eye. I fell in love with poetry as a teenager in part by hearing poets read. I went to readings at the Poetry Center of the 92nd Street Y in New York. And I listened to the great recordings of Dylan Thomas. Poetry is given life by the voice because it is, basically, a transcription of voice and of breath—and of the silences between. When a poet reads, the creative process is somehow recapitulated. We almost hear the muse whispering in the poet's ear.

Our age is rich in poetry recordings and poetry readings, so perhaps the poetic impulse will survive all our neglect. One thing is sure: Poetry cannot be killed. We do it for love, not money. Arts practiced without ulterior motive are the most durable arts of all. No "marketplace" or lack thereof can shout them down. The medium of exchange is love—and its helplessness against time.

Poetry preserves the living moment and our lust to inhabit it fully. As the seventeenth-century poet Bashō says:

Having sucked deep

In a sweet peony

A bee creeps

Out of its hairy recesses

Is all poetry about lust? Sometimes it seems so. Lust is the opposite of death. And since we know that death will gobble us in the end, we lust for lust. We suck on words as Bashō's bee sucks on honey. The sweet peony makes us hungry where she most satisfies.

*The ideal of happiness has always taken material form in
the house.*

—SIMONE DE BEAUVOIR

"I am thrilled to the spine . . . and I feel as if I were going to
get married—to the right man at last!" Edith Wharton wrote to a
friend about her delight in renovating a ruined fortress above the
Mediterranean at Hyères, France. And indeed she was to have her
most prolific period in the 1920s, while dividing her time between
this Mediterranean retreat and a grand house, Pavillon Colombe,
outside Paris. Clearly both houses were more than just dwellings.
They were constructions that mirrored some inner geography and
had the power to release her creativity.

A writer's house is a many-gabled dwelling. Its bricks are made
not of clay but of imagination. Its windows are the writer's eyes.

Its chimneys smoke with our desires, and its fires blaze with the trees we chop down in our secret gardens.

Studying Edith Wharton's quest for the perfect house—from her parents' "cottage" in Newport, to her own house in Lenox, "The Mount," to those two French locations where she spent the prolific years of her late fifties and sixties—we see that writers' houses are hardly roofs against the rain. They provoke the sort of ecstasy we associate with falling in love. They play Cupid, midwife, Judas, and even grim reaper. The general reader may think the writer copies houses, but actually we invent them as much as any architect does. We put several houses together in our dreams, alchemize them again in the trance of fiction, and build a house that embodies mother, daydream, nightmare, aspiration.

The splendid Elizabethan house in Virginia Woolf's *Orlando* is a perfect example of such alchemy. It is based partly on Vita Sackville-West's Sissinghurst Castle (an Elizabethan ruin that she bought in the thirties and lovingly restored with her husband, Harold Nicholson), Knole (where Vita grew up and which, to her bitterness, passed to a distant male relative), and Long Barn, which Vita occupied before she restored Sissinghurst.

The Elizabethan ambience of *Orlando*'s fictional house owes something to each of these great piles. The silver candlesticks, the flaming logs, the velvet draperies that surround Orlando are Virginia Woolf's evocations of the splendor in which it seemed to her Vita Sackville-West lived.

Woolf herself lived in relative penury. She was a literary novelist, after all, and came from a literary but not wealthy family. Sackville-West lived like an heiress to the Elizabethan past. But as a woman, she could not inherit her ancestral home, Knole. And so, banished from its splendor by a feudal vestige, she re-created a legacy for herself in Sissinghurst. In the process she became the inspiration for Virginia Woolf's male/female hero/heroine.

But what *is* the connection between the house and inspiration? In one of her poems, "Housewife," Anne Sexton compares the house to a woman. She describes the housewife "on her knees all day, / faithfully washing herself down." Her meditation on houses becomes a meditation on mothers: "A woman *is* her mother. / That's the main thing."

In Marge Piercy's novel of the future, *He, She and It,* the protagonist's house is a mother/robot who welcomes guests, educates the young, and knows everything about the history of the tribe. Either she *is* God or she is programmed by God. She is both educator and moral arbiter, both source of warmth and source of education. She is, in short, a maternal deity of sorts, a female Higher Power.

Sexton and Piercy clearly show that in the unconscious, the house *is* mother. Probably many psychoanalysts could corroborate this. (Poets and psychoanalysts are seldom far apart in their perceptions.) We are particular about our houses because we unconsciously understand their meaning. "Womb with a view," we joke. Houses give birth to us—or at least to our best selves.

So we are hardly surprised by the coziness we feel in a red room. Warm, passionate, snug—a red room beckons us back. We take for granted an umbilical connection between home and its dweller. We scarcely *know* a person without visiting her home.

We are also fascinated by haunted houses. Do the ghosts dictate stories? Naturally, we assume so. *The Amityville Horror,* with its extraordinary durability as a bestseller and a film (not to mention all the sequels), testifies to this fascination. The original story is of a couple driven out of their home by eerie phenomena (caused supposedly by the murder of a whole family by one brother in the years before their ownership). And nearly everyone has a tale to tell about a haunted house. Perhaps it had to be sold because the ghosts whispered too loudly; perhaps there were strange drafts, noises, and apparitions in the night; perhaps there was a figure of a headless woman standing on the widow's walk at night.

Most of the writers I know claim to have *lived* in haunted houses at one time or another. Is there a special affinity between writers and haunted houses or do we simply have better ears to *hear* the ghost stories in the walls? Do we *move* to haunted houses because we are drawn by the stories themselves? Is the haunted house another version of mother—who talks to us long after she is dead?

I once claimed to own a haunted house in New York. Friends were fascinated. "How did the ghosts appear?" they would ask.

"Well, I always had a splitting headache in that house. I couldn't write there, and I was always escaping to the country."

"Come on," they'd say, "that's not *haunted.*"

"But I dreamed the wrong dreams," I'd say.

Interest would grow.

"You dreamed the *wrong dreams*?"

"They were dreams full of people I didn't know and situations I couldn't recognize."

"Tell us more!" they'd clamor. "Tell us the story!"

Were *ghosts* really responsible? It sounded good, but I didn't want to think about it too deeply. The house had previously been owned by a psychoanalyst, above whose conjugal bed hung the motto MENTAL HEALTH IS OUR GREATEST WEALTH. I told myself that I was dreaming the dreams of his patients—not all their dreams but only the repressed, uninterpreted ones. Perhaps the people in my dreams were really ghosts. Secretly, I hope so.

Writers tend to be addicted to houses—haunted or not. We work at home, indulging the agoraphobia endemic to our kind. We are immersed in our surroundings to an almost morbid degree. Not only do we see terrifying apparitions that the rest of our families miss, but we sometimes hear loud whispers and feel unearthly chills on our backs. Sometimes there's organ music or the tinkling of a fountain—even on the twenty-seventh floor. In our books, we mingle dreamed and actual houses; we renovate them with the tools of our imaginations.

Mother, womb, ghost hotel—no wonder it takes an interesting house to make an interesting novel. A house loves and nurtures us. It hates to let us go.

When Vladimir Nabokov taught literature in America, he always emphasized the design of the house in which the action of a book took place. He believed that if you started with a house, put characters in it, and set them in motion, you would wind up with a novel. Whether it was Gregor Samsa's house in Kafka's "The Metamorphosis" or Dr. Jekyll's house in Robert Louis Stevenson's *The Strange Case of Dr. Jekyll and Mr. Hyde*, Nabokov knew that only certain characters lived in certain houses and only those houses allowed those particular events to occur.

We instinctively know that Nabokov is right. When we enter Edith Wharton's The Mount in Lenox, Massachusetts, or 18 Villa Seurat in Paris, where Henry Miller completed *Tropic of Cancer* and *Black Spring*, or The House of the Seven Gables, which inspired Nathaniel Hawthorne to compose the novel of the same name, we sense that we are coming upon *more* than a dwelling: We are entering the writer's source of inspiration.

Many writers visit my house in Connecticut. It sits on a ledge of rock overlooking a steep ravine. Below is the Aspetuck River. Although the area has partially succumbed to the developer's ax in the many years I've been here, my ledge is still remote enough to insulate me from the world.

When visiting writers find themselves able to work here, I am delighted. Fay Weldon was recently my houseguest for a weekend. Quite early Sunday morning, after a cup of tea, she vanished back to the guest room without saying a word. Soon her friend appeared, to brew another cup of tea. He went to her room with it, bringing also a toasted English muffin.

"Shh," I said to my husband. "Fay must be writing."

"Shh," Fay's friend said to me. "She's writing."

I puttered about the kitchen, feeling a delicious sense of anticipation. It was almost as good as writing myself! It was as if the *house* were writing. Everyone felt the frisson of creativity. I wanted to write myself—even though houseguests usually block me. But I stayed on in the kitchen, playing hostess (or muse) for another creator.

At last we all assembled for a late lunch.

"I wrote a story!" Fay said, to no one's particular surprise. "This is a great place to write!"

We all knew better than to ask "What's it about?" And we sat down to eat thinking our various thoughts. I knew not to worry about whether or not my house would appear in Fay's story. If it appeared, it wouldn't be my house anymore—but *her* house, built of *her* imagination. This house is mine only by title and by the titles of the books I have written here.

"I am glad to be the steward of a house that inspires poetry," the lawyer Michael Kennedy wrote me when I sent him and his wife, Eleanore, two poems I had written at Kilkare, their beach house on the Atlantic. Kilkare stands like a nineteenth-century schooner facing the sea. The ocean winds cannot tear it from its moorings, though with each hurricane the beach recedes. For me this house and this beach constitute an object lesson about permanence and impermanence. The billionaires may build their beach houses here, but they still can't control the ocean.

But a house, after all, *exists* to be a steward for our dreams. And the practicalities always matter less. If you sleep well there, you can wake up and write. If someone you love brings you tea, so much the better. And the sound of the sea doesn't hurt either.

As Edna St. Vincent Millay said:

Safe upon the solid rock the ugly houses stand
Come and see my shining palace built upon the sand!

I like trees because they seem more resigned to the way they have to live than other things do.

—WILLA CATHER

Home is the place where you feel safe, where despite disquieting news that arrives by cable or optical fiber, you can leave the door on the latch and wander outside in your old terry-cloth bathrobe and a pair of muddy clogs to check on whether or not the crocuses are poking through the snow.

As a child, not knowing there is an alternative, you never really appreciate home. As a young adult, home is what you want to leave as soon as possible, brandishing a new driver's license and a boyfriend.

Only in midlife—our sexy new term for dread old middle age—does home beckon seductively again, inviting you to pleasures running away can never supply. Home is where your books are. Home is where you keep those bell-bottoms from the sixties that may just come back in time for your daughter to wear them. Home is where you know all the quirks of the plumbing, but they comfort rather than irritate you. Home is where you get out of bed at three A.M., wink at the full moon through the bathroom skylight, and go back to sleep perfectly contented, knowing no demons can follow you here. Home is where the trees are all part of your history: the weeping cherry planted for your daughter's birth, the Scotch pine that once was a Christmas tree, the birch that was hit by lightning and came back the next spring, the oak that seemed to die the winter you were divorced but revived three years later with patience and pruning.

Home is where the same bird's nest on the front-door lintel receives new robin's eggs year after year after year. Home is "something you somehow haven't to deserve," says Robert Frost in "The Death of the Hired Man." Amen.

I travel so much that often I wake up with a start, wondering whether I am in Rome or Hong Kong or Auckland, but in my house in the hemlock woods of Connecticut, I always know I am home no matter how jet-lagged.

I bought it twenty-two years ago: my first house with my first real writing money. I carried my daughter into it in my arms when she was three days old. Built on an outcropping of rock over a river, it is made of old Vermont barn beams, fieldstone, and glass. It has never been "decorated." It contains instead the collections of my life: my grandfather's paint-splattered easel, my father's old upright piano, antique quilts bought on drives to Vermont, majolica plates sent home from Faenza, wineglasses I watched being blown in Venice, a motley assortment of family portraits painted by my painting family.

I have a writing room on stilts—a tree house connected to the main house by a raised breezeway. The breezeway is lined with shelves, which contain all my books in foreign editions. My desk wraps around me in a U-shape. It is always piled high, with books for the current project. (Only between novels do I clean my desk.) On a raised platform facing a wall of windows, my desktop is polished oak the width of an old tree. A wall of poetry books is to my left, and all my archives of photographs and manuscripts are in the cabinets. I am never happier than at my desk in Connecticut. This is where I heal and dream.

In the fall, the squirrels play acorn football on the roof of my study. In the spring, birds nest in the eaves and wake up with the first pink light of dawn. I even enjoy having insomnia in the country, so that I can be up before the birds and await their serenade.

From the deck of my tree house, I can see the white-tailed deer tiptoeing up to eat my roses. They wait until the tender buds appear, then chomp them savagely, leaving the bushes bare. I do not shoot. Every year, I vow to put in a deerproof fence, but I never do it. At least the deer leave the mountain laurel and the blackberry brambles to me.

Midsummer will come, and there will be blackberries glistening up and down my steep driveway and throughout my woods. Like the deer among my roses, I will burst their redness upon my tongue, searching for ruby jewels amid the thorns.

I know I am home because Poochini, the bichon frise, has curled up on the stair landing between the first and second floor. I know I am home because Basil, the cat, is racing up the huge ficus tree in the living room, looking for a perch in its swaying top. I know I am home because my desk is heaped with fresh legal pads and stacks of marked-up books. I know I am home because my heart is calm and my pen is moving over the page to its tranquil beat.

Last summer, I put in boxwood hedges to fool the deer. (Deer hate the aroma of boxwood as much as I love it.) I replaced the roses the deer had decimated and prayed for the best. I planted peace roses, pale yellow with blushing edges. Last spring, I had the roof redone. Cedar-shingle chips rained all over the decks for months, imparting their tart aroma on top of the resinous smell of the hemlocks.

I have been planning to build a pool for almost twenty years. But the cycle of a writer's economic life is such that by the time I have paid the taxes on the last book and the bills that accumulated while I was writing it, there is never enough money left. I live on that see-saw (best known to freelance writers) between flush and broke—so I am glad to have the house even if it lacks a swimming pool.

The pool is no minor matter since the house is built on a ledge, so that blasting will be required to gouge a pool out of the cliff. Every year, it gets more expensive.

"I'll build it next year," I say to myself, before turning to the next writing project. If only I could *write* a pool! I imagine it as an outdoor Roman bath surrounded by pillars bearing statues of the world's most inspiring women. Sappho, Boadicea, Elizabeth I of England, Mary Wollstonecraft, Colette, Emma Goldman, and Golda Meir would look down upon my swimming mermaid self. In the summer, it would be a *tepidarium,* in the winter, a *caldarium.* I would swim naked, of course, attended by towel-bearing young male masseurs.

What's wrong with this picture? The pool doesn't match the house—which is homey and warm, if not humble. It's a cocoon for writing, dreaming, sleeping, having long talks with my daughter, entertaining friends, and making love. The hot tub on the deck doubles as a cauldron for witches' brews. It has known several incarnations in twenty-odd years—from redwood wine cask to insulated fiberglass that keeps the water hot all winter.

In that tub I have planned my life and books for as long as I can remember, summoned (and dismissed) lovers, and conjured up adventures. I wouldn't trade this magic house in the woods for The Mount, Hadrian's Villa, or San Simeon. Its spacious simplicity suits me. The house had mothered me as I mothered Molly and my books.

I suspect there is one more house in my life, but where the ultimate one will be I have no idea. Near the sea, but whether the Adriatic, the Aegean, the Atlantic or Pacific, I don't yet know. In theory, it is drastically modern, a glass Bauhaus box with futons instead of beds, tatami instead of rugs, and a raked sand garden imitating eternity.

The truth is, I admire such houses, but I could never live in one. What would I do with the clutter of manuscripts, pictures, collections? What would I do with my walls of books? What would I do with family and friends, arriving to paint on the deck or compose concerti at my father's old piano in the guest room?

Words can build many houses. I am thankful that this one is mine.

One of the oldest human needs is having someone to wonder
when you don't come home at night.

—MARGARET MEAD

Ten years after we were married, my husband and I burned
our prenup. We burned it in a wok at the end of a dinner party to
which we had invited our dearest friends—and our lawyers. Either
that's the most romantic gesture ever made, or the stupidest. I prefer to see it as romantic.

Marriage is about trust, and trust takes you quickly to the matter
of money. It is very hard to trust someone and share all your
worldly goods with that person, but the alternative is worse. During the better part of a decade when I was single and recovering
from the bitterest of divorces, I usually felt fine until I saw the term
"next of kin" on a form. These three little words shook me up more
than "I love you." Leaving the space blank meant there was no one

to look after my daughter if something happened to me, no one for doctors to consult in case of emergency, no one to bury me if I dropped dead, no one to decide which manuscripts to burn and which to sell. Leaving it blank meant I was an orphan from the human family. Yes, I had sisters, but their enmity toward me and my writing was, alas, not reassuring. Things are better now, but then I felt alone.

Marriage fills the blank and does more. A good marriage replaces monologue with dialogue, enhances your life expectancy, and gives you somebody to blame for whatever is wrong with your life. If you want to stay married, you don't hold the grudge. You realize that whatever you gave up in order to join your life with this other person's was more than compensated for by the things you got. But that doesn't mean you lose the right to complain. Healthy complaining—even the occasional unhealthy rage—also keeps marriages together. It's the endless silences that torpedo them.

When Ken and I met, each of us had been married before— twice in his case, three times in mine. We stamped the phrase "A Triumph of Hope Over Experience" in red on our wedding announcements right over the line "Erica and Ken are astonished to announce their marriage." We joked a lot because we were terrified. We both thought we had come to our last chance. We didn't want to blow it.

My own marital history made great copy but was hell to live through. My first husband went crazy and thought he was Jesus Christ. My second was the psychiatrist I married to protect myself against madness. The third was my dearest soul mate until he became my bitterest enemy. No wonder I never wanted to marry again. By the time I met Ken I had figured out how to have men in my life without making a commitment: either they were terminally commitment-phobic or otherwise committed. I tried to have two or three at once so as never to have to depend on one, but I quickly learned that three men add up to less than one. I thought the system worked just fine for me. Until I met Ken.

On our first date I insisted on bringing a car and driver so he wouldn't be able to drive me home. (It was spring break, and my daughter and I were ensconced in the "country" house.) After our second date I devised a business trip to Los Angeles to get away from him (but then I called him as soon as I arrived, and left my number). After our third date I escaped to Europe, supposedly to attend a cooking school in Italy—though I never cook. There was also a boyfriend in Italy—one of those otherwise-committed charmers who liked to drop in unannounced and then flee back to home and hearth. While I'd be waiting by the phone for him to call, Ken would call instead. He was on his way to Paris and sending me a ticket to join him. Meanwhile the Italian hadn't been heard from. By the time he slithered into the dining room of the cooking school I had made other plans.

I am reporting the events but leaving out all the anguish. Unless you are a cold-blooded psychopath, it's not easy to juggle partners. And at times the effort of keeping these multiple fires burning turned my life into a French farce.

Ken had lived his own version of this comedy—through two marriages and one long-term cohabitation that was much like a marriage. Instead of feeling free as a result of his escapades, he often felt trapped. Instead of feeling sated, he often felt lonely.

During that first weekend in Paris, we talked so much we never slept. We also fought, but our fights never ended the conversation; we discovered we always had more to say. When sex entered the equation, I became so scared of intimacy that I went home early. Left to my own devices I would have sabotaged the relationship, but even at our darkest moment Ken was optimistic. After our first fight, he went for a walk and brought me back a first edition of Colette's *La Fin de Chéri* as a farewell present. I was so touched by his knowing it was one of my favorite books that it became a hello rather than a good-bye. It was his generosity and risk-taking that won my heart.

When we got back from Paris we had dinner together every night. We used to look up from the table at each other and be surprised to find restaurants closing around us. Everyone's deepest hunger is to be known, and we were determined to know each other. The more we learned about each other, the more connected we felt.

When we had been together two months or so, we went to Vermont for a weekend. We stopped at the Putney Inn for dinner, and I blurted out my worst fear. "It seems okay now, but pretty soon you'll be telling me what to write—and threatening me if I don't write what you like. And I can't live with that."

Ken grabbed a napkin, scrawled something on it, then handed it to me to read: "I trust you completely. Do whatever! Write whatever you want! I release you! Ken!"

I folded up the napkin and kept it. I still have it. A month later we decided to get married.

Why did we write a prenuptial agreement? Ken, who is a divorce lawyer, wanted to waive it, but I felt I needed the protection of a legal document. I had worked hard for what is called in Hollywood "fuck-you money" in a very unstable profession, and I had no intention of jeopardizing my future or my daughter's. Also, I had no faith in my own judgment. I had been wrong about men in the past. I fully expected to be wrong again. So we both prepared net worth statements. And we both agreed to keep our monies separate. If we walked away from this marriage, we'd both take our marbles and go home. I hired a lawyer to put all this in writing.

But here is the strange thing about marriage: either it gets better and stronger or it withers away. With every year that passes, the matter of money seems less important. Inevitably funds get mixed, you buy things together and write wills protecting each other. Little by little, prenuptial agreements become obsolete. Do you sit down and renegotiate after ten years—or do you quietly agree that the document has served its purpose and let it lapse? Because a prenup *does* serve a purpose. It says, "I hope I'll be able to trust you, but I'm not sure yet." When we discovered after ten years that we trusted each other more, not less, we decided the prenup was outdated.

"Will you still be happy to have revoked it if he runs off with a twenty-five-year-old next year?" my lawyer, Ellie Alter, asked, posing the unanswerable question.

It's in the nature of life that we protect ourselves against things that never happen and utterly fail to contemplate things that do: About a week after we burned the prenup, Ken collapsed with what at first appeared to be a mild heart attack and turned out to be a dissection of the aorta. The first thing I thought was, We should never have burned the prenup. Somehow it had gone from being a legal document that would protect us from each other to an amulet that could protect us from the vicissitudes of life. Maybe it had been an amulet all along.

During the hours I sat outside the operating room and the weeks I spent in the hospital, waiting, I realized that my life was irrevocably bound with Ken's—prenup or no prenup. We had crossed that invisible barrier between being two people and being one. And while I had failed to protect myself against grief and loss, I had succeeded in building the real marriage I had always wanted.

If you join your life with someone else's you become a hostage to fortune in such a way that no legal document can protect you. Marriage is primal stuff—two people confronting their own mortality. It is not for the faint of heart. It is not for beginners.

"I didn't see a long tunnel with a blinding light at the end and my mother and father waving," Ken said when he recovered from his near-death experience. "I didn't see my body on the operating table connected to a heart-lung machine and hear angels choiring in the background." But he is different, and so am I. (And it isn't only because of his new Dacron aorta.) The time we spend together is infinitely more precious. We are arranging our lives to have more of it.

I would not be telling this story honestly if I did not admit that by writing this I feel as though I am tempting the gods. Early in my life I got married without having an inkling what being married meant. I was lucky to have survived three marriages and to have healed enough to write about them. Now I want to protect the marriage I have with silence.

"I hope you're taking notes," my husband always says to me when we go through a hard time. He relies on me to be his chronicler. He was mostly asleep during his crisis, and I was awake. I am supposed to be his Boswell and he my muse. Marriages have been based on worse contracts.

Marriage is, of all human arrangements, the chanciest. We know all the things that can go wrong but are still delighted when they go right. We never tire of hearing how couples met, or of the obstacles they surmounted. We pride ourselves on being hard-boiled and pragmatic, but deep down we long to be gooey and romantic.

As we search for new rituals for the millennium, burning the prenup is probably fated to become a trend. Vintners will create special wines and bakers will devise special cakes. Priests and rabbis will be asked for new vows. It will become the commitment "I do" was for our grandparents.

"Darling, do you love me enough to burn the prenup?"

If you refuse to accept anything but the best, you very often get it.

—ANONYMOUS

When Random House's Modern Library imprint issued a list in 1998 of the one hundred best novels in English published during the twentieth century, surely I was not alone in noticing that only *nine* books written by women were among the designees. The list created controversy—as lists are meant to do.

There was plenty of printed reaction to the Modern Library announcement, but none I saw seemed to offer an alternative list. The Random House Web site was deluged with reactions from angry readers who wondered where their favorite novels were, but nobody (not Harold Bloom with his Western Canon, nor Camille Paglia with her six-shooter, nor the Modern Library itself) thought to come up with a list of women writers in English who published

novels in this century. Surely a century that produced Isak Dine-
sen, Virginia Woolf, Colette, Doris Lessing, Simone de Beauvoir,
Willa Cather, and Edith Wharton has been an extraordinary one
for women authors. Released from compulsory pregnancy every
year, liberated from having to pretend niceness, goodness, meekness (not to mention amnesia toward our own anger) women have
produced an astonishing literature in English—and a host of other
languages. The twentieth century has been the first in which women
collectively roared. Why then have the good people at the Modern
Library not heard? Well, women's achievements tend to be overlooked even by the enlightened who think themselves sensitive to
such things. A woman's name on a book practically guarantees
marginalization—which is why so many geniuses, from the Brontë
sisters to George Sand and George Eliot, chose to use male noms
de plume.

And yet I find myself thinking—in 1998!—that we have abandoned that practice at our peril. Oddly, books written by women
tend to be marginalized by both male and female reviewers. Yes, it
is true that certain hunky male authors like Sebastian Junger and
Ethan Canin (as for Hemingway and Fitzgerald before them) have
been reviewed for their jacket photos, but generally the practice of
reviewing the writer's photo rather than her text, her personal life
rather than her novel, her love affairs rather than her literary style,
is the fate reserved for women authors. A recent example of a writer's life being reviewed even before her book is published is Joyce
Maynard—but many authors, from Charlotte Brontë to Colette,

have met this fate. Why this automatic response? Surely, given the works of Sappho, Emily Dickinson, and Jane Austen, it should be clear that a vagina is no obstacle to literature. Yet in a sexist society, both women and men automatically downgrade women's work. A poetess is never as good as a poet. An actor is more serious than an actress. An aviator navigates better than an aviatrix. The response today may be more unconscious than deliberate, but, alas, it remains. (I suggest that some compulsive scholar do a computer search of the typical weasel words in reviews of women's books. They are: "confessional," "narcissistic," "solipsistic," "self-aggrandizing," "self-indulgent," "whining.") For a woman to claim to have a self is, I suppose, narcissism.

I have been the recipient of this sort of literary "criticism" for so many years that it makes me snort and laugh rather than smart and weep, but my heart goes out to the novice female writers who run this gauntlet with their first novels and are so wounded that they never show up for the second act. This is, of course, the point. Boo the women off the stage with catcalls and rotten tomatoes and get them back to their proper womanly duties—editing men's books, feeding the egos of male writers, writing theses about James Joyce, William Faulkner, and Ernest Hemingway—as if we didn't already have enough. Political correctness has rapped us on the knuckles for doing this to writers of color who are female. As a result, those artists are starting to be reviewed on their merits rather than their gender. This is a welcome change. Around 1970, Toni Morrison's first novel, *The Bluest Eye*, initially was turned down by Random

House (where she then worked as an editor) because at the time, it was assumed that African-Americans did not buy books and that nobody else would want to read novels about black people. The arrogance of those assumptions has long since been dispelled. But while it is clearly racist to attack writers of color, women writers who appear to occupy no minority niche are still fair game. Women are the scapegoats of the human race, and if scapegoats don't exist in nature, they have to be invented. The Modern Library list contained only eight women because a ratio of 92 to 8 probably seems normal to literary folk. (Edith Wharton accounted for two of the nine titles.) Diversity has come to mean racial diversity rather than gender fairness. Wherever possible, the token women on a committee, a panel, a list, is apt to be endowed with melanin. This is a condescending way of including two "minorities" in one fell swoop. But women are not a minority; we are 52 percent of the population. We are, in fact, an oppressed majority. If we didn't already know this the Modern Library list would have made it abundantly clear.

I've no particular wish to dump on the Modern Library. That venerable venture, started by legendary twenties publisher Horace Liveright and sold to Random House long before it was a vast agglomeration of formerly independent imprints, always has had a worthy mission: bring good books to the people inexpensively. The Modern Library was clever to devise the one hundred best list as a way of getting column inches for reading. It worked. Anything that gets people talking about books in a video culture is to be applauded. The composition of the original list was hard not to quarrel with.

1. *Ulysses* by James Joyce

2. *The Great Gatsby* by F. Scott Fitzgerald

3. *A Portrait of the Artist as a Young Man* by James Joyce

4. *Lolita* by Vladimir Nabokov

5. *Brave New World* by Aldous Huxley

6. *The Sound and the Fury* by William Faulkner

7. *Catch-22* by Joseph Heller

8. *Darkness at Noon* by Arthur Koestler

9. *Sons and Lovers* by D. H. Lawrence

10. *The Grapes of Wrath* by John Steinbeck

11. *Under the Volcano* by Malcolm Lowry

12. *The Way of All Flesh* by Samuel Butler

13. *1984* by George Orwell

14. *I, Claudius* by Robert Graves

15. *To the Lighthouse* by Virginia Woolf

16. *An American Tragedy* by Theodore Dreiser

17. *The Heart Is a Lonely Hunter* by Carson McCullers

18. *Slaughterhouse-Five* by Kurt Vonnegut

19. *Invisible Man* by Ralph Ellison

20. *Native Son* by Richard Wright

21. *Henderson the Rain King* by Saul Bellow

22. *Appointment in Samarra* by John O'Hara

23. *U.S.A.* (trilogy) by John Dos Passos

24. *Winesburg, Ohio* by Sherwood Anderson

25. *A Passage to India* by E. M. Forster

26. *The Wings of the Dove* by Henry James

27. *The Ambassadors* by Henry James

28. *Tender Is the Night* by F. Scott Fitzgerald

29. *The Studs Lonigan Trilogy* by James T. Farrell

30. *The Good Soldier* by Ford Madox Ford

31. *Animal Farm* by George Orwell

32. *The Golden Bowl* by Henry James

33. *Sister Carrie* by Theodore Dreiser

34. *A Handful of Dust* by Evelyn Waugh

35. *As I Lay Dying* by William Faulkner

36. *All the King's Men* by Robert Penn Warren

37. *The Bridge of San Luis Rey* by Thornton Wilder

38. *Howards End* by E. M. Forster

39. *Go Tell It on the Mountain* by James Baldwin

40. *The Heart of the Matter* by Graham Greene

41. *Lord of the Flies* by William Golding

42. *Deliverance* by James Dickey

43. *A Dance to the Music of Time* (series) by Anthony Powell

44. *Point Counter Point* by Aldous Huxley

45. *The Sun Also Rises* by Ernest Hemingway

46. *The Secret Agent* by Joseph Conrad

47. *Nostromo* by Joseph Conrad

48. *The Rainbow* by D. H. Lawrence

49. *Women in Love* by D. H. Lawrence

50. *Tropic of Cancer* by Henry Miller

51. *The Naked and the Dead* by Norman Mailer

52. *Portnoy's Complaint* by Philip Roth

53. *Pale Fire* by Vladimir Nabokov

54. *Light in August* by William Faulkner

55. *On the Road* by Jack Kerouac

56. *The Maltese Falcon* by Dashiell Hammett

57. *Parade's End* by Ford Madox Ford

58. *The Age of Innocence* by Edith Wharton

59. *Zuleika Dobson* by Max Beerbohm

60. *The Moviegoer* by Walker Percy

61. *Death Comes for the Archbishop* by Willa Cather

62. *From Here to Eternity* by James Jones

63. *The Wapshot Chronicle* by John Cheever

64. *The Catcher in the Rye* by J. D. Salinger

65. *A Clockwork Orange* by Anthony Burgess

66. *Of Human Bondage* by W. Somerset Maugham

67. *Heart of Darkness* by Joseph Conrad

68. *Main Street* by Sinclair Lewis

69. *The House of Mirth* by Edith Wharton

70. *The Alexandria Quartet* by Lawrence Durrell

71. *A High Wind in Jamaica* by Richard Hughes

72. *A House for Mr. Biswas* by V. S. Naipaul

73. *The Day of the Locust* by Nathanael West

74. *A Farewell to Arms* by Ernest Hemingway

75. *Scoop* by Evelyn Waugh

76. *The Prime of Miss Jean Brodie* by Muriel Spark

77. *Finnegans Wake* by James Joyce

78. *Kim* by Rudyard Kipling

79. *A Room with a View* by E. M. Forster

80. *Brideshead Revisited* by Evelyn Waugh

81. *The Adventures of Augie March* by Saul Bellow

82. *Angle of Repose* by Wallace Stegner

83. *A Bend in the River* by V. S. Naipaul

84. *The Death of the Heart* by Elizabeth Bowen

85. *Lord Jim* by Joseph Conrad

86. *Ragtime* by E. L. Doctorow

87. *The Old Wives' Tale* by Arnold Bennett

88. *The Call of the Wild* by Jack London

89. *Loving* by Henry Green

90. *Midnight's Children* by Salman Rushdie

91. *Tobacco Road* by Erskine Caldwell

92. *Ironweed* by William Kennedy

93. *The Magus* by John Fowles

94. *Wide Sargasso Sea* by Jean Rhys

95. *Under the Net* by Iris Murdoch

96. *Sophie's Choice* by William Styron

97. *The Sheltering Sky* by Paul Bowles

98. *The Postman Always Rings Twice* by James M. Cain

99. *The Ginger Man* by J. P. Donleavy

100. *The Magnificent Ambersons* by Booth Tarkington

Ulysses by James Joyce, a formerly banned book that is now safely verified as a masterpiece because nobody reads it in its entirety, was the safest of safe top choices. Vladimir Nabokov's *Lolita* gave the list a bit of derring-do, circa 1955. Evelyn Waugh's *Scoop*, a personal favorite of mine, is a wonderful satirical novel about how the press starts wars, then covers them, but it is in no way as large a portrait of the world as *The Golden Notebook* by Doris Lessing. The Modern Library did make an attempt to include writers of color—V. S. Naipaul, Ralph Ellison, Richard Wright, James Baldwin—though women were not among them. Of the women on the list, Edith Wharton's *The Age of Innocence* and *The House of Mirth* are inevitable rather than courageous choices. (I would probably give a limb to have written *The House of Mirth*, but it hardly takes imagination to praise Wharton this long after her death—in 1937—and more recent transfiguration into film.) Of course all these books are worth reading and would enrich anyone's life, but so would the ones below.

The Random House readers who posted their choices on the Web site wound up with a list that puts four Ayn Rand novels in place of *Ulysses*, *The Great Gatsby*, *Catch-22*, and *Darkness at Noon*. Since Ayn Rand is not my cup of tea, I must abstain, but the readers' list is far more gender neutral than the original and doesn't discriminate against sci-fi or horror authors. (Robert Heinlein and Stephen King figure prominently.) The attempt to create a women's fiction list proved a fascinating exercise. I wrote the 250 or so distinguished women writers and critics whose correct addresses I have in my database. I posted a notice on the rather lively writers' forum that used to be on my Web site (www.ericajong.com) until it was spammed out of existence, and then, for good measure, I wrote to about thirty male novelists, critics, and poets whose judgment I respect and whose addresses I happen to have. The results of this informal survey were instructive. Because I promised anonymity to my respondents, they were frank with me. They apologized for liking certain books that they deemed to be important in their own lives—*Gone With the Wind* and *Interview with the Vampire* are two examples—but that they suspected Helen Vendler and Harold Bloom might pooh-pooh. The scholars responded quickly—as if they had been list-making all their lives. The poets' and novelists' lists dribbled in more slowly. Pretty much everyone I wrote to tended to take the project seriously. They congratulated me on raising the question of a women's list at all—whether or not they had seen the original Modern Library list. Sometimes they included lists from their best friends, members of reading groups or seminars.

Here are the books most frequently repeated (after 1. Margaret Mitchell's *Gone With the Wind* and 2. Anne Rice's *Interview with the Vampire*):

VIRGINIA WOOLF

3. *To the Lighthouse*
4. *Mrs. Dalloway*
5. *The Waves*
6. *Orlando*

DJUNA BARNES

7. *Nightwood*

EDITH WHARTON

8. *The House of Mirth*

9. *The Age of Innocence*

10. *Ethan Frome*

RADCLYFFE HALL

11. *The Well of Loneliness*

NADINE GORDIMER

12. *Burger's Daughter*

HARRIETTE SIMPSON ARNOW

13. *The Dollmaker*

MARGARET ATWOOD

14. *The Handmaid's Tale*

WILLA CATHER

15. *My Ántonia*

ERICA JONG

16. *Fear of Flying*

17. *Fanny*

JOY KOGAWA

18. *Obasan*

DORIS LESSING

19. *The Golden Notebook*

20. *The Fifth Child*
21. *The Grass Is Singing*

HARPER LEE
22. *To Kill a Mockingbird*

MARGE PIERCY
23. *Woman on the Edge of Time*

JANE SMILEY
24. *A Thousand Acres*

LORE SEGAL
25. *Her First American*

ALICE WALKER
26. *The Color Purple*
27. *The Third Life of Grange Copeland*

MARION ZIMMER BRADLEY
28. *The Mists of Avalon*

MURIEL SPARK
29. *Memento Mori*
30. *The Prime of Miss Jean Brodie*

DOROTHY ALLISON
31. *Bastard Out of Carolina*

JEAN RHYS

32. *Wide Sargasso Sea*

SUSAN FROMBERG SHAEFFER

33. *Anya*

CYNTHIA OZICK

34. *Trust*

AMY TAN

35. *The Joy Luck Club*

36. *The Kitchen God's Wife*

ANN BEATTIE

37. *Chilly Scenes of Winter*

ZORA NEALE HURSTON

38. *Their Eyes Were Watching God*

JOAN DIDION

39. *A Book of Common Prayer*

40. *Play It as It Lays*

MARY MCCARTHY

41. *The Group*

42. *The Company She Keeps*

GRACE PALEY

43. *The Little Disturbances of Man*

SYLVIA PLATH

44. *The Bell Jar*

CARSON MCCULLERS

45. *The Heart Is a Lonely Hunter*

ELIZABETH BOWEN

46. *The Death of the Heart*

FLANNERY O'CONNOR

47. *Wise Blood*

MONA SIMPSON

48. *Anywhere But Here*

TONI MORRISON

49. *Song of Solomon*

50. *Beloved*

STELLA GIBBONS

51. *Cold Comfort Farm*

SYLVIA TOWNSEND WARNER

52. *Mr. Fortune's Maggot*

KATHERINE ANNE PORTER

53. *Ship of Fools*

LAURA RIDING

54. *Progress of Stories*

RUTH PRAWER JHABVALA

55. *Heat and Dust*

PENELOPE FITZGERALD

56. *The Blue Flower*

ISABEL ALLENDE

57. *The House of the Spirits*

A. S. BYATT

58. *Possession*

PAT BARKER

59. *The Ghost Road*

RITA MAE BROWN

60. *Rubyfruit Jungle*

ANITA BROOKNER

61. *Hotel du Lac*

ANGELA CARTER

62. *Nights at the Circus*

DAPHNE DU MAURIER

63. *Rebecca*

KATHERINE DUNN

64. *Geek Love*

SHIRLEY JACKSON

65. *We Have Always Lived in the Castle*

BARBARA PYM

66. *Excellent Women*

LESLIE MARMON SILKO

67. *Ceremony*

ANNE TYLER

68. *Dinner at the Homesick Restaurant*

69. *The Accidental Tourist*

NANCY WILLARD

70. *Things Invisible to See*

JEANETTE WINTERSON

71. *Sexing the Cherry*

LYNNE SHARON SCHWARTZ

72. *Disturbances in the Field*

ROSELLEN BROWN

73. *Civil Wars*

HARRIET DOERR

74. *Stones for Ibarra*

JEAN STAFFORD

75. *The Mountain Lion*

STEVIE SMITH

76. *Novel on Yellow Paper*

E. ANNIE PROULX

77. *The Shipping News*

REBECCA GOLDSTEIN

78. *The Mind-Body Problem*

P. D. JAMES

79. *The Children of Men*

URSULA HEGI

80. *Stones From the River*

FAY WELDON

81. *The Life and Loves of a She-Devil*

KATHERINE MANSFIELD

82. *Collected Stories*

REBECCA HARDING DAVIS

83. *Life in the Iron Mills*

LOUISE ERDRICH

84. *The Beet Queen*

URSULA K. LE GUIN

85. *The Left Hand of Darkness*

EDNA O'BRIEN

86. *The Country Girls Trilogy*

MARGARET DRABBLE

87. *Realms of Gold*

88. *The Waterfall*

DAWN POWELL

89. *The Locusts Have No King*

MARILYN FRENCH

90. *The Women's Room*

EUDORA WELTY

91. *The Optimist's Daughter*

CAROL SHIELDS

92. *The Stone Diaries*

JAMAICA KINCAID

93. *Annie John*

TILLIE OLSEN

94. *Tell Me a Riddle*

GERTRUDE STEIN

95. *The Autobiography of Alice B. Toklas*

IRIS MURDOCH

96. *A Severed Head*

ANITA DESAI

97. *Clear Light of Day*

ALICE HOFFMAN

98. *The Drowning Season*

SUE TOWNSEND

99. *The Secret Diary of Adrian Mole*

PENELOPE MORTIMER

100. *The Pumpkin Eater*

That is the preliminary culling. It gives us, at least, a starting point. An equally long list could be made of memoirs, poems, and novels in languages other than English.

All lists are highly arbitrary. And this, like all such efforts, is a work in progress. I invited my readers to write their favorites to me at my e-mail address, so that I could include books I and my respondents had missed. So many worthy books were sent to me that this little essay could well turn into a book. Perhaps it will.

Ranking the listed books seems to me like a useless exercise. Books are not prizefighters. They don't compete against one another. It may even be that many worthy volumes escaped the notice of my helpers because they were printed in tiny editions and disappeared into the pulping machine before they were even discovered. Many good women's books doubtless go unpublished. What the list chiefly teaches us is the extent of our own ignorance. I don't claim to have read all these books, but it strikes me that this list would make a fascinating beginning course in women's literature. If we could only begin to immerse ourselves in the riches of the writers who came before us, we would see that we had an excellent broth to nourish our future efforts.

It interested me greatly to learn how hard it was for most of my respondents to name a hundred books. I received scribbled notes that said things like: "Don't forget Angela Carter!" Or "What about the short story writers whose novels are less good?" Since the list was of novels written in English, I had to exclude favorites of mine—like Colette, Simone de Beauvoir, and Marguerite Yourcenar. Memoirs like Maxine Hong Kingston's *The Woman Warrior* were excluded because there will eventually be a separate list of memoirs. Poetry was excluded because that, too, must wait for a future tally. (Women poets in English in this century could fill a very large library.)

Assembling the preliminary list, I kept being reminded of Emma Goldman's wise words: "When you are educated, when you know your power, you'll need no bombs or militia and no dynamite will hold you."

Old age is not for sissies.

—BETTE DAVIS

There was a time in the not so very far past when women of a certain age accepted, often with relief and pleasure, their new status on the margins of the sexual dance. They nurtured the younger generation. They gave advice. They taught table manners, which fork to use, how to waltz (or Charleston), and how to write a bread-and-butter or condolence note. They were the great repositories of social knowledge. The fact that they were not going to nab your boyfriend was obvious. They had said good-bye to all that.

My grandmother was in her late fifties when I was born. Considered a stylish beauty in her youth in Russia and England, she now dressed to go out in black velvet suits with white silk blouses, pearls, white kid gloves, and sensible, low-heeled black shoes. She almost never wore color. No makeup—except for a swipe of pink on the lips for going to the New York Philharmonic and out to dinner. She dressed in the elegant way of ladies who accepted their age. Her flirting days were over and her clothes showed it. She was a lady. In her bureau drawers was an almost infinite supply of white kid gloves of all lengths. In her closet, silk blouses in cream or white. Her hats were becoming, black, and never full of feathers or fake jewels. Her pearls were real and came in various lengths. Her demeanor said: I am a grandmother and I love it.

Her calm, her sweetness, her sense of herself as matriarch gave my sisters and me a great sense of security. In no way was she in competition with us as we grew up. When boys called the house or arrived to pick us up, there was no hint of impropriety in her manner. Our mother was flirtatious, stylish, dressed to kill. She never gave up on designer clothes until, in her nineties, she exchanged them for nighties and caftans. Our grandmother was the rock on which we stood.

Think of Colette's aging courtesans like Lea in *The Last of Chéri* or Gigi's grandmother in *Gigi*. These women were not antisexual. They were just past it and happy to be past it. That gave them time to educate the younger generation.

Of all women writers, Colette understood this female transition from sensual being to grandmotherly teacher most accurately. Lea is still sexual in *Chéri*, when she takes as her lover the beautiful young boy she calls Chéri. Chéri is willful, gorgeous, indefatigable in bed. He is nineteen and a walking erection—but that is not really the point. The point is that he loves his aging "Nounoune" (as he has called her from childhood) and she is life itself to him.

Half mommy and half mistress, Lea knows that Chéri must marry a girl of his own generation sooner rather than later, and that she must let him go. Meanwhile, she enjoys him to the fullest and he enjoys her coddling him as much as the sex, which is only ever implied but clearly omnipresent. He loves to wear Lea's marvelous pearls against his naked body. He is a sleek, muscular Adonis in bed with an aging Aphrodite.

Lea is forty-nine to Chéri's nineteen. And we know she is old enough to resort to various stratagems of dressing and grooming to make her look younger. She wears pink silk around her face, winds diaphanous fabrics around her lined throat, and keeps her bedroom decorated with rosy silken fabrics—though such decoration is out of date. She is a woman in the full ripeness of her years and she knows what she knows. She would rather be fully dressed or utterly naked—nothing in between. She is proud of her marvelous breasts, which still stand up. But she understands they will not last forever. Nor will her liaison with Chéri.

In *The Last of Chéri*, Chéri has married the appropriate girl of his own age and he is wretchedly unhappy with her. She knows nothing of his needs. She is vain and silly. She cannot nurture him and satisfy him as his Nounoune did. He tries to come back to his aging Aphrodite, and for a moment he does. Then Lea takes it upon herself to quit the sexual dance—in part to force Chéri to grow up, as she knows he must.

She cuts off all her hair, abandons her regime, grows fat, and wears asexual clothes. When Chéri comes to see her, he is horrified—though the reader knows that Lea has retreated from love in part to make him grow up. Her renunciation of sex is not only her own healthy acceptance of age but also her wish to make him a man by withdrawing her coddling.

Chéri is shaken by her transformation. He now has no place to hide. He doesn't want to grow up. He wants his Nounoune, his childhood, his carefree existence. He doesn't want to be a husband and a father. He is Adonis, so of course he can never grow up. He is fated to die young. The second Chéri book ends with him about to put a bullet through his head.

> In the end, he stretched himself out, resting on his folded right arm, the muzzle of the pistol in his ear, the gun half smothered by the cushions. His arm began to grow numb, and he knew that unless he hurried his fingers would refuse to do their part. He uttered one or two stifled moans, for his forearm, cramped by the weight of his body, hurt. The last thing he knew in this world was the movement of his index finger against a tiny steel rod.

And now we come to the present day. Colette is long gone (she died in the fifties) and the baby-boom generation is at the crest of the hill and about to go over it. I pick up an amusing memoir by a woman now in her seventies, but in her sixties when she wrote it. It is called *A Round-Heeled Woman* by Jane Juska and it recounts the story of a woman in her sixties who, after her son is grown and gone, after she has retired from her career as a teacher, decides to have some "late-life adventures in love and sex."

Jane Juska is appealing to me. She reads Trollope and admires good prose. She writes her story with a light, ironic hand. She is able to tell tales on herself—the sign of a real writer. And, blessedly, she doesn't take herself too seriously.

She has had real unhappiness in her life: a first marriage that was painful but left her with a son she adores, a period of being freakishly overweight (more than one hundred pounds) in order to hide from her sexual yearnings, a history of illness induced by obesity, a struggle to lose weight for the sake of her health. She has a psychological breakthrough—the right therapist coming just at the right time when she is open to change—and she decides to experience sex before it's too late. So she turns—where else?—not to the Internet but to the *New York Review of Books*.

She places an ad that reads:

Before I turn sixty-seven—next March—I want to have a lot of sex with a man I like. If you want to talk first, Trollope works for me. NYR Box 10307.

And then she describes what happens. She describes the winnowing process, the meeting process, the anxiety, the disappointments, the bad eggs and the good guys she meets after having been out of the world of sex for forty years. What a brave woman she is to embark on this at sixty-seven! I think of my own intervals of dating—between marriages, at twenty-three, at thirty-nine, at forty-seven—and how sexual mores were totally different each time I found myself single, and I want to salute JJ for her daring. To date again at sixty-seven, even to take your clothes off with a stranger at sixty-seven—what guts! Or what idiocy! And then to write about it! That takes courage. I admire courage far more than I admire circumspection and repression. Courage makes the world go round.

JJ becomes a risk-taker—something she has never been before. She becomes an inspiration to all her women friends as she explores the various partners the *New York Review* sends her way. Hurray for Jane! I like her—and not just because she's a Democrat and a constant reader. She's got pluck and she seeks to know herself. She's a teacher teaching herself. She believes, like me, that the unexamined life is not worth living.

Where do we learn more than we do in bed? Bed is where we learn what frightens us, what delights us. Bed is often where we discover who we are.

Jane is a teacher and bed becomes her classroom. She learns and she teaches. What she finally learns is a lot like what I learned in my eight and a half years of singledom between my third and my fourth marriages: Men are not the enemy. They are as scared as we. Possibly more. Sex only really works when you are friends as well as lusters-for-each-other. Men can be fun and they enhance a woman's life. But they are not essential. Women friends are essential. Men are not the main course. They are dessert. Women friends and children are the main course.

Of course that's only my opinion. It does not necessarily reflect the views of all women. Some right-wing women hate my affection for Juska's courage. Men think themselves essential and bully for them if they think so. But wisdom for women usually means knowing you can take care of yourself—with the help of your trusty women friends and your loving, if self-centered (as they must be to make their lives), children and grandchildren.

Lately I have read more than one whining male-authored magazine article about how independent women have become the new men. These men complain in shock and amazement that the new woman doesn't want commitment, loves to sleep alone, treasures her privacy in her own home, enjoys her ability to run her own life even though she *does* want men for companionship and sex.

She refuses to be faithful to one partner or compromise about money, children, or even home decor. She likes men but doesn't want to be mastered by a man. She wants to live alone. Shocking!

Men seem utterly flummoxed by this new independence. "Women now act as men once did!" they complain. It's not fair! And men now act like *women* once did, trying to trap their girlfriends into marital monogamy. They cook for women, cosset them, try to get them into living together arrangements in which they promise not to fuck other men. But the new woman doesn't want this. She treasures her "space." She *does* want a man in her bed a few nights a week, but she's perfectly happy to let him leave after they have sex. O Brave New World that has such women in it!

Jane Juska's story is hardly unique. Suddenly there are post-menopausal women going to bed all over the place and not wanting any strings attached. There's "Erica Barry" [*sic*] played by the marvelous Diane Keaton in the absurdly named *Something's Gotta Give*. Erica Barry is a rich playwright who lives in the Hamptons and falls (unbelievably to me) for her daughter's boyfriend played by Jack Nicholson. The appeal of this lover is that he gobbles Viagras like M&Ms, keeps having heart attacks, and is amazed to be turned on by a woman over thirty. I found his character rather repellant despite Nicholson's animated eyebrows; I myself would have opted for the dishy young doctor played by Keanu Reeves. But Diane Keaton's performance is a wonder. She also looks great (despite having been born in 1946) and from the fuss made about her looks in this movie, you'd think fifty-eight was Methuselah's age.

The costuming of Keaton in *Something's Gotta Give* is also bizarre. She plays a woman who seems to feel that if she takes off her turtleneck, her head will fall off. Swathed in white cotton up to the chin, she begins the movie as a nun of some sort of weird order clothed by L.L.Bean. When she finally takes off the white turtleneck and appears fleetingly nude in one scene, movie critics responded as if she'd invented the cure for cancer. Is the flesh of women in their fifties and sixties considered so unacceptable in our society that we must never take off our turtlenecks? This movie was hailed as liberated for presenting the older woman as a sex object, but I found it full of unconscious misogyny.

Which bring us to *The Mother,* written by Hanif Kureishi, directed by Roger Michell and starring Anne Reid as a widow who thought nobody would ever touch her again except the undertaker.

The Mother is a far subtler piece of filmmaking than *Something's Gotta Give* and it ultimately rends your heart. We follow May, an aging housewife of the fifties, on a trip to visit her grown children in London. During the family fun, her husband suffers a fatal heart attack.

After his death, May tries to return home, but finds she cannot stay there and waste away by the telly like her friends until it's time to enter the old-age home. She decides to seek the cold comfort of her son and daughter's ménages. Her daughter is having an affair with a married bloke—Darren played by Daniel Craig—who is also renovating her son's house.

Darren is one of those sexy drifters who appeals to women of all ages. His tenderness and skill in bed conceals his rage at the world and at women. May surprises herself first by kissing him, then by inviting him "to the spare room" where they make outrageous love together. May's daughter, Paula, is also obsessed with Darren—a very tasty hunk of manflesh but hardly suitable for the long term.

Paula wants Darren to move in with her and she solicits her mother's talents as a go-between. Paula simply cannot conceive of her mother having needs of her own. She uses her as a baby-sitter, go-between, confessional, and emotional trash bin until, convinced that her mother is poaching on her stud, she gives her mother an impressive black eye.

Even more shocking than the sex between a woman in her sixties and a man in his thirties—probably as old as civilization—is the viciousness of the unresolved mother-daughter fury.

May is a woman who sacrificed her whole life to husband and children—just because it was "done"—and never gave herself a chance to discover who she wants to be. Her drawing, writing, and taking a young lover constitute her first tentative feints at self-knowledge, while her daughter Paula takes self-expression as her right yet can do nothing creative with it. She tries to write plays but winds up burning them and blaming her mother for the conflagration. It turns out she is even more in the thrall of patriarchy than her mother.

May has begun to glimpse freedom for herself, but Paula is utterly blind to her own needs and thinks attacking her mother is somehow therapeutic. May's son is equally selfish. As for Darren, he is fucked up on drugs and full of rage, but at least he has given May fleeting pleasure and a new understanding of herself as a creature apart from slavery to family.

Daniel Craig's Darren, with his irresistibility to women and his incurable self-loathing, reminded me of a man I spent entirely too much time with at a certain point in my life. He became my lover, housemate, and dependent. Though the sex never flagged, my patience with caring for him did, especially when he began drifting

into other women's beds. When I kicked him out, he left his bar-
bells, cameras, books, and glossies in my attic. He eventually turned
up again after a failed marriage left him with two little children. He
brought them to me, probably hoping I'd take them in as I once had
him. He could only see me as a caretaker or a sex object and he
hoped his two sweet kids would worm their way into my heart. It
was pathetic but I sent him and the children on their way.

Craig was utterly convincing in the role of sexy drifter, as was
Anne Reid as the grieving mother who needs to be touched before
the undertaker comes.

Since I live in New York, I was fortunately spared the prurient
British tabloids' response to this film, but I can well imagine them.
The Mother is not shocking for the raw sex but for the naked revelations of family misunderstanding and rage. The generations not only
can't communicate, but the younger are so lacking in empathy that
their progenitors have no choice but to die on the spot or walk away
to preserve themselves. *The Mother* is a harrowing movie and a true
one, unlike the flossy and amusing lies of *Something's Gotta Give.*

Why all these postmenopausal women having sex in books,
movies, and on TV? Well, baby boomers have always expected the
world. Why should they give up the benefits of sex just because
of a few wrinkles? They are the generation who always got their
way, who pushed the envelope in the sixties and hardly expect to
give up pushing now that *they* are sixty. Do they see sex as akin to
vitamins—something you do for increased longevity? We know
that coupled people live longer than single. We know that our gen-

eration is health-crazed. Why should we give up intimacy and sexuality just because it shocks our kids that we still need it. Fuck 'em! We will go on having our way until we are carried out feet first.

Is the news that older women are enjoying more sex a trend caused by our aging populations? Will we see the elderly increasingly engaging in youthful behaviors of all sorts—from Rollerblading to composing love songs? I think so. Our kids will have to get used to the idea that they can't corner the market on lust and love. It won't be easy for them. They want us as kindly old grandmas and -pas ready to baby-sit for free. They don't want to find us in the spare room with some Darren. Not only does it shock them, it cramps their style.

Evolution dictates that we stand aside and help to raise the next generation rather than have adventures of our own. Our adventures will not result in babies—so we must let the babies have their due. Grandparents have always been vital as caregivers and teachers. Since human babies are so slow in becoming independent, it takes a village to raise them and we are that village. Should we be fornicating in the spare room when the toddlers may need us? Absolutely not. But most of us don't live in extended families with our kids so we don't need to resort to hot-sheet motels with our lovers. Just as we fled from our parents we now have to flee from our children— pleading pottery classes or shopping or doctors' appointments. We may be liberated but our kids are not. Having suffered from our derangements and divorces, they are far squarer as a generation then we were. They want white weddings and diamond rings and happily ever after. Good luck to them and God bless. Remnants of the seventies, we still want a whiff of Woodstock in our later years. But we'll have to hide it from our progeny. That we know. Fortunately, we have our own digs.

Will sex ever be free of secrecy and repression? We think we are so liberated, but now we find ourselves sneaking around to deceive our children. It is just not in the nature of things for the generations to celebrate sex simultaneously.

Our children believe they have cornered the market on sex and let them think so. They don't want to imagine granny in a hotel suite one delicious afternoon a week. Perhaps that's why there has been so little open discussion of the subject of postmenopausal sex. One giggles about it with close friends, but it seems not fit to print in family newspapers. Nobody wants to acknowledge publicly that sex has no age limit. Perhaps it's a question of oedipal suppression. Kids hate to think of their parents having sex.

For the parents, however, the urge to merge may be a response to many things. Sexual craving may be less of a factor than the nearness of death. Sex is a way of convincing yourself you're still alive. I think of all the distinguished old men—poets, novelists, professors who wooed me when I was a miniskirted twenty-two. I felt sorry for their ardor, which I could not share. Now I understand their desperation. They wanted reassurance that they were still part of the dance of life. They wanted proof that the angel of death was not hovering too near. They thought they heard the dark wings beating overhead and they hoped my youth could protect them.

Sex is a very profound drive for human beings because it can serve so many purposes. It can convince us we can still feel. It can fill us with hope. It can enliven the mind as well as the senses. If we take a broader definition of sex than intercourse alone, a Lawrentian view of sex, we discover that sex is the secret key to letting the world in. It is a universal curiosity, a need to reach out and give ourselves to others as well as a need to take others in. No wonder we learn so much from sex. If we will only allow ourselves to understand sex as something beyond reproduction we will have a clue to its enormous power. In their sexual meditations, Tantrists find union with God. They use the body to get beyond the body. We can discover this exercise of sexuality at any point in our lives. Perhaps, in truth, we are better at it when hormones alone do not rule us. The Greeks knew that Eros and Aphrodite ruled even the other gods. Perhaps it is time for us to rediscover their wisdom.

May your every wish be granted.

—ANCIENT CHINESE CURSE

On Sunday, the *New York Times Book Review* called my new book, *Seducing the Demon*, "disheveled" and "trapped in time." That review wasn't as scary as the one in the *Chicago Sun-Times*, which called me "a delusional car wreck."

Ever since I published *Fear of Flying* in 1973, some reviews of my books haven't just been bad, they've been apoplectic—as if I'd committed a crime that had nothing to do with words. Being called a "giant pudenda" by Paul Theroux still sticks, three decades later.

For most of my career, after reading a bad review I would take to my bed, refuse all calls, drink wine straight from the bottle, eat chocolate cake, swear off writing, and consider going into social work and fantasize about doing bodily harm to critics. I considered hiring a hit man, but since I've always pretty much hung out with liberals and eggheads, I never had access to that phone number. So my revenge of choice would be public humiliation. Four inches taller in my black velvet boots, I would splash cold vodka in my critics' eyes at the PEN gala. Blinded for the evening, they would still see the errors of their ways, repent, fall to their knees, and write letters of retraction.

Yet I never was able to inflict my fantasy. I am neither Gore Vidal nor Camille Paglia—the only two writers who make vitriol both illuminating and entertaining. I have stood face-to-face with my detractors and said nothing but "How are you?" while they shuffled from foot to foot, bracing themselves for a punch or that vodka. Am I cowardly or wise? Wise by default. I know that revenge springs back on the avenger. Also, ever since my prescribed Wellbutrin kicked in, I'm able to be a lot more mellow when I get bad news. What used to be body blows are now slaps. So instead of seeing the review as a personal vendetta or sexist attack, I'm living with the fact that the critic simply thought my book sucked. So how can I write a better one?

Here's how. Become less self-centered. One thing my critics, my husband, my daughter, and my editor all make fun of me for is my narcissism. How do I get over myself? Being a grandmother helps because it made me realize what a self-absorbed mother I was. The nanny changed my daughter's diapers. As some kind of penance, I now insist on changing as many of my grandson's as my daughter and son-in-law will allow.

Besides, I've always wanted to improve and evolve as a writer. I'm now writing a novel about my doppelgänger, Isadora Wing, as a woman of a certain age, and I've finally, at age sixty-four, gotten to the point where I realize that there are lives and characters more interesting than mine—and Isadora's. After inhabiting a writer's mind for decades, I'd like to inhabit the mind of my readers and, God help me, my critics. To love them instead of demanding that they love me.